Captured

Yesterday

Captured Yesterday

The Wartime Diary of Tony B. Lumpkin

Tony B. Lumpkin

Copyright © 2017

All rights reserved. No part of this book may be reproduced or transmitted in any form by any means without written permission of the author.

ISBN: 978-0-692-89253-4

Table of Contents

Introduction & Acknowledgements 1
Chapter 1   Destination: Ireland 4
Chapter 2   War-Games 26
Chapter 3   To England 48
Chapter 4   Aboard the Duchess of Bedford 60
Chapter 5   Landing in Algeria 71
Chapter 6   Success against Italians 96
Chapter 7   Krauts Break Through 107
Chapter 8   Captured Yesterday 138
Chapter 9   Tunisia to Poland 145
Chapter 10   A New POW Camp: *Oflag 64* 171
Chapter 11   German Plans go *Kaput* 201
Chapter 12   D-Day and a Celebration 230
Chapter 13   Camp Population Swells 239
Chapter 14   Gottfried Dietze: An Unlikely Friend 249
Chapter 15   Forced March and Escape 263
Chapter 16   Warsaw to Odessa 299
Chapter 17   Odessa to Newfoundland 307
Chapter 18   Debrief, Visit Fort Hunt, and Finally Home .. 318
Afterword 321
   Appendix A – The Germans 333
   Appendix B – Rations and the Effect of Hunger 342
   Appendix C – Internal Organization of the Camp 346
   Appendix D – The Russians 349
Glossary 355

Table of Figures

Figure 0-1 Pages from the original diary 3
Figure 1-1 Captain Lumpkin on board the Queen Mary en route to Ireland 8
Figure 1-2 Castlewellan Castle in Northern Ireland 14
Figure 1-3 Officer's group photo at Castelwellan 19
Figure 3-1 Tony Lumpkin in front of bombed out section of London 51
Figure 4-1 Convoy on way to North Africa 62
Figure 5-1 Captain Lumpkin (center) among a group of officers and soldiers somewhere in Algeria 76
Figure 5-2 Roman ruins 94
Figure 6-1 M3 medium tank dubbed "Missouri Military Academy" 97
Figure 6-2 T-5 Steiner and Capt. Frederick Hughes (both later captured) 102
Figure 6-3 Famed WWII correspondent Ernie Pyle 104
Figure 7-1 Remains of downed German Ju-88 Stuka 108
Figure 7-2 Capts. Venerie and Ernest "Buck" Hatfield outside Oran in the back of General Ward's half-track 117
Figure 7-3 The new "Jeep" negotiating terrain 122
Figure 7-4 T-5 William Nikolin "Nicky" 132
Figure 7-5 Captain Lumpkin's volunteer patrol in a pass outside of Maknassy, Tunisia with their "home-made" gun fashioned from a 20mm canon from a scrapped British Spitfire airplane 136
Figure 9-1 Telegram received by Capt. Lumpkin's wife almost two full months after his capture 163
Figure 10-1 ID papers of captured German soldier that Captain Lumpkin managed to keep hidden throughout his captivity 173
Figure 10-2 One of many letters Capt. Lumpkin wrote to his wife, Betty. Each passed through German and U.S. censors before being delivered 200
Figure 12-1 German newspaper wartime propaganda cartoons depicting allies as barbaric gangsters. 232
Figure 12-2 From left to right: 1st Lt. LeRoy Ihrie, Captain Tony Lumpkin, 1st Lt. Henry Haynes, and 1st Lt. Amon Carter Jr. in the "Parcel Hut" at Oflag 64 234
Figure 13-1 Captain Lumpkin's POW ID. He distorted his face whenever photographed by the Germans in order to make later identification more difficult. 245
Figure 14-1 Poster warning that those who attempt escape will be shot 259
Figure 15-1 Captain Lumpkin's photo in a Polish newspaper. The caption reads: "Soviet troops liberated from German camps a thousand British and American prisoners of war. On the photo: Soviet officer talks with US officers." 279

Figure A-1   Tony B. Lumpkin 321
Figure A-2   General John Waters 322
Figure A-3   Amon Carter Jr. 323
Figure A-4   Henry Söderberg 324
Figure A-5   Gottfried Dietze 325
Figure A-6   Georgy Zhukov 328
Figure A-7   Ernie Pyle 329
Figure A-8   "A Captain Is Captured" – Ernie Pyle (continued next page) 330
Figure A-9   Continued – "A Captain Is Captured" 331
Figure A-10 Ernie Pyle Donates ID Bracelet 332

Introduction & Acknowledgements

This is the wartime diary of our grandfather, Tony B. Lumpkin. Tony was the commandant of the Missouri Military Academy in Mexico, Missouri until going on active duty after the attack on Pearl Harbor. He kept the diary, made up of several small notebooks with tiny, barely-legible handwriting that he kept hidden from his German captors.

For the most part, he could make an entry in the diary each day. However, there are periods while he was unable to make entries because it was either impractical or the notebooks had to remain hidden because of rumored Gestapo searches, etc. Also, at times, the entries in the diary become brief and cryptic as his circumstances grew more difficult due do hunger, cold, etc. Unless we were able to verify spelling, there are cases where names are spelled differently which were intentionally left as they were in the diary.

The diary makes several references to "security parcels" which refers to a then top-secret program operated by the Department of War called MIS-X. MIS-X used the cover of fake aid organizations such as the "Prisoner of War Benefits Association" to smuggle in secret equipment such as maps, compasses, and radios into POW camps. Coding on the packages indicated if they contained contraband material and efforts were made to keep these packages from being searched by the German captors. In the case of *Oflag 64*, even .22 caliber pistols and ammunition were smuggled into camp. This program remained classified until the late 1980's.

During a reunion of *Oflag 64* POWs in the 1970's, several former POWs made notes in the diary that are included as footnotes in this publication. Since the MIS-X program was still classified at that time, you will see comments suggesting removal of any diary entry that refers to "security parcels."

Our grandfather crossed paths with many notable individuals during the war. Before capture, he became good friends with famed correspondent Ernie Pyle and was the subject of one of Pyle's nationally publicized columns. While in prison camp, his fellow prisoners included John Waters, General George Patton's son-in-law, William Wright Bryan, longtime editor of the Atlanta Journal, and Amon Carter Jr., son of Amon G. Carter who was the creator of the Fort Worth Star-Telegram. During his escape, he also came face-to-face with Marshal Georgy Zhukov, who remains the most decorated military leader in the history of both Russia and the U.S.S.R.

Both my sister, Dr. E. Noel Lumpkin and I, Tony B. Lumpkin III, have labored over the course of several years but there have been many other hands involved that helped us get the diary published. Ruth McMonigle, our grandfather's secretary, got the effort started unknowingly in the 1970's when she converted the P.O.W. section of the diary into typewritten form. Our aunt and Tony Lumpkin's daughter, Anne Sudduth, painstakingly organized most of the documents and pictures used to supplement the diary. The title of this book, *Captured Yesterday*, was her idea as well. Also, our cousin-in-law, Nicky Westover-Sudduth, spent numerous hours converting the P.O.W. section of the diary from typewritten pages to an electronic format.

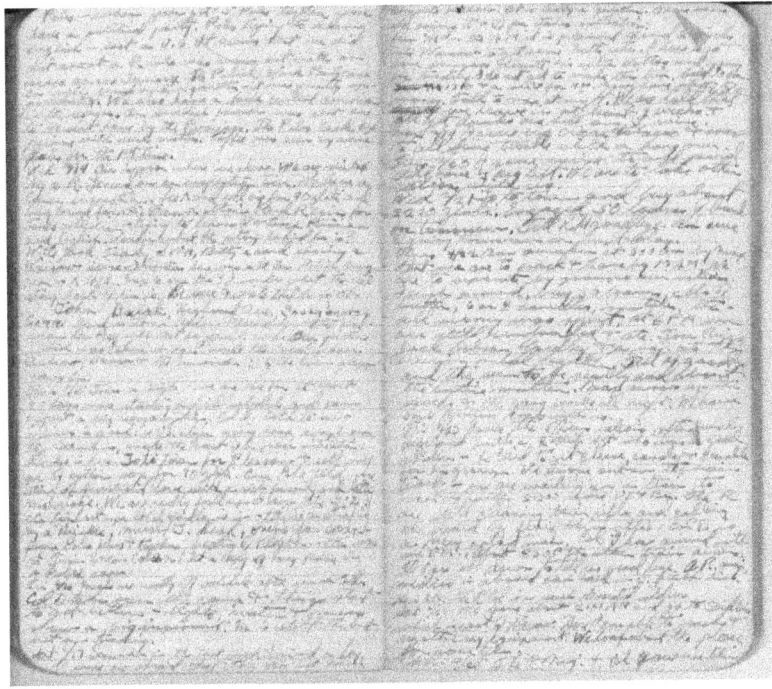

Figure 0-1   Pages from the original diary

Chapter 1

Destination: Ireland

May 3, 1942 – **Fort Dix, New Jersey.** For the past week, I have been trying to get oriented in duties as Assistant Commandant. The officers of this Headquarters Battalion (HQ Bn.) of the First Armored Division (1st AD) are certainly swell. They all try to make you feel at home. They all also seem to know their administrative jobs well but are not too good with basic training skills. There is quite a bit of red tape and not thinking the problems through – i.e. this morning it was found that 50-caliber mounts and 30-caliber guns are mounted on the jeeps. General Orlando Ward and Colonel Hasbrouck are fine chaps. Col. Hasbrouck is a very capable executive. He is one of the best that I have ever seen. There seems to be a General Daily, the Commanding General (CG) of V Corps who is a #$%@&, but he has made this unit more alert. Capt. William S. McElhenny is and has been a real help. Both he and Lieutenant Hatfield are aids of the Gen. Ward. The General sure knows a hell of a lot about leadership. This is a very flexible set-up, but a good outfit. There is quite a problem in getting all of my equipment, money, etc., etc. Susserman, the local Provost Marshall is sure a dinger for his prerogative. The General and the C-S raised hell with him for raising hell with me. Sunday was spent in Division Headquarters. Col. Hasbrouck asked me out to fire the 75mm (75-millimeter gun) in the medium tank. We had one hell of a good time. He and Col. Maraist are sure swell. Boy is that gun great. You could knock the eye of a fly out at 1,000 yards. This was my first ride in the medium tank (M3).

May 4, 1942 – I had a hell of a time drawing 50-caliber tracer ammunition to be used on the range for Division Headquarters. Finally, Majors Hoy and Brown went out on a limb and saw that I received ammunition. After all of the stewing about, we did not shoot because the range caught on fire from the tracer ammo.

May 5, 1942 – Shipped our lockers. The time is near. I wish that we were on the water now. This job is certainly a whizbang – lots of work, lots of grief, and lots of bosses. Some are swell to work with. It has one drawback. There is not enough time to do one job well! I must learn to do things more quickly or learn to shake jobs off on others. Could HQ and Service Company be closed to Division Headquarters?

Father Martin had a hell of a time rolling his bedroll for Red Cross men! They seem to be okay, but, like me, are helpless at times.

May 6, 1942 – Trying to get firing done. One hell of a problem. Must have: gun's ammunition, targets, range transportation, safety precautions, etc. Finally, today we get it all lined up and ... no firing. It seems we have a map problem and a cross-country run tonight. The declination was not considered and I wind up 200 yards off. A hell of a lot of these officers know nothing of maps.

Corregidor has been taken by the Japs.

May 7, 1942 – We are to leave very soon on the *Queen Mary*. Col. Hasbrouck raised hell (and I don't blame him) for the lack of firing. It is almost impossible to get all of the prerequisites together at one time. Col. Martin, the chaplain, is some character. The firing went off better today. All of the officers are buying swagger-dagger sticks. I'll put my trust in a 45-caliber. I tried to buy some English Pounds but failed. Cols. Farmwick and Ginn are good eggs. Some officers seem more anxious to buy swagger sticks then in buying equipment that is reported as being needed.

May 8, 1942 – The firing was better and smoother today. I heard one soldier say, "Gee, I sure miss my wife. She sure could make me happy." I had a hell of a time trying to get to the pistol range. Finally, used one near the HQ after it had been denied to me several times. The Army certainly does some things backwards. Too much red tape in connection with equipment. I had dinner with Major Chuck Miller, his wife, son, and some friends. This son is a real boy. He's about 8 years old.

A prisoner tried to haggle himself to keep from going. His IQ was 38.

May 9, 1942 – It seems that all details regarding entraining and detraining must be carefully adhered to. All equipment must be unloaded prior to shipment and crated up. Most articles had been wired to the trucks. Funny thing – my field glasses are poor. The Ordinance Officer at Dix gave me a note to exchange them, but the Supply Sergeant would not allow the exchange. Upon calling the Ordinance Officer, I find that he could not issue it either.

We must tag bags showing: rank, name, serial number, unit code, and symbol number. I am to leave on #11 at 11:00pm.

May 10, 1942 – Finally left Fort Dix at 8:30pm from Bldg T-6-30 (officers' quarters.) I brought along forward echelon and HQ Company. The equipment strapped to us was something very funny. Especially a lieutenant of the Medical Corps who had all that I had plus his medical kits in case someone was hurt on the way up. I saw the *SS Normandie* on its side in the water.

We boarded the *Queen Mary* at 4:00am. There are six of us the stateroom, M-28. Captain Hugelet is the only one that I knew before, however all in the room are from the 1st AD.

May 11, 1942 – I am Police Officer of the boat, which has me in charge of policing the ship. There must be a million jobs on the ship. Several of the officers are very interesting. Major Bube, the Chief Mess Officer, Mr. Wright, the ship's Deck Officer, Mr. Foggarity, the 2nd Mess Officer. They have 9,975 troops and about 1,000 sailors aboard. The boat needs paint and is chipping very badly. She has just returned from Australia.

I am too tired at night to do anything.

May 12, 1942 – I had one hell of a time trying to keep details moving. The 1st AD is part of the VAC and the policing detail is with the 13th. Maj. Russell is doing a very good job and working like hell. Maj. Cairns is trying too hard. We had a mix-up in instructions, but I may have them wrong. Maj. Pritchard is okay. He's a graduate from West Point in 1933.

The boat is armed with several guns. The largest is 6 inches. Trash is emptied twice daily. She has 10 or 12 decks for quarters and are they crowded! Soldiers are even sleeping in the swimming pool. Boat drill is a mess. If it should be needed, I bet that 75% will not make it.

The inspection of my areas is very difficult. One man defecated on the floor of the cocktail lounge after he could not find his way to the toilet. The meals are excellent. The cavalry seems to have an edge on all jobs here.

May 13, 1942 – Stewed about trying to get ship policed. I made blackout inspections with the 3rd Officer, John Hughes. He is a very likeable chap. He has two sisters and one brother. His address is: John Hughes, Senior 3rd Officer, "Queen Mary" – 38 Mayville Rd., Liverpool 18. His father is D.P. Hughes (Staff Manager) The New Zeal and Shipping Company, 18 Water Street, Liverpool. Home phone: Wavertree 2384. Hughes is very much interested in horses. He has a horse in Australia now.

The *Queen Mary* is 1,008 feet long and 109 feet wide.

Cigarettes on board are 7 cents. No convoy now.

Several are getting sea-sick. One man was so sick that he tasted hair.

<u>May 14, 1942</u> – Still no convoy. A real wind is blowing. We have a good bunch in our cabin. Capts. Quest, Blodgettt, Moore, and Hugclet.

One man said: "Why don't they tell us where we are going (Ireland) so that at least we will know where we would have gone if we are sunk."

Rumor has it that we land in Glasgow on Saturday. An MP was asked by an officer: "Where is this group of men from?" He replied, "Sir, they just got on – okay!"

This police job is just plain hell. I hope Betty is not worrying. I am glad she does not know what boat I am on as it is rumored that we are reported sunk.

Figure 1-1   Captain Lumpkin on board the Queen Mary en route to Ireland

<u>May 15, 1942</u> – A British convoy came up. Four destroyers and one cruiser. I had another talk with Hughes last night. He gave me a bottle of beer. The cleaning job was better today. We had some trouble because of duplicates of duty and

responsibility. However, some lieutenants had no sense of responsibility and no sense of duty.

<u>May 16, 1942</u> – We finally reached the roadstead at Lubnock, Scotland on the Firth of Clyde. It is one of the most beautiful countries I have seen yet. There were two awe-inspiring moments to remember. One was on reaching land, about four hours before dark and seeing the very neat and green hillside of the valley with the bright sunset and clear air, the ships, etc. The *Aquitania* and the *Britannic* are here. The barrage balloons are up and very pretty. A motor blimp took out to sea. Another very memorable scene – at officer's call, General Ward thanking us for the work of bringing the group through safely and Father Martin offering a prayer of thanks to God for a safe trip.

Some British came aboard and messed up all plans. Some of us go to the *Aquitania* and some go to Ireland. I am fortunate and am with the General and his Ireland group. I am surprised at the amount of counter-decisions made by this group. They decide to do one thing and publish an order and then before the ink is dry, it is passed down to the men – then they publish another. There were four changes of policy made on one item yesterday. Will this continue throughout the war or will we get smart? The trouble is not thinking the problem through.

<u>May 17, 1942</u> – After much stewing about cleaning the boat, etc., we were able to leave the *Queen Mary* about 3:15pm on a "butterfly" tug named the *"Isle of Mann"* that had been used at Dunkirk. Four of her crew of ten had a Distinguished Service Cross. We spent the night on the boat and arrived at Belfast at 9:00am the next morning. I found that I had lost my raincoat. This is sure bad as it was almost new and Ireland is reported as being very wet.

<u>May 18, 1942</u> – As usual, the plans are all messed up. They drove off and left the Division staff and were they burnt up!

However, we finally got on one of the dinky trains. These trains reminded me of my kid's electric train. The Navy had a lunch for us at Belfast Station. It was delicious but served by two of the most homely women yet. The coffee was good and I was hungry as hell. I couldn't buy a paper since I had no English money.

Arrived in Ballykinlar. This place had been used as a concentration camp for Germans. No mattresses, blankets, sheets, or pillows. There were no preparations made for us. The food is very plain. The British certainly have us in line with their plans.

May 19, 1942 – We completed the obtaining of equipment for officers and quarters. We had to move some AT's (British women soldiers) out to make room for General Oliver and his combat command (CC). Maj. Price, of the British Army, was very pleasant to deal with. Of all things to beef about – no toilet, no coal, no toilet paper. Drove the MP "Beep" (smaller jeep.)

Col. Hasbrouck said the firing at Dix was okay. We will try to finish up when we get ammunition. I helped Col. Ginn, the Division Surgeon, start his fire. He is from Richmond, Virginia and is okay.

I heard today that we can have cameras after I had sent mine back.

I had a bath – the first since leaving the boat – and it was cold and wet.

May 20, 1942 – Quite a day! A thousand details to correct. Came on duty as Staff Duty Officer. About midnight, someone, possibly the IRA, tried to cross the sentry line. He was fired upon several times but got away.

Maj. Hoy and Howze are sure swell. My equipment came in (trunk, bedroll, and suitcase.) A friendly patrol boat entered Dundrum Bay and I had to warn all of our troops – some job.

May 21, 1942 – Rooming with Capt. Frank Wilcox. He was a cop at one time. It is not dark at 11:30pm. We eat at 7:00pm.

The British are hard to deal with at times. They take care of everything in time – only it is too late. They need to hustle along. The houses of the farmers are poor – thatched roofs, etc. We are learning the English money system by playing poker. Some try to time raising the pot 1 shilling 6 pence.

There really was a problem when it was found that Maj. Cochran had left off names of three officers. Col. Hasbrouck has directed me to write a letter thanking the British for the bedding, etc.

May 22, 1942 – Good day. Solved several problems. Coming back from headquarters, I saw a parade by one of the units of the 13th. It almost brought tears to my eyes to hear the *Star-Spangled Banner*. It was a time to remember – at twilight against an English military post setting, the US and British flags in the breeze, and the horse (called "Whin") and the Tommies with their funny salute. Had some more dealings with Bugs Cairs. He lacks something, but I do not know what. Col. Hamilton is sure a peach. He is a real soldier and has leadership, brains, and tact. Capt. Sawyer has some goons for platoon leaders. I hope to hell that I never get that company. It is a good thing that I keep this diary. I can write things down and it keeps track of the days.

May 23, 1942 – Rained almost all day. Chuck got in late from Belfast. His descriptions are a scream. For example, this morning, "Go get one of those goons to screw it up." I thought that I would die laughing.

May 24, 1942 – Had a swell trip with Maj. Cochran and Tyson to Dundrum, Newcastle, and another small town, Kilkeel. They have the most beautiful shrubs in this section. Stopped and had lunch at the Royal Downs Country Club and met a Mr. Battle. He was a very pleasant fellow and was much interested in horsepower and fishing. The beer was okay, but had a different taste from any that I had ever had before. This guy Cochran is okay after all. He is a fine chap and smart. Tyson is true blue. Saw some of the Irish lassies – are they homely. They should stop the war and take a bath and police up. The goons have screwed the detail again – they forgot the General and C-S room and was it a mess!

It did not rain today for the first time in many days.

May 25, 1942 – The General gave his staff hell for being late to drill (exercise.) We had it coming. There were too many late. Today worked better in many respects.

May 26, 1942 – General Ward has a crow all boxed up. Chuck and I are thinking of getting a goat to use as a scavenger, a plow horse, and a general nuisance.

This is some country: very pretty, very cold, very damp, women are unattractive, and food is scarce.

The British do everything the hard way. All coal is dumped in one pile and packed out to units. A truck passes by us and cannot stop but must go down to pile and dump and then fill up and return to us!

May 27, 1942 – Drove the light tank – real fun. I wish that I had more time to follow through on this. We are definitely moving to Castlewellan, a 98 room castle with huts for 600 men on the place. Some layout.

May 28, 1942 – Had some real fun this morning. We went to Newcastle, about 30 miles, to see Maj. Hill, a British officer. We had cakes and coffee. The first attractive lady that I've seen in Ireland came in the shop. The shop has a very pretty view of the Irish Sea. Had a long talk with Mr. Annesly, the owner of the castle. He would not let us use certain rooms. A typical Englishman, but seems to be okay. Miller is a hell of a lot of fun. The Provost Marshall of the British Army came down today and we all had a conference. Things are picking up. No one wants to move into the castle at present as heat and toilet facilities are nil.

<u>May 28, 1942</u> – Won 3£ at poker.

<u>May 29, 1942</u> – I went to Belfast to help buy china for officer's mess. Met a Pat O'Brien who could certainly soak it up. Got back at 3:00am. It was a good idea to have someone to soak it up as they were ready to get drunk.

Wired Betty and Col. Stribling.

<u>May 30, 1942</u> – What a grind – got to bed at 1am after preparing for inspection.

<u>May 31, 1942</u> – Inspected by General Ward and Maj. Howze. The troops were lousy – it was a sight.

<u>June 1, 1942</u> – I went to Castlewellan with Maj. Miller, Lt. Ulmer, and Lt. Jacques. It is some place. Capt. Bothwell, the British HQ Commandant, showed us about and explained some of the problems: Water must be chlorinated, light system is overloaded, heat is by hearth only. A very pretty place with a 100-acre lawn. Shrubs, trees, plants, etc. are worth at least $1,000,000. Some are in bloom and are very pretty. Almost all shrubs are tree-high. The formal garden has about 20-25 acres and full of boxwood, flowers, vegetables, etc., etc. – something from every climate – Australia & New Zealand. We are just out of Castlewellan (town) and four miles from Newcastle which is on Dundrum Bay.

Played poker with Col. Zutter, Majs. P. Brown, Hightower, Cochran, and Pritchard, and Lts. Green and Schmidt. Won 17 shillings.

<u>June 2, 1942</u> – Had a half day off and went to Holywood with Capt. White, Lt. Eddy (who knows Tom Hook) and three others. Came back through Belfast and at the Abercorn. Stopped by Embassy Club and talked to some people who had been blitzed. One Madge O'Neil had lost her home and

Figure 1-2 Castlewellan Castle in Northern Ireland

father and still had a rare sense of humor. Saw a Negro dancing with a white girl! She was a cabaret singer.

June 3, 1942 – Tired.

June 4, 1942 – Nothing eventful.

June 5, 1942 – Visited Castlewellan again.

June 6, 1942 – Visited Castlewellan once more. It really is a beautiful place.

June 7, 1942 – Worked on getting castle ready. Much dirt. The British are not clean.

June 7, 1942 – Same as 06-07.

June 9, 1942 – The General was well pleased and complimented Maj. Miller and me for the work in getting the staff moved. We sure put the dog on. Orderlies, guards, trumpets, etc.

June 10, 1942 – Usual duties.

June 11, 1942 – Belfast to take laundry and try to get canvas for a painting. Met a British captain and his wife, "Candy Bar", who had been a commando. Came back at black-out with no lights on car at all. It was hell at night.

June 12, 1942 – General Ward marched us up to the top of a mountain – a real view, but it wore us out!

June 13, 1942 – Stole a gong (used during air raid) from the 13th. They will scream to high heaven.

Got four letters!!! Betty, Ferguson, Stribling, and Bohannon.

June 14, 1942 – Job is getting easier. Made a reconnaissance with Maj. Miller – some job those light tanks. He is a real egg.

June 15, 1942 – More mail – usual routine duties.

June 16, 1942 – To Belfast with McElhenny and back at 4:30am – some trip. Drove back in a bus with a large bag of gas on top – went up on Belfast & County Down Railroad. Some train – reminds me of an electric train.

June 17, 1942 – A Chinese General visited with 1st AD – we are getting to be a showplace. Tired as hell – have a "crick" in my neck.

June 18, 1942 – More mail and letters of Anne and Tony – good snaps. Heard from Betty that she had received my cable and that Stribling had read his at Commencement.

Went to Newcastle for a mop-up demonstration in a village by the 6th – very good. The demonstration with canister in a 37mm was a flop. Had one hell of a time arranging and quartering Col. Fritzscle. Had to move several officers. Went to Newcastle at night for a dance – could not find it. McElhenny and I came back after Chuck looking for me.

June 19, 1942 – Made a reconnaissance for air raid shelters and found none. Went to Belfast in afternoon. Met British Commander & Mrs. Baidwood and Lt. Gazel, a Polish naval lieutenant. They went nuts over an orange. Would like to see an onion. I promised them one.

June 20, 1942 – One of our tanks, in prep for the King and party, tore down a wall – it was rebuilt by an old lady about 65-70 years old. She was paid – but what does that mean to her? War is sure hell on the poor folks!

June 21, 1942 – Preparing for His Majesties. Who is responsible for what? They sure plan and change plans of this. Road to area passes through a bog. A medium has torn it up. An Engineer Battalion was up all night getting it fixed and the goons drove over it again. Now it is torn up but there is a promise of fixing it up again. It was reported as a "small hole" but it was over 2,000 yards long. Went to Belfast – took 3 onions in to the Braidwoods – they were not in.

June 22, 1942 – Preparing for His Majesty. Doing quite a bit of Hqrs. Commandant work. Borrowed large tent and put it up backwards.

June 23, 1942 – Road to Doogloo busted again – engineers fixed it again – that outfit catches hell.

June 24, 1942 – Wrote fire order – posted as General Order #1 Camp Castlewellan.

June 25, 1942 – Big day here. Assisted Maj. Hoy at Tyrellen Range. King and Queen seem to be very nice. Met Mr. Marcel Wallenstein, 3 Johnson's Court, Flut Street, London, E.C.4. Phone Central 3671. He knows Sid Houston (with Kansas City Star), Frank Poindexter and all of the Kansas City outfit – promised to send kids a hello. This was some day. They practically tore the place down for them. Tanks, guns, battles, equipment, reviews, drills, etc., etc.

Quite a joke about Andy McAuttey, the local barman who we think is Bn. Commander for the IRA.

Found out that Maj. Hoy visited Cole L. Blease at Boscobel in 1925. There was a whole bunch of the press present. The Queen was very pleasant and the King quite a soldier. Lady

Spencer was present also – quite attractive in a pale way – not much life.

Visitors present: King and Queen Lascelles, Winant, Piers Legh, Morrison, Generals Bradshaw, Bates, Ward, Hartle, Hollar, Collins, Oliver, McQuillan, Martelli, Crawford, and a whole slew of others. The column was almost snafued by the 2nd convoy starting early. It was solved by having it backed into a side road.

Today is my birthday – 34 years old.

Major Juffod, the Special Services Officer, is going to the Beach Landing School – they tell me that he did not want to go. My increase in salary for foreign service is $20. There is talk to counting inactive time as full time – I certainly hope that it is true.

A plane came over very early this morning – about 20-25 thousand feet over. Reported as German. No sound but left a streak from exhaust – enough to make the General ask the C-S to have the orders published relative to bombing and air raid – they have recently been changed.

The Maintenance Battalion (Col. Grubbs) is sending a wrecker over to hang a gate at entrance – one of the medium tanks eased through the gate too fast and the gate was smashed. Col. Grubbs could pass as the brother of either Mary or Jake Gilmer (my in-laws.)

June 27, 1942 – Went to Mourne Park to see Engineer Bn. have its demonstrations. Tank mines, rifle grenades, mine detection, etc. – very interesting. Came back to find that all hell had broken loose. Chuck is in Belfast – we are to go on maneuver on Monday and practice a bivouac. We are short of rolling stock. Rumor is thick that we move out into a new position – maybe into a jump-off position. Went to a show, "Rebecca," the first in months, with two Red Cross men. A French military party came over to look at our equipment. About 50 men were gassed badly while driving a convoy of tanks, etc. from the docks. Might have been from the exhaust or maybe sabotage.

June 28, 1942 – Went to church this am – first time since over here. It reminded me of Vesper Service at the Academy (MMA.) Wrote two letters to Betty and lost them. Chuck back and everything is going okay – for how long? Remember the church service – a Catholic priest in a Mission Hat and about 10 men present. "Onward Christian Soldiers", etc.

June 29, 1942 – Went to Newcastle – had drinks with Capt. Campbell and Mrs. Cotton (Blondie) who is a great and good friend of Chuck's – remembered his leading the King's convoy. Capt. Campbell is in the British Army. Maj. Haut of the French Hqrs. was along – he is a good guy.

June 30, 1942 – Had a march and bivouac overnight – a very good experience. There seems to be several (Wilcox, an expoliceman of Cleveland, Lyman, and others who are beefing about the food.) Many errors made on the march.

July 1, 1942 – Got paid – received a box of cigarettes and a coat from Betty – sure sweet of her to wrap and send them. The coat fits me to a tee. Met with Hqrs. Co. on practice bivouac and march tomorrow. Several new promotions. Best – Brown P., Cochran, Howze, Curtis, et al. Worst – Wilcox who is not quite a gentleman.

Made a reconnaissance for the selection of a bivouac and found a hunting lodge on the estate – walls about three feet thick – richly furnished in its day. Wish that Betty could see it. The jeeps can certainly travel over any terrain. Got a card from the Braidwoods – want me to come up for tea! Met a Capt. Seabright who is the British Claims Officer.

July 2, 1942 – Made a march in the rain – put the tops on and then had to take them down – the C/S ruling.
Wet through and through but problem worked okay. Used the convoy radio today – almost got some of the words mixed up:

Figure 1-3 Officer's group photo at Castelwellan

From left to right: 1st Row: Maj. Sidney Clarke White Jr., Maj. Kenneth W. Tracy, Lt. Col. Hamilton H. Howze, Lt. Col. Grant A. Williams, Col. L. Holmes Ginn Jr., Col. Robert V. Maraist, Major General Orlando Ward, Col. Robert W. Hasbrouck, Col. Clarence C. Benson, Lt. Col. Homer P. Dittemore, Lt. Col. Edward R. Martin, Lt. Col. Percy H. Brown Jr., Lt. Col. Loris R Cochran, Lt. Col. James R. Pritchard; 2nd Row: Capt. Tony B. Lumpkin, Maj. Wm. R. C. Ford, Maj. Wm. C. Farmer, Maj. Wm. S. McElhenny, Maj. Franklin W. Patton, Maj. Chas. W. Miller, Lt. Col. Max Franklin McAllister, Maj. Joseph E. James, Lt. Col. Cecil C. Wilson, Lt. Col. M. M. Brown, Maj. Alfred M. Koster, Maj. Frank Pomeroy Wilcox Jr., Capt. Walter S. McClennan, Capt. Loren D. Buttolph; 3rd Row: Maj. Roy L. Hickox, Capt. Thomas L. Griffith, Capt. Wm. L. Schmidt, 1st Lt. Theodore Dastoli, Capt. Harry E. Lyman, Capt. Frederick K. Hughes, 1st Lt. Edward O. Jacques, Capt. Gilbert F. Broders, Capt. Sydney S. Combs, 1st Lt. Boswell R. Ulmer Jr., 1st Lt. Paul P. Byrne, 1st Lt. Ernest C. Hatfield, 1st Lt. Kermit J. Wilson, Capt. Paul Wesley Hanshew; 4th Row: 1st Lt. Edward H. Come, Capt. Herbert L. Cantrill, 1st Lt. Robert L. May, 1st Lt. Henry Gordon Green, Capt. Richard F. Cecil, Capt. Robert H. Oppelt, Capt. Homer E. Long

"Roger" for received, "Wilco" for will comply. Our Staff Duty Officer, remainder of echelon arrived with rest of tanks and half-tracks – this puts most of our equipment over here. "Atlantic," a problem about attacking North Ireland is coming off soon.

Looks as though the time is near and we are to start out. Chuck starting his diary from mine. Col. Taylor, Capt. Patton, and Capt. Koster arriving. Koster is okay. Maj. White also here.

British have a phone that shows by a light whether the wires are tapped or not.

As the new officers are arriving they are demanding more and more. As they become acclimated to the conditions, their demands drop off and they fall into the routine of the matter – there seems to be no end to the demands made by some.

July 3, 1942 – Clawed about trying to contact Mr. Anesly and have use of his large mirrors – no luck. McQuillan and the General went to England. Chuck to Belfast in the C-S car.

July 4, 1942 – Went to Belfast with Buck Halfield – had coat repaired – had one hell of a good time. Met up with some people who have invited us to the beach for the weekend. Remember some steaks that were too tough to eat – we traded and ate cold tongue. Saw some of the sights of Belfast. Met a captain who is General Hartle's aid – was he screaming because he could not obtain a drink at 1:00AM in the morning! Woke up the whole hotel. Remember the home we visited and the small living room. Rode on a "tram" – a 2 ½ story street car – came back in a taxi using a large gas bag filled with gas. Bag of gas is slightly larger than a can and is good for about 30 miles. Natives are short fruit, onions, sugar, and candy. Heard that Gen. Kelly had been called up.

The Commander-in-Chief of the Polish Forces visits us tomorrow. He is General Sikorski[1].

Getting ready for "Atlantic," a maneuver for Northern Ireland.

July 5, 1942 – Getting ready for my first field maneuver. Made a trip with Capt. Griffith and the Signal Company Officer for a bivouac for forward echelon. Used an area occupied by the British – an old race track with a nice steeplechase course – very little cover. The Jeep drove down a gully that a mule could not have made. After much reconnaissance and arguing, we finally selected the arrangement. A Battalion Sgt. was there – he was certainly an "old timer."

July 6, 1942 – More visitors – we are getting to be a show-off group. War has started and our guards are alerted. Much preparation and ready to move at 1000 hours. Order finally came through – we leave at 1930 hours. Much leaving the Hqrs. Commandant out of the light as to when, rules of war, etc. Eat at 0530 and leave at 0730 promptly – Chuck put me in charge of the column! We travel 450 yards and find the first "Snafu." The 13th has not crossed our I.P. – their column is about 2 ½ hours longer. We finally leave after being fired upon by planes. Chuck takes over the column. One group of which has gone ahead. Hoy called Howze to inform him of the first snafu. Used the field set. We travel in blackout and arrive safely to find that the forward echelon of the group has already moved and the arrangement has to be changed slightly. Finally checked everything as to outposts and get in bed about 0230 hours – slept in a mission hut with Eddy, Chuck and Mullins who has the platoon of 6th Infantry for C.P. security.

---

[1] Tragically, General Sikorski would be killed in a controversial plane crash in Gibraltar exactly one year from this date. His body was exhumed in 2008 as the investigation into his death continues.

July 7, 1942 – Up and at them rearranging the outposts and their sitting around. Hasbrouck raised hell because I did not accompany the first group. However, I find that the screaming does not seem so bad after the actual fight starts – the primadonnas have something to do! After arguing for 30 minutes, they decide to move out at 2030 hours. Griffith and Hughes and Signal Officer and I are sent ahead to reconnaissance a bivouac area. We had to bust through several columns – mediums gong like hell fire down a narrow road in opposite direction – it was some time. Finally decided that H.Q. could not reach there and so we start back – Griffith and one of the "Rover Boys" are captured – in the meantime Chuck has selected a position further back and we turn out of the column to join him. Right at a R.J. – planes are overhead – we move in. After dark (about 2100 hours) we are told to select another position. So, we start out and run right into the enemy. Finally, we get back with one prisoner. So they argue whether to go or remain and get further from the road – finally decide to go. Got the group alerted and ready to pull out – ran 1 ½ miles at top speed to catch up with my car – Chuck leading in jeep. It is almost midnight.

July 8, 1942 – It is darker than hell. We are actually back of the enemy lines and plan to go still further back. Scout car leading the column and following are Chuck's jeep. The scout car leaves the road once and Capt. Sawyer pulls past to take the lead. Rest of column did not follow – someone asleep. Luckily, I catch it before very long and halt. In the meantime, Chuck has passed an RJ and I do not know which way to go – so call him and explain. Send a cycle back for column. Finally get to together again. Run into several other columns and are delayed further – big problem is in getting other drivers and occupants awake. One column ahead was lost – someone went to sleep and did not follow. Finally sneak past lines of patrols and break into the open. Bivouac on the road. Trains come in behind us – everything is in the trains except motor cycles – there seems to be a little of everything collected or having been lost. We form a large loop in the road net. Halt is at 0600 hours and ready to move again if it is necessary. One car reported to ask another if they were moving and got this answer: "No you are just in front of me." Breakfast at about 0800 hours. Game called off – set up outposts – pitched a tent and fell asleep with Hoy and Chuck. Hoy is sure a swell guy. Tired as hell. Trains still coming in – Kent arrives with five tanks. They decide to move out so we load up and wait about three hours to tail in behind part of the 13th. Pull out and go about 1 ½ miles and wait another three hours to get road priority. Really get going about 1700 hours but held up again at 1800 hours. Have supper while halted and move out. Chuck turns over the column to me and I miss a turn outside of Lisburn. So, we turn around a small road and start again – raining like hell. Chuck and I trying to follow the route. Run into the 13th again – a narrow road, black-out, raining – some time. Got into the Castle at 0200 hours of next day.

<u>July 9, 1942</u> – Tired as hell – Tex Hightower says that he is going over to the 1st Armored Regiment.

Reflection on lessons of the last few days:
- Do not follow front car necessarily
- The <u>Practical</u> and the <u>Theoretical</u> are not aligned
- Reconnoiter area before making a bivouac
- Do not try to do other man's job
- Tanks slow down a column and should be fairly close together, maintain a constant speed and keep distance

Work from 1000 hours on – the 13th tried to pass some Prisoners of War over to us – are they nuts? Prima Donnas are too tired to do much beefing today – the prize of all – a Lt. trying to have one man awakened to carry his bedroll up.

<u>July 10, 1942</u> – Chuck goes to Belfast with laundry. I have been appointed on a special court martial and a summary court martial all in the same order #147. Buckingham from the 13th

came over. He seems to be an okay guy. Mailed package to Tone, Anne, and Martha – hope that they get there.

July 11, 1942 – Someone got into Lord Annesley's wine cellar – Chuck and I had to scent and chase it down – his articles stored there were priceless. China, glasses, champagne, etc. – and Lord A. is slap happy if there ever was one. General Ward had a critique on the problem.

T5 William Nikolin is now clerk in Terry's place. (Terry died while we were on maneuvers.) Nikolin is a graduate of Sorbonne.

A good letter from Betty: Kelly is on active duty, Beans overseas; Stribling is now assistant PMS-T. Some job for him after all of the cracks to me when I was there. Col. D., the I.G., is certainly a stickler for exact terms in reports.

July 12, 1942 – Quite a day – "Lord" Annesley and a couple of the British – Mr. King and Mr. Norton – came over so that we could requisition the rest of the Castle – Lady Mabel Annesley would reel around the mug at the way we discussed moving her articles. A stuffed python would have made a real object d'art to put in "Seuss'" bed. It was coiled and ready to strike. We may move our office. Nice talk and some bull-slinging done at mess.

July 13, 1942 – Both Hqrs. and Service Co's give a going over – it seems to have done some good. Lt. Eddy gave me some lessons in motor-cycling – doesn't seem to be too hard – except the control of the gas feed – the motor has a tendency to race – however it can be mastered. Long bull session with Sgt. McWhinney, The Royal Ulster Constabulary, gave us some sidelights on the life of the people – 100 per month is a very good wage here – no one ever gets drunk – all seem to be more highly civilized in that respect. He is a sort of father and guardian of the flock for the town of Castlewellan. Seems to be on our side.

July 14, 1942 – Quite a time. Mr. Annesby and Mr. King came over preparing to move. Had a long talk with the local saloon keepers relative to the prices and sale of whiskey to our boys. Got some pictures, from Betty, of the children – wish that I had one of Betty. Went to the show last night with Al Koster. Maj. Hughes and a Lt. from the CWS – pleasant men and seem to be okay. Remember the python, lion's skull, and wine cellar of the castle.

July 15, 1942 – Made several arrangements with moving quarters about the Castle and grounds – quite a bit of fun with Lady Mabel Annesley's invitations to a tea from 3:30-6:30 August 12, 1926. Had about 20 war correspondents in for dinner – sat next to Ed Beattie of the UP & Quentin Reynolds of *Collier's Weekly* – very interesting talk. Reynolds had been in Africa and had some interesting experiences – both were out of cigarettes so I gave them a couple of packs – seem to appreciate them very much. Some real talkers – was very sorry to see them go.

Col. Dittemore is raising a stink about our way of doing things – says that we are not coordinated – ah well – what the hell. I've had a cough for the past few days – hope that it can clear itself up soon. Hope the hell that I can read all of this one of these days and understand what it is all about! Chuck is kicking to Cochran about organizing this as a battalion. Hope that it goes through.

Chapter 2

War-Games

July 16, 1942 – Day spent in trying to get everything lined up for the rat race, CPX (war-game) "London." Orders are vague and incomplete. The thing is so clear to the G-3 Section that they think that it is clear to the others. Special Services had a show – they have a lot to learn about running a machine! Got all maps together – marked the route from an overlay that did not fit our scale maps – what in the hell are we going to do when we run up against the "real McCoy?"

July 17, 1942 – Ready to leave at 0600 hours and had to wait on – of all people – the Bull (C-S)! Pulled out at 0615 and had the route changed at 0730 – what an army. Parked on the road and was the General and C-S up in the air! Maj. Curtis and I were sent ahead to find a new bivouac area – which they did not use. So we pull out and go after another area. Finally locate one and put them in rather a tight fit but got them in and set up an outpost about 400-1,000 yards out. Put them to bed. Felt like hell all day. Had a cold and a cough and touch of intestinal flu.

July 18, 1942 – Had a commando raid pulled on us – lost 1 tank, 1 ½ track, 10 trucks, 40 men, and 100 wounded. Outpost by mortar squad of 6th Inf. was too close. Another raid later in the day resulted in a complete victory for us. We captured the entire lot. Decided to pull out at 1500 hours. Curtis and I went ahead and tried all fields – finally found one about five minutes before the column got there. Put them in and had supper. Radio system would not work so we decided to move the C.P. This time Col. Howze, Maj. Hoy and I go forward. Hunted until dark and finally put them in a field entirely different from the field that I had selected – was glad that they found that it is no way an easy job to find a field large enough for our vehicles and umpire vehicles and the liaison vehicles and all stray vehicles that come along. Pulled all tanks and trucks in but the last ½ track busted the gate to hell and back. What a CP! It started to rain and one scout car caved into the ditch. Some of the sights – a medium tank in a peat bog – the cutting of peat in the mountain. Talk with the man at the lodge at one of the castles – the word "plantation" is used here for a way under the Castle-Grange.

<u>July 19, 1942</u> – General called the CPX off and we head for home. "Chief" let me take over – sure glad that he did. Pulled through a very pretty valley just east of Castle Dromore. Peat bogs everywhere. Ran into Trains, Hqrs., and Supply Battalions and 701 – they seemed to be everywhere. Finally got in at 1930 hours. One of the best remarks yet – Osbourne – our scout car driver was hungry and he said: "If they don't hurry up and feed us it will be too bad – I've sure been looking at some of these fat kids." Quite a character – like a livery horse – he steps on it when headed home.

<u>July 20, 1942</u> – Recovered from the CPX all okay – took laundry in at 1300 hours. Had a nice time just walking the streets – quite a number of commandos about – ran into one from Scotland – about the Firth of Clyde. He and a Royal Engineer ("Honi Soit Qui Mal Y Pense" – motto) had a good time. Engineer's wife along and was she full of the baloney – works at the U.S. Embassy and tried to impress all that she was

hot stuff – was a no good stuffed shirt if there ever was one. While eating at the Abercorn, met a Mr. Blunder (ph. 25831) – nice chap – was in road building business – several people came in and brought their dogs who remained under the table! A good day and a good time doing nothing.

July 21, 1942 – A rest day – spent day learning to ride a motor cycle – can now ride cross-country. Went to show with Buck Hatfield – a good guy from New Hampshire. Making several moves about the Castle – the AG section is wanting to spread again – it seems that they cannot be satisfied with any space that is allotted to them. At least 10 loads of mail have not been received – hope that it gets in.

July 22, 1942 – One hell of a day. "D" is sure gunning for Chuck and myself in this office. He is snooping about trying to catch us out on a limb. Have tried all day to get a few moves made and complete the taking over of the remainder of the castle. One man was caught out in woods with a girl from Belfast – hiding in a cabin – what will these soldiers think of next.

July 23, 1942 – Practiced an "alert" – Hqrs. and Service Companies did okay. Got the rest of the moving done. Received notice to sit on a court martial tomorrow at 1:30pm – Capt. Sawyer is to be sent to Base Command. Chuck says that the General wants me to be put in his place. Aunt Mame's package comes.

July 24, 1942 – No letters – they must have been sunk. Bill Ruther is acting Chief of Staff – he sure is a swell egg – knows Mac Graham. Capt. Sawyers is to be relieved. Moved office into castle.

July 25, 1942 – Letters from Mother, Tone, Mark & Jack! We made Honor Rating! What a relief – would have been a pity to have lost it last year. Hear that Jack Carn has had a stroke – too bad. We sure butt our heads about in this Hqrs. All seem to be trying to squeeze the most rank from the war – some actually hope that it will last more than this year – I hope that the damn thing is over pretty damn soon so we can get back to the school (MMA.) Got $150 for uniform allowance – bought a blouse for £7-180 – not as good a grade of cloth as in my old one. Soldiers have too much time on hands. Frank Capra of *Collier's Weekly* was other guy with Quentin Reynolds.

July 26, 1942 – Nice trip on cycle to Newcastle, Kilkeel, and return – cycle riding is some nuts – rode in rain until water entering shoe finally came out of collar. Larger part of day spent in rewrite of alarm, gas, call & air raid orders. Heard from Tone, Jack, and Mark.

July 27, 1942 – Rewrite orders again – gave Hickox a buzz on cycle – to the consternation of all. Had a CPX posture on grounds and vehicles cut ruts in road. Went to Kinkeel with McElhenny – getting better on the cycle.

July 28, 1942 – A British Stock Company gave us a play & song & dance act – very good. Had a hell of a party after – Wilcox, Farmer, Lyman cracked it – Chuck and Ulmer did the work and C. would not give in and join – girl ate in our mess – certainly livened things up. The comedian had been in Hollywood – the piano player was a funny person – out with the drummer.

July 29, 1942 – Here we go again – in Newcastle – McE, Chuck, and I at Cotton's with Davis and Campbell and a couple of the Stock Company players. Lead man was exactly like Fred Astaire. Party started with a bang and went on and on – home about 3am and at them immediately.

July 30, 1942 – Practiced a parade-run combination – some argument as to how it was to be done. Went to Belfast with Lt. Jacques to take cleaning and laundry and buy some electrical supplies – Jacques ran into a very cute number in the electrical shop and stayed in. I ran into an Irish Commando and did nothing except walk the streets. Saw a sorry sight – a girl about 8 years old carrying in a baby in a shawl almost her size – both in rags.

July 31, 1942 – Got up at 6:00am and paraded for the General. Everything went off okay. We have an Irish cat in the office that was left by the British that is a scream – wants to be petted all of the time – howls for attention just like a dog – jumps in your lap – sleeps in the "out" basket and is a pest in general – but we keep her just the same – sure wish that we had a tom for her.

August 1, 1942 – Did not take pay this month will let the govt. keep it for me as they can do a better job than I can. On duty as the Staff Duty Officer and nothing happened. Raining like hell – unable to see Col. Benson today – hope that he can help me out.

August 2, 1942 – Battalion went to church – did nothing about desk. Breakfast was a few minutes late – sweated a few of the details out – found that it is awfully hard for some officers to say: "I do not know!" Got another card from Braidwoods.

Rather a dull day – rained. Morale starting to go down – we have nothing to lead up to. Lt. Davis in charge of Hqrs. Co. now and is doing okay. Wrote a letter to firm in Belfast relative to boilers and a tank made for water.

August 3, 1942 – Had a visitor (British Brigadier General) to spend night with us. Mc got all excited about whether he had a bedroll or not – finally turned out that he did. Maj. Sid White from Texas is sure a swell fellow. Chuck is sick – has a cold and feels like hell.

August 4, 1942 – Chuck sick and ying-yanged with White and Gillours regarding the CPX "Defiance" – are they giving me the run around or not? Got a letter from "Beans" Cutter – he is in England!

August 5, 1942 – Getting ready for CPX. Chuck is up but feels like hell – hope that he is better. Looks like I am to try running this one. Hope that I do not snafu this one – he is so anxious to have this recognized by all as a battalion. Col. H. is going back to the States as a brigadier general – Fritsch is going back on account of his health. It looks almost like they are leaving the sinking ship? Hope that I can wrangle an artillery position out of this somewhere. Finally pulled out at 1730 hours for Long Kish – the same old race course as we stayed before. Kelly (tanks) and Davis (Co. Com. Hqrs. Co.) went with me. Just as we pulled into bivouac we found that some British were already there. However we shoved in and made room.

August 6, 1942 – Major W. B. Malone % Cox and Kings, Pall Mall, London or Hqrs. Guards Armored Division, Horne Forces is with me in our scout car – an interesting character – an "idler" before the war but paying for it now – not married and seems to be a hell of a good egg. He is no trouble at all and seems to be getting a hell of a kick out of it. Went in to Grand Central one night. Today spent in arranging outposts and usual garrison duties. Windshields should be down and latrines should be dug immediately. I was sent forward to reconnoiter a new bivouac area on Lyles Hill – the 1st was just moving out when I got there. Cover was good so we decided to move in. Came back and got column started but ran into the Division Trains. Finally pulled them and put them in about 2300 hours.

August 7, 1942 – Arranged outposts and set up camp a little better. Eddy and Kelly and Davis and 6th Infantry officers were a hell of a lot of help. We are winning the battle but Maraist says that they are not using artillery correctly. Lost two gas trucks and had to use Signal Company trucks for the job of bringing up gas.

August 8, 1942 – Maj. Malone left us. Started in and ran into Mtn. Battalion. Changed routes and came in over an unimproved road. (Scared hell out of Cochran who had logistics.) Got in for lunch. Chuck had certainly cleaned up the Castle – painted the floors and it all looked swell.

August 9, 1942 – Went to church in the Graze – Chaplain Hanshaw held the services. Our "wine merchants" seem to hit quite a bit of publicity in the papers even though we kept it a hush-hush affair.

August 10, 1942 – Parade for Col. Hasbrouck, the C-S, who is to go back to the States as a brigadier general – Chuck and I were almost "plastered" during the parade. However, Col. Hasbrouck was very appreciative – party that night and a show. Chuck says that I am to move up to his place and he is out. Col. Benson is acting C-S. Had my eyes examined in Belfast and came back for parade.

August 11, 1942 – Court today and nothing much happened.

Almost forgot – made a night reconnaissance with Chaplain Martin – stopped at a small town near Newry (on the border) and entered the tavern – the owner came out and insisted, after he found out that Father Martin was a Catholic, that we come up to his quarters – had coffee and fruit cake – with his sisters and boy was the food good. Got a real sight into the Irish question – it is all on religion and is it bitter!

August 12, 1942 – Went to Belfast – Braidwoods was out but Dickey was back – had a good time at G.C. and O.C. Doc Ginn is sure a swell guy. Ran into some French Commandos – told them that I was a Missouri Commando. Doc was bowled over when I gave his wife some flowers – one nurse at dance was sure a swell dancer. Came back with Tyson – another swell egg. Most of these boys are okay.

August 13, 1942 – Had an inspection by the General – over the entire castle. Then got everything ready for the CPX Kilkeel.

August 14, 1942 – Here we go again – a rat race just across the lake and everything went too smoothly – even the latrine bench for the General was okay. Some Negroes are mainly at Ballywillwill – call themselves "American Indians" and "Cape Cod Indians." We may have trouble yet as the Irish do not draw a color line.

August 15, 1942 – Broke up and came in – made a reconnaissance with "Boxwell" Ulmer – is he a scream. Went to Newcastle and back at 2130 hours – visited in a very neat farm house set in a mud puddle. Bought eggs there. There were two daughters who were very hot on the behavior of our boys – said that they were too rough and loud and drank too much. Doc said problem was with some non-commissioned officers.

August 16, 1942 – Two British officers gave a demonstration of German arms and equipment. One of the officers was a lecturer at the University of Oslo and has taught at the University of Wichita – a small world after all. A good talk and an excellent presentation.

In the last few days, I have heard from Aunt Audie, Betty (2), Else, Hocker, Mother, and received a carton of cigarettes from Betty. Went to bed at 8:30pm with a cold. German planes over Belfast again – looking for the aircraft carrier that is being built at the docks. Hope that they do not come too close.

August 17, 1942 – Went to Belfast on the train and spent the night at the Grand Antial. Slept until noon the next day. Saw Tim Lake (1st Bn.) who is with 34th Div. Had too many drinks – went to a dance and then came home.

August 18, 1942 – A real day – loafed about Belfast – took a train to Bangor – nice town – bought a pair of shoes and a pint bottle to fit into gas mask. Doc is mad as hell at me for last night. However, I guess that is for the best. Spent the night in Grand Antial – came back with Sid White at 6:00am.

August 19, 1942 – Started the day off okay. Am driving a tank now – a "Honey" – real fun and are they powerful! Chuck left for Belfast for some reason or another – later we are to send Div. M.P. into Belfast. Saw two shows (pictures: "Babes on Broadway" and "My Favorite Blonde" in the Castle. Visited enlisted men's dance at TMCA hut. Two Polish officers are visiting us. Two French (free) are expected in tomorrow.

August 20, 1942 – Sweated out a problem of canvas covers for the back of the scout cars and half-tracks. What will they add next to the load of these vehicles? The last was a portable toilet for the officer's latrines and a large storage tent for the officer's mess. A case of reported rape at Newcastle came to an officer today. Too bad as I am afraid that the Irish do not understand our American soldiers too well anyway. Days are getting shorter and nights longer. Germans over Belfast again. Hope that I can read this diary when I get home and between the lines!

August 21, 1942 – Talk with Cochran relative to joining a combat unit – wants me to see him sometime. Show at night – date with Miss Jane Lupino – sister of Ida Lupino of Hollywood. Very attractive young lady – whole family is theatrical – she sings and dances – excellent ping-pong player. Just a nice time in YMCA hut – coffee and sandwiches. Another "rat race" coming off Monday and Tuesday. Strange plane over the Castle last night – AA lights up and at them intermediately. Did not sound like a German plane. Northern track to the mountains.

"Tamerlane" Smart borrowed some lights for the dance tonight – he is a swell egg from Detroit.

August 22, 1942 – Usual ying-yanging in the AM. To Drumbeg and Belfast at night. With McElhenny and "Buck" Hatfield – had some drinks and came home at a rather decent hour. Tyson not in and Brown just coming in. What a scream! Loaned McL and H. £1.50.

August 23, 1942 – Coast Guard sent us an air-raid warning – our first real daylight one. All clear in a few minutes or so. Our air raid alarm must be rewritten.

August 24, 1942 – Leave on another CPX (Terry) – way up on tip of Ireland in County Antrim. Locate CP in a large field and get them all bedded down when they decide to change it. Finally put it in a community ball north of Ballymena at 2:00am in the morning. One half-track went off a bridge and everyone just stood around and watched it. Lady at the first CP location came out and brought us hot bread and butter – the natives are sure swell.

August 25, 1942 – Was sent ahead to reconnoiter another location for CP and exercise was called off – some talk with a group of kids – bought some cookies from a traveling bakery. Came home and went into town to see the grocery store – bed at 11:00pm – tired.

August 26, 1942 – Belfast – met up with a bar maid – are these people naïve and are they excited over religion – will hang six IRA for shooting a car. Everyone up in arms.

August 27, 1942 – Went cycling to Mount Panther – some colored troops stationed there – really glad to see a Negro again. Came back by Ballykinlan and saw Hoy – these regulars are certainly aching for promotion continually – is it true throughout the divisions? Hope not as they are not interested in training but in promoting.

August 28, 1942 – Miller again off and I am trying to hold the fort – met a Maj. Wilder – nice guy. Betty sent me 48 air mail stamps! The General went to Dublin yesterday – while in civvies I almost crowned him – thought he was IRA. Cycle ride to Newry and Mourne Point – met the IRA bartender and his sister again. Nice trip – about 60 miles.

August 29, 1942 – Remember "G.I. Jesus." Went to Belfast and met up with an East African Commando – danced with his wife – one of the best dancers over here.

August 30, 1942 – Took last month with pay – almost broke – loaned 20 pounds to McElhenny and £2.18 to Buck Hatfield – it put me near the edge – had borrowed £5 from Suess and £5 from Chuck – all paid now.

August 31, 1942 – Rumored that we go to England soon – hope that is so.

To Belfast. Behaved very well – saw Doc and bought some presents for folks – met a tall blonde and Maj. Rudolf – was he plastered! – finally took him home with me. Met Brown (ordinance) and his friendly.

September 1, 1942 – Slept late and really enjoyed leaving. Came home on train – to Newcastle – caught a ride on in. Rode train with a British medical major and his wife. Went to Seaford House to a talk by Pet Haines – back from London – will we team up with the Poles? Later to a dance at Nancy Neals and Tyraller House at Ballykinlar – nice home but girls are awfully young. Some fun and a good time was had by all.

September 2, 1942 – Cycle ride to Ardglass – saw some sunken wrecks – "tea" with Mrs. Smith Pam and sister – had a hell of a time with cycle. Two letters – one from Betty and one from poker gang. Rumor is that we team up with Poles and beach head it at Bust – maybe in a month or so. Spy in battalion is really working the boys over. Looks like the real McCoy – must establish the second front in order to help Russia. Remember in the climb to Slive Donnard the truck load who would not let others on – "This truck for men only!" – They really can make some screaming remarks. Belfast in a turmoil over a hanging – people in the streets praying, etc.

September 3, 1942 – To Belfast to see Braidwoods and they were gone – ran into Capt. and Dorothy Rogers and stayed the night with them – what a time – real people – never so well treated before – Irish and the felt business – Mrs. (Dorothy) very charming – maid thought that I was going to scalp her – a very good time.

September 4, 1942 – Had some time trying to get back to Castlewellan – got back and hit the ball for some time. The General is back – looks like the real thing this time – in about 30 or 60 days – rumors are fast and furious. Went to a dumb show – the British pictures are very poor.

September 5, 1942 – Battalion is out. Chuck to Belfast for a house party. I went in at 6:00pm and had a hell of a good time – came back with Col. Harry "Cyrane" Tyson and Buck Hatfield. Poor Chuck and the "Iron Firemen" did not make a go of it – I hear from Col. (Doc) Ginn (who by the way had a swell looking dame) that things are certainly coming to shape up for the big push. General is worried – everyone taking inventory – even the natives said we are leaving!

September 6, 1942 – Harshaw was better this A.M. – Took a cycle ride to Ardglass – very pretty shoreline – attractive people – they certainly spruce up on Sunday. Had a show in the Castle – "*Andy Hardy*" and another – poor entertainment. The rumor now is Africa! Maybe we can tie in to Rommel yet.

September 7, 1942 – Did practically nothing all day long. Played poker and won about 35p from Chuck Miller. Ray Cochran, Holmes Ginn, Percy Brown, Suess Patchard. Sent Tone a cable on going to school.

September 8, 1942 – Easy day – bought some Hershey bars! At night with Cochran, Ginn, and Miller went to Ballykilar to see a U.S.O. skit and had one hell of a good time. Al Jolson, Allan Jinkins, Frand McCue, Patricia Morrison, and Merle Oberon were in the cast. Merle O. was so beautiful she made me home sick to see an American girl! Patricia Morrison was really a glamour girl and had a beautiful voice. Jenkins and McCue we good. Al Jolson really stole the show as far I was concerned – he sang all of his old-timers *"Sunny Day," "Mammy,"* and a host of others – *"Brother, Can you Spare a Dime."* This troupe really deserves the best support that can be given by the U.S. public – if I ever get back I hope that I can repay these four in some manner or means as they did take me out of the dumps. Jolson is a post master at handling his audience – his jokes were for men only but they were good.

Remember: "Belfast" "The T. C. is an unpholetual sewer." and "I like the people and the country but they can pour their beer back into the horse!"

September 9, 1942 – Col. Krautwald, Chief of Polish Artillery, returned. Lt. Gen. Daufrefore, the Commanding General Belgian Army, Cammandant Kronacker, Commandant Monjorie, and Count De Borghame all of Belgian Army visited us. Went in a tent with Buck Hatfield – "here we go again" – the 47th Medical battalion had a dance at the Officer's Club in Belfast. I took Buck's friend's friend to dance – she was not too sincere and only eighteen – however the first one that I've seen who could recite English literature. Quoted Edgar Rice Burroughs *"Tarzan"* and Milton's *"Paradise Lost"* in the same breath!

September 10, 1942 – Had one hell of a time today – finally went to sleep on the lawn tennis court of the castle. Went to a picture show at night with Buck – he is a hell of a good egg.

September 11, 1942 – Went to a dance in Kilkeel at the 27th (Col. Rockoff) – a real time. The boys play rough. Went with Col. Ginn, McElhenny, Tyson, Hatfield, Butolse. Came back in a 6x6 truck – McElhenny. Left Tyson and myself. Saw a lot of people whom I had met – are we Americans wild! Chuck in to Battalion. Nikolin, our clerk is some boy – had a good head on him – quite a talker – a comment on everything – to everybody – almost too much.

September 12, 1942 – Went on walk with General – he sure took us for rough trip. A truckload of Negros stopped in Castlewellan and were very untidy so I drove to Clough and Mr. Panther to talk to their C.G. Few of the "Caribou" (invasion) boat commanders are here as dinner guests tonight. Looks like the time is near!

September 13, 1942 – Went to Belfast with McElhenny and Hatfield – caught a train to Bangor to see the Rogers – they were not home – left orange juice, peanuts, etc. – ate dinner at a very pleasant hotel with Mr. A. Payne of Jolly & Sons Ltd., Bath, England (linen), he had been at Dunkirk. Came back to Belfast and registered at G.C. Called the Kennedys (Dick and Molly) – they were busy and so time hung on my hands – went to the officer's club and was bored stiff until I met Lt. and Jane Payne – he had a Distinguished Service Cross. Later met Lt. and Lillian Wilkes – all of RAF. Then had a hell of a good time. To bed about 1:00am.

September 14, 1942 – Got up about 10:00am and collected China from Googg and Co. – took Lillian Wilkes to lunch with another couple. Had some beer and lemonade. Went for a train ride and had some honest drinks at a small inn way up the west bank of the estuary. Back at 6:30pm and home with Junior James and Al Koster – one hell of a good time. I visited on the 8th to a dance at Mowbatten Club. Hope to make it.

September 15, 1942 – Not too much doing. Walked home from Newcastle. Saw Bill Coultan, Kay Davis, Annesby, Capt. Hill, Col. Johnson, and a couple of others. If I could write, there is a story here. Remember the blonde hussy and the dance at the 27th and the look on their face when I showed up – a skunk at the wedding! Wendy Dawson is some character – an artist or is it artistic? Remember the butter and take a chance!

September 16, 1942 – Am getting to be some stepper – to Belfast and a party at Lt. Wilkes – everyone busted in and all got mad. What a night – home about 3:00am and dead tired. D'Astoli, Buck, McElhenny, and Chuck there. At no time could I get away from the crowd.

September 17, 1942 – Lt. Col. Bill Nutter had to go to London again so blouse needed cleaning – finally got the job done by swearing & cursing & pleading – Bill was late and scared the pants off of me. He is certainly a fine fellow and a damn able officer. He was at Riley when I was there and is about age of Staley – a Cav. but a good egg. Out Battalion put on a parade for Col. Hamilton (armored trains) and had a good show. Went to Belfast with Chuck – took he and Lt. Lloyd Gabler out to a party – Lt. Harrison and wife very nice – was some party Tamelton playing the piano – right in the IRA area. I went to "400" and had one hell of a time trying to find the place afterwards. Tullipane was the driver – he had to stay by Omau Road to tell girlfriend he would be late. Some night!

September 18, 1942 – Letter from Gus, Helen, Sgt., and two from Betty – I sure miss them all. Was bumping all day long but took the laundry in – Chuck needed help with a blind date who came with his date – so I pitched in – nice girl – a telephone operator. Lights in Belfast picked up a plane over the city – a real sight – searchlights ranged over the city for some time – looked almost like a premier in Hollywood – a sight to remember – Is the fear that they have in Belfast of the raids? – it really must be a horrible experience – hope I can tell more about it later on – as it is, we do not fear it enough I think.

September 19, 1942 – Preliminary Administrative Instructions came out relative to our examination "Krant." I studied some of the boys – Elmer and Davis. We don't know where or how but we are sure that it is soon. My bet is that Nikolin will come through better than any. To bed early – wrote some letters. Rogers called up.

September 20, 1942 – Not much to do – went to church this AM. Mack Brown returned from London. The boys are sure wondering where and when we go.

September 21, 1942 – Went in a mail truck to Belfast and caught a train to Patrush and trolley to the Giants Causeway. A foundation of stones five and six sided some concave and convex – an interesting freak of nature but very much ornated. It rained like hell and I had a talk with a British soldier stationed near Lurzen – had some drinks on the train and gave crew some peanuts. Got off at Belfast and went to Bangor – stayed at Rogers – nearly scared maid to death – they are a real family. They cannot understand why we get up so early.

September 22, 1942 – Returned to Battalion on the bus and train (changed at Hollywood) – a million kids on the bus. Breakfasted at Thompson's & returned on the mail truck. Back to work and rather tired. Miller into Belfast at night with Doc Ginn.

September 23, 1942 – I almost forgot to mention the water in Bangor – there are three taps in each home – 1 hot, 1 cold, and 1 drinking. Remember the holes in the cliffs at Portrush – it was very pretty but rained like hell all of the time. This am, the grind stared again. The Prime Minister of VAC called relative one of our (1st Armored Regiment) drivers who hit a tram in Belfast. CCB goes soon and we follow in a fortnight. Everyone is trying to decide about packing, etc. and are asking one million questions. Lt. D'Astoli (engineer officer) is sure a nice egg.

Went to Ballykinlar and Belfast with McElhenny – came back with Doc Ginn – behaved almost too well.

September 24, 1942 – Went to Newcastle to see Lt. Commander Moloney (his ship named *"Misoa"*) and his fleet of caribou boats. Too many people coming aboard the vessels. They are something to remember – can take tanks, etc. through the end and draw very little water – the *Misoa* draws only about seven feet – the others only about three feet. Had one hell of a time driving back through the sand. Came back and went to Belfast with Chuck and came back with Lt. Col. Percy Brown – sure had a good time at officer's club and 400. Met Mr. McDumutt – a school superintendent in Belfast school – he was tighter than a tick! Remember Sadie Hawkins and Doc Ginn. I later found out that in getting Percy Brown out of a mess I almost "chose" "Philadelphia Jack" – one time champ of the U.S. Fleet – he was running the Army down to Percy in the 400 and I horned in – angels sure watch out for fools and drunks!

September 25, 1942 – Chuck took laundry in and I was on duty – what an afternoon – a million details came up – wrote a last letter for Betty "in case." Had visitors tonight – Bruce Bairnsfather – the English cartoonist and originator of "Ole Bill" and also the commander of the "caribous" and tank roads. Saw the "Maile Animal" – a good picture – Betty would like it.

September 26, 1942 – Mess around – drove a scout car to Hog Head Park for 37mm shooting at moving target. Shot both towed mount and tank. Scout car really rolls. At last moment went to Belfast to a dance at officer's club – saw the Wilkes – did not have much fun – wish Betty had been there.

September 27, 1942 – Chuck still gone – got wind of a movement and cannot locate him – rumor may be haywire. More than likely we go to a staging area in England first. Got two letters and saw a show in the Castle – took a bath – the first in ten days.

September 28, 1942 – Got a tooth filled – Dr. used the field equipment. The doctor was a Col. – a Fighting France Officer – in the Ministry of Ordinance – father was Chief of Staff of the French Navy in World War I. Gave a talk on France: Maginot Line costly – country was unprepared – country ready to rise up – will take three armored divisions and ten infantry divisions to make a beachhead and hold it.

September 29, 1942 – Miller got off to London – McElhenny may be demoted because T-O. Had a show last night – an interesting talk with an Irishman from Dublin and a young lady from Bristol. These people are interesting and queer. Capt. Eicher is not assigned to this office and is getting restless as a "crutch" – he is okay and will gradually fall into the situation. Some of the boys are feeling the rank – they get it for the position they occupy and then think that the respect automatically follows. I've changed my opinion on some of them – Cochran is okay, there are several others that are okay.

September 30, 1942 – Col. D. inspected Hqrs. Co. – everything seems to be okay. Was "ying-yanged" by Lt. Col. McAllister about a jeep – found out later that he did not know it was us anyway. Went to Belfast with Cols. Brown and McPheeters – some time. Ran into a British naval Lt. Hughes – surgeon on the "Delhi" – he was drunker than two hoots! This war has certainly played hell with a certain type of person: Lt. Hughes was with Mrs. Vickie (Micky) Scherwein whose husband has been gone two years – has a daughter 13 years old and is playing the field! – ready for any fun she might find. She was as stewed as Hughes – who was thanking me for helping him with the "Philadelphia Jack" fight. This "P.J." is same bird that I ran into with Percy Brown and is not such a bad egg. General Huntsburg of the Canadian Army visited here and I released him at the gate.

October 1, 1942 – Busy day with lots of details being corrected. To bed early after a bull session with Mac Brown and Harry Tyson and Butyls – my roommates – all are excellent fellows and damn good eggs.

October 2, 1942 – Cochran has a job – 1,000 new replacements coming in and needs help of MP's – to meet boat – bring them via rail, and hike to Ballykinder – much plans made and then they postpone detail. Had Ray worried somewhat. Took laundry in and went to Bangor to see Rogers – Crawford had left but Dorothy was there – so sad and crying – gave her a drink or two. Came back to Belfast to officer's club and 400 ran into Col. Dittemore who introduced me to Marshall – nice people – act as though they had never seen any U.S. soldiers. Got an invitation to a British Engineers dance at Shive Donnard at Newcastle. No go. U.S. 16th have on at Kilkeel tomorrow night – will go.

October 3, 1942 – A young lady, Partricia Convery, age 16, has run away from home in Belfast and is reported to be here – Lt. Dempsey is mixed in it – ROC has it and P.M. at Corps has it – what a mess. Took Dempsey to Kilkeel to a dance to see if girls were there. Father Martin there in it also. She was not at dance. I went with Buck Hatfield and really hung one on – had one hell of a good time – no good-looking ladies (except Lady Elizabeth) – but plenty of good whiskey!

October 4, 1942 – Slept through – the first time for this. Went to church – Chaplain Donshue (Capt.) from Kansas City gave the talk – he was good. Arranged about firing of forward echelon. Father Martin and I went to Kilkeel to meet Mr. and Mrs. Convery and take young Patricia back home – just a lovesick, adolescent, stupid kid that didn't know down from up. However, I will talk to Dempsey again. Mr. and Mrs. seemed to appreciate all that we did. Hope that Anne and Martha never give me that trouble – but they probably will think of something else.

October 5, 1942 – Usual running around and not a great deal of interest.

October 6, 1942 – Had to divide Service Co. into two echelons – one to go with Hqrs. Co. and one to follow. Went to Belfast with McPheeters. His is a swell guy – he had a date with Margie Delancey.

October 7, 1942 – An awful thing happened. Mary Jane Martin of Ballywillwill found dead in her hut and as it was near one of our camps, I was called in. Looks bad – Inspector Reid and Regan of R.U.C. are in on job and we expect to pin it on a Clark of the 1st Armored Division who is AWOL. Her notes implicated him.

October 8, 1942 – Clark is in the clear as he was on duty. Death by strangulation – no rape but all signs of that being the motive. All day on case. Chuck not in but due in.

October 9, 1942 – Clark lying – also implicated are Harris and Reold and a Mr. "X." Minnie was deaf and dumb and her lights were blacked out at 12:30AM by command of guard – she was seen at 7:45PM – spent all day on case – Chuck back – Nick took laundry in – on duty as Staff Duty Officer tonight.

October 10, 1942 – R.O.C. taking case over. Chuck Miller back and I've brought the entire list of events up to date for him. Had 30 officers dumped on us and no warning.

October 11, 1942 – Played rummy with Chuck and Doc – took off with McPheeters for a day off. Went to Bangor and visited the Rogers'. Some time! Came back to Belfast early and slept.

October 12, 1942 – Finally contacted the Braidswoods – the commander had to leave so Roumay and I took a walk to Crawfordsburn (about halfway between Bangor and Holywood) – a real nice time – she is very much a literary type – wants me to see her family when I get to England. Her father is a retired army officer (India) and she is certainly a fine person to talk to – reminds me of Betty and Anne Elizabeth. All in all it was one of the most pleasant times that I have spent in Ireland and one of the most sober! Sure wish that the decent things will continue after all of this is over.

October 13, 1942 – Went to Crossgar with Jimmy James – a smart fellow – original thinker and very logical. Still no mail from anyone.

October 14, 1942 – Col. Maraist said this AM that I might be able to go to AA school in England – sure hope that it can be worked out – it looks as if it is the break that I've been waiting for! Sid White sold me on going to Newcastle to the D.C.R.E. dance. Very poor – too many elderly people. A Miss Pimm from Dublin was very much interested in horses. The C-S was about to tie one with an Englishman – so I waded in and settled the argument. Chuck and I published a poem *"Snafu"* – a fair take off on *"Excelsior."*

October 15, 1942 – Still no word from home – guess that it will all hit at once. Early to bed. Important meeting in General's office.

October 16, 1942 – To Bangor to see the Rogers – probably last time that I'll see them. Came to Belfast and Newcastle on an early train – tired but had some fun.

October 17, 1942 – Trying to gather the odds and ends together. Fired the 37mm and 50 cal. at Ballykinder. St. Kinser held his eye too close to sight and recoil almost caught his eye for good.

October 18, 1942 – Send a poem "Appeal for Reason" to the General. T5 Lawrence McKenzie of 1st Armored Regiment, Co. G. confessed to the murder of Mary Martin – so winds up the case. Inspector Regan and Reid were my guests for dinner.

October 19, 1942 – Took Cochran's blouse into the Sixty Minute Cleaners in Belfast in the AM – did nothing in afternoon – to Belfast with Tyson – back at 3:00am – a good time. Not a W.A.R.F. who could really dance and a "bare shoulders" who couldn't also. Did go on hike with General – another poem about the hike – a take off on *"The Children's' Hour."*

October 20, 1942 – The General is really hopped up about the morning walks. We form in three groups and the race is on. This morning was really a killer-diller! I was supposed to go to England to Northwich with the advance party to prepare for Division Headquarters – at the last moment Chuck went and I'll bring up the Headquarters. I understand that we land at Liverpool and will live in an old country home. Will be there about a month and then to Africa – either Dakar or Liberia.

October 21, 1942 – Chuck was on some tool in Belfast last night. Left for Laine at 2:00pm and I am now "sweating it out!" Who and when we leave is something I do not know. Some fun packing (&*#%) and taking up the slack on the prima-donnas!

October 22, 1942 – To Belfast to get the last cleaning and laundry – in a sedan – bought a book of Keats' poems. Order for movment came through and was very difficult to understand. Did some final packing. Ford of Special Services and Martin (Chaplain) were certainly dumb about move.

October 23, 1942 – Finally got everything all straightened out. Arranged schedule of leaving and all details of cleaning up. Had sandwich and coffee about 11:00pm. Train pulled out Annesborough (Castlewellan) at 2:30am.

Chapter 3

To England

October 24, 1942 – Lt. Davis and I had a compartment alone – no sleep – arrived at Larne 6:45am – walked to breakfast – boat left at 9:50am – had a pep talk by Captain referencing an emergency – boat a device to detect planes – had sandwiches on boat – took some pictures on boat. Trip a bit rocky. Landed at Stranraer – remember the bird island just before landing – nothing but birds on the island. Landed at 12:45pm and walked about one mile for coffee in a NAAFI camp. Had to collect 2d for coffee at Carlisle – then British decided not to charge us – train left at 4:05pm – thought that I had left Col. Martin and Dittemore but they were in another coach. One man became sick and I left him in hospital at Stranraer – Col. Grubs took over as train commander from Stranraer as he was ranking man.

<u>October 25, 1942</u> – Arrived at 2:15am and no sleep – sweated out baggage and bags until 5:30am – up at 10:30 and behold what a mess! We are at Marbury Hall, Northwich, Cheshire – in an old golf club – very dirty. Combat "B" just moved out and left everything – four rounds of 37mm and 12 tanks and loads of everything – war seems to be that way. Am rooming with McClellan, Byrne, Schmidt, Moeller, Cecil – a

good group. This building rambles over the entire grounds and has some old statutory.

October 26, 1942 – This is a very dirty place. Was a club at one time – many members – once owned by Lord Marbury – went into town with Davis – no whiskey but lots of beer – very weak – met the tavern keeper and his two daughters – both very young.

October 27, 1942 – Still a very dirty place. Have lots of men working it and it seems to be no end to the dirt.

October 28, 1942 – Met a Sadie Silverstone who is manager of a dept. store. Some gal – quite a talker – sent several men to a concert. It is very hard to write this as Capt. Eicher is here talking – and talking too loud. Grounds have several statues on grounds – one is a man holding a ball in his hand and we call it Joe de Ball! Lost in fog on way home and walked about 8 or 10 miles trying to find Hall.

October 29, 1942 – Went to a reception in Chester – the British really tried hard to make it a good party but no one there except us and the grandmothers – one lady sang. Met a young lady who is a wood chopper in the Delamere Forest – a girl but built like a boy – almost too English.

October 30, 1942 – Looks like I'll go to AA school in London – this is really the break that I've been hoping for – hope that I can produce. McPheeters is with the group to the school and three others. Am now rooming with Pritchard in a new room. Spent the night reading up on AA fire. Mr. Robert Oliver Holt (ph Northwich 4304) 185 Runcorn Road, the local Air Raid Warden called. There are three signals here: purple – raiders expected in 10-30 minutes – turn all lights out; red – sirens blow and watch out!; white – all clear. It is all funny but since a huge chemical plant is about ¼ - ½ mile off – we could get it any time. The plant makes the products of salt – chlorine and ammonia, etc. for explosives – will be bad if it hits. On duty last night.

October 31, 1942 – Did not walk this AM as was on duty last night. Invited out by Sadie Silverstone – manager of a dept. store – very dull. Col. Bill Nutter is going back to the States and Percy Brown is now G-4. Going to AA school tomorrow.

November 1, 1942 – Left Marbury Hall at 10:15am and on trail at Crewe for London. Phillips, Morison, Daily, McPheeters ("McP") and Gaylord in party. We are to go to the Naval Dome Range AA School. Arriving at Euston Station, we take two "GI" sedans and go to Northwick House to see Wrideman and Griffith – driven by two female chauffeurs. Passed the Amopath and Will Pitt's statue and many bombed areas – Bond Street Picadilly Circus – we (McPheeters and I) are in the same room in the Park Lane and it is nice as hell. Ran into a WAAF officer whose father was an importer of wool – Myrtle Phillips.

November 2, 1942 – To school in the AM – is very interesting and full of good ideas – the British are great on educational films and teaching aids. School is on two ships: *"President"* and *"Chyethem"* – near the Blackfriars St. Victoria Embankment. Saw Cleopatra's Needle, Trafalgar – St. Paul's cenotaph – Scott's *"Discovery"* is tied up very near. This is some town and I really think that a man could kill himself very easily here.

November 3, 1942 – Had a steak at "Jacks" on #10 (or #16?) Charles Street – Met a Betty Knotts from Kansas City – she is a newspaperwoman and actress – very clever – she was with Beatrice Farnum (2nd ANC) from New Hampshire. Check with Bab White on this place. Also a Finn was there – was with Geo. Gaylord. Went to school the AM and still think that it was okay. British are really nice and try to give us anything that we ask for. We go to school from 9 to 12 and 1 to 5. Bought a new cap at the office PX. Lugh Hunt is stationed here in the Allied Command Headquarters – still screaming about his promotion. Funny how promotion is so paramount on some minds.

Figure 3-1 Tony Lumpkin in front of bombed out section of London

<u>November 4, 1942</u> – Last day of school – it has been most interesting. Have just wound it up. McPheeters is trying to fly to Nutt's Corners to see Sid in Belfast – he is sure a swell guy and is nuts about a very swell lady. Tried to see the changing of the guard at Buckingham Palace but it is held every other day and should see at 10:30 tomorrow. Rode buses with McPheeters to see Tower and St. Paul's and Madame Tausand then walked and walked and walked. Got back to hotel – had a couple of drinks and Amon G. Carter called McPheeters and I to have dinner with him – knows everyone (including Amon C.!) and is a very good talker and a plentiful talker. Gave an autographed $1.00 bill as a calling card. Saw some funny signs: "Pied Ball" – "Potter's Fields" (a street) – women run the buses – remember the "Ho tile"-"Hold Tole"-"Ho tiles" about that they put up and the big hat who gave us directions to the Tower. The blitzed areas are something awful – buildings just completely wrecked

– solid blocks in some areas. Queen Mother's home near a large area of that type.

<u>November 5, 1942</u> – McPheeters left to ying-yang a flight to Belfast and Sid – rather complicated arrangement – hope that they work out okay. What a day! Went to Buckingham Palace to find no guard mount on account of rain – to Wellington Barracks and a long talk with Sgt. Maj. and a Capt. in Grenadier Guards. They are intensely proud of their Regiment and showed difference in uniforms – spacing of buttons, etc. Then to Westminster Abbey where I picked up a Mr. Hallen, formerly of the London Police Force. Saw the Norris tomb – Dickens, etc., etc. to House of Parliament and across Lambeth Bridge to Lambeth Castle – to Cheshire Cheese Ho. where Dr. Johnson, et al, held court – remember the stuffed panat and the worldwide obstrares on the wall – to Fleet St. Strand, to Bow St. Church in the center of the Cockney's area to the Town and Bloody Tower – Sir Walter Scott – Anne Boleyn – the Raners on the roster – the Yeoman (Beefeaters) – the grave of the various royalty (34 names on plate and all rich in history.) This was a kind of a Royal Prison – Sir Guy Faulken – Col. Blood (later on staff of Charles II). Then back to hotel after getting twisted on the subways – and the sharing of a taxi with Lady "Something or Another" who wants me to stop and chat with her – she is doing RFC work and is about 65 years old – I sure make an impression with the old ladies! Also saw Drury Law Theater and the old section of city – London, proper, covers a small area – Westminster (accent on "west") is newer part of city. After getting back to hotel and a few drinks met Mimi Dennis and husband – she was a card. Mr. is in public service – a gas attack expert. Had quite a time with them. Amon Carter called.

<u>November 6, 1942</u> – Up early and packed. Phillips and Gaylord and I went to Savoy to breakfast with Mr. Carter but no answer – found out later that he had slept through. Took a

walk about Trafalgar Square and shot some pictures. To officer's club for lunch. Bought Betty some handkerchiefs at Selfridges – cannot buy a thing on account of coupons and rationing. Got a crown and a 5 franc coin at the Bank of England. Walked in Hyde Park and took pictures of gilded gates at Duke of Wellington – ducks and swans in Hyde Park. To station for 5:30pm – Mac had called and had me buy three tickets (£3 and 1s) for a party of his coming by plane. They did not make it. Dinner on the train – everything served by a gun crew – fast and efficient. Brought all soup, then dinner, then salad, then coffee. A sedan at station. Daley had made no reservation on train or for transportation at Crewe – not much sense of responsibility there I am afraid.

November 7, 1942 – Up and at them – rewrote AA paper for Col. Maraist. Betty had several letters and two boxes and two *Saturday Evening Posts* waiting for me. She sure is a swell and grand little lady. I'll write tomorrow as I really owe her several letters. One of these days I hope to make it up to her for what she is doing.

November 8, 1942 – Busy as a beaver in PM but nothing to do in AM. Getting list of passengers in each vehicle in C.P. – saw a show "Texas" at night – We have received radio of arrival of CC "B" in Africa – sure put everybody in a better frame of mind. Went to church in mess hall. No time for a cycle ride – hope to do it tomorrow. Wrote to Betty on the typewriter – hope that she can read it – will try to write more tomorrow. Harry Tyson has developed bad legs and will probably be sent home – same for Bill Nutter. Policy on Negros changed by "Ike" – they are to be treated as equals – buck can go with white girls and English with Negro girls – what a life.

November 9, 1942 – Ying-yanged passenger lists all AM and part of PM – to Knutsford with Chuck to see Peters Haines III and Col. Buck and to get some whiskey for a farewell party.

Had a long talk with McPheeters and he still hopes to get me in Artillery Section yet.

<u>November 10, 1942</u> – Bought two bottles Scottish Royal George from Mr. Lighton at Knutsford. Nothing much today – Chuck is planning a good party tomorrow night – played the General a game of ping pong. Looks like we move at end of week and to Oran or Algiers!

<u>November 11, 1942</u> – Just got news that General Oliver had signed armistice terms to Vichy French at Oran – Germans reported at Tunis and Corsica. Radio full of messages from Canada to soldiers in British Army. Chuck had a hell of a good party for his officers – met a May McGorty and Lady Martin and about five other attractive young ladies – the boys had no idea that a party was to be had – they thought that a staff meeting had been called! Quite a surprise to all. A note on the British people and country: They are very reserved but bend over backwards trying to be nice to us – as the party or tea or reception at Chester on 10-29. Their army is full of tradition: the buttons on the guard regiments, the back strap on the blouse of the regiment that did not get new in India to cut their quixie. Their houses almost always name: "Casa Mia" – Barrymore (Marbury Hall). Their houses are neat – brasses are shined, windows cleaned and very neat lawns – groceries in most of them now. They are full of determination and are capable of severe rationing (1 ½ oz. of meat per week), 3 oz. of candy per week – and they take it with a cheerful grin – no coal fires allowed and we are freezing with a merry blaze. Most of interior rooms are dark but interesting: room and ceiling at inquest in Ballywillwill Ho., Tryella Ho, Marbury Hall Golf room. Their fields are very green – even the bark on the trees. They are very thorough teachers – teachers can always check pupil. And almost always good sailors. They are as a whole very pleasant, very gullible, very nice, and have little use for the

French. They all want to come to USA – phone service is terrible and toilets are worse (hard to work.) They lacked oranges and peanuts – no dry cleaning and poor laundry (due to shortage of soap.) Freight cars are small and engines to "peep" or "Wheep." Remember the orchestra singing *Chattanooga Choo Choo* at the 400 club in Belfast! Belfries in London wear different hats for different countries. Their directions are poor: down the road about 4 or 5 minutes may be 1 to 1 ½ miles. Drives all vehicles on wrong side of road. Terms used are somewhat different: torch is flashlight; shields are mud guards; cheerio is hello, goodbye, so long, etc.; "pudden" is pardon; tram is streetcar; wind screens are windshields; robots are traffic lights; bonnets are hoods; "aye" is yes, no, maybe, perhaps or anything else to an Irishman; frock is dress; scheme is maneuver; spirits is whiskey; petrol is gas; chips are fried potatoes; flesher is meat market; pub is saloon or tavern; tea is a break in the afternoon from 3:30 to 6:00pm; they eat from 7 to 9pm, get up late and are wed to long days in summer and long nights in winter; wireless is radio; intensely loyal to King and Queen and upper class. All in all, pretty good eggs. An anime is a motion picture. Water closet is a toilet. Tin opener is a can opener. "But One" is one after next.

November 12, 1942 – Nothing at all.

November 13, 1942 – On the walk this AM (We walk about 4 or 5 miles each AM) I saw a very beautiful English home. House of about 20 rooms – three formal gardens, well kept lawn, gardens, etc. Came back and worked on the arrangements of the C.P. Going to Liverpool tomorrow with Putman. "*H.M.S. Formidable*" in dry dock there.

November 14, 1942 – To Liverpool with Putnam ("Puttie Put") – drove up in a jeep – passed long column of 150mm – crossed from Birkenhead to Liverpool via the Musey Tunnel – took a car ride along the docks – severe bomb damage there but docks busy – White Star was bombed – "Pasteur" in max – several dry docks there – much of our equipment on docks. People in town do not smile much – guess the bombing has taken all laughs from their life. Financial district hit severely – took several pictures of area – also one of two small boys – bought a French dictionary – most stores closed – Lee Department Store almost like Stix-Barr-Fuller. Had tea at Zagub Hotel – stores seem to be well stocked but people all look poor – no middle class. Had dinner in Chester at Blossom Hotel and home about 2100 hours. Puttie's friend at Chuck's party was Gladys Martin.

<u>November 15, 1942</u> – To church and had communion – ringing of bells (church) in rejoicing our victory in Africa over Afrika Korps and Rommel – Bow St. Church, Big Ben, Cathedral at Coventry, Westminster Abbey. They have issued sulphanilamide tablets to all in next movement.

Saw a show – "*Broadway*" with Geo Raft. Lt. Col. Marshall of 6th killed in action at Oran – the 6th Infantry must have caught hell – two companies lost by sinking of landing craft. Read a murder mystery through.

<u>November 16, 1942</u> – Wrote up a S.O.P. for bivouac and alarms. Took a cycle ride over the countryside and almost froze to death – saw a hedge of holly – a real military road – a grave yard with tombstones in line – a real talk with an English pub keeper ("Things will be better after the war is over") – they are almost too idealistic. The General had a CP in lounge on Africa and it was really good. Had a beer uptown with H. Tyson – he is a "card" – gave his girl in Belfast a box of candy sent to him by his wife – coming back on bus met an English nurse who tried to be nice to me and talked – it was late and I found out that she had not eaten (10:15pm) – these people are crazy at times. The railroad viaduct in this town is beautiful – has 13 arches in it. The town has two canals – one is on the side of the

hill and has quite a bit of traffic on it. A radio over here is a wireless.

November 17, 1942 – Got two boxes – one from Betty and one from Glynn – both for Christmas but since I cannot pack them along I had to open – there were presents (to cat) from all including Jock! The C-S has us on a CPX in the lounge room. AM was used in working on CP layout. Went to a show in Northwick (all towns ending in "wick" are in salt area) to see "*They Flew Alone*" – an Amy Johnson and Jim Mallison story. Saw the British nurse (Lt. Allen) again and an interesting character – also wants to come to U.S.A.

November 18, 1942 – Worked on CP again – to a dance at Horsley Hall, Gresford, W. Wrexham – held by Hqrs. Coy #2 M.T.T.C. – a very interesting experience. All ladies in uniform and called Lt., Sgt., Corp., PFC, etc. Had a cabaret scene – two good singers – to poor dancers – a dance of seven veils and a good show all in all. Whiskey at Officer's Bar gave out and I teamed up with St. H.P. Sheridan and go to Sgt.'s mess to get more. She was from Dublin and had a pleasant personality – was a nurse before the war. Lt. Moore put on the cabaret and was a dancing teacher in London – she danced a doll dance and a Scottish fling which was good. Both were very good conversationalists. The real payoff was a Lt. Col. "The Queen Bee" – the commandant of the camp (Lady Michaels in private life) – a real sense of humor and keen judge of human character – "had fought them two wars and would quit after this one!" Sgt. Sheridan had a sticker to put a hot water bottle in her bed – what an army can come to in an "all-out war."

November 19, 1942 – Moped about in the AM and to Manchester with Capt. Putman in the afternoon – had dinner and looked for some presents but everything was so scarce and rationed. Many areas blasted – especially in financial district – had one hell of a time trying to get out of city. Was mistaken for a Britisher when ordering a double scotch with plain water and no ice! Bartender was quite a talker. Lights went off and on many times.

November 20, 1942 – Just waiting – a draper is a dry goods store – they announce a program of "cinema music" on the air – a plantation is a small field. Problem still going strong – had a picture show *"The Corsican Brothers."*

November 21, 1942 – We just sit and wait. McElhenny is promising again to get me in the artillery – bought from town some flints. Boxes from Mother, Betty(2), Wiza – this newspaper item cut from the *London Daily Mail*. I bet Adolf Hitler cussed a blue streak when Combat "B" (500 ships) landed at Oran (remember the wild tank of Oran) and not at Dakar where his was expecting it. A good job of keeping it quite. I broke my horn rim glasses and am now wearing the G.I.'s issued to me at Fort Dix.

November 22, 1942 – Went to Catholic Church and saw impressive ceremony by Father Martin. Two cartons of Camels from Missouri Military Academy Seniors. I've more cigarettes that I can use or carry. Christmas is sure nice and everything is swell but I do wish that the boxes would be spread over the next few weeks. Everyone is getting candy, nuts, gum, soap, cakes, etc.

A good letter from Betty relative to birthday party of kids. Tone calls her "Mrs. Guggenstocker", "JapRat" and about a dozen other. Went to see the Silvertons and had a poor time – talked about the salt deposits and towns ending in "wick" are in salt area.

500 packs of mail reported in. Hope that I get some more letters.

November 23, 1942 – Issuing orders to move the officers of 1st AD to Northwick RR Station to Crewe to Liverpool to boat – plans may be changed as 20 were reported lost in return from medical convoy. Attached is a ration coupon issued to the U.S. troops for use in purchasing clothes in the British Isles. 88 to each officer for the year. One for a pair of socks, three per pair of shoes, three per shirt, everything had coupons and there were several types of coupons: clothing (as shown), food, confection. My book number was: ZB 391998 Form # Clo. B2a. – good till 31 May 43.

<u>November 24, 1942</u> – Packed last night and tried to get all that I could in my suitcase. This AM there were 10,000 questions on who, when, and what and how it goes. I will be glad to leave Marbury Hall, Northwick, Cheshire, England – Even if it is four miles north of Whales in the midlands – about 25-30 miles south of Liverpool and Manchester. Packed up suitcase and read roll. A party of eight had dinner and were charged $64.00 – a holdup if there ever was one. Foggy night and almost fell into upper canal at Northwick. All set to go tomorrow.

Chapter 4

Aboard the Duchess of Bedford

November 25, 1942 – Still trying to get pictures that were left to be developed. This is sure a war of waiting – we hurry up to wait at trucks – hurry up to wait on train – on docks and on boat. Rode up with Chuck and Pritchard in a nice train compartment. Left about 1330 hours and arrived Liverpool at 1630 hours – embarked on *Duchess of Bedford*, a Canadian Pacific Line, from the Canada docks.

All night long troops arrived. I am in #148 with Capts. Sternburg from Ohio, Eicher from Iowa, and Cantill from Springfield, Ill. Cantill seems to be a very good guy. So far, I have not drawn any special details and hope that I do not get the police detail (remember the *Queen Mary*!) Felt sick with flu and went to bed early.

<u>November 26, 1942</u> – Thanksgiving Day and turkey for dinner at night – good food so far. All day spent in ying-yang. 30 nurses, 32 different units, 4,069 soldiers aboard. Have a copy of room menu for Betty. Mail from Wiza. Hope to get AA detail but gods are against it – I guess.

November 27, 1942 – Up and at them – I am on table 43, 1st setting. Father Martin doing his usual bit of getting into everyone's hair. General Ward is Commander of Troops – so far his G's are doing a good job of it. Looks like a real good trip so far. We have had on boat drill to find the assigned places. After lecturing against tying the back straps of life preservers, someone tied his and the General called him. The harbor at Liverpool is hemmed by locks to keep water at proper level. The boat left at noon and scraped its hull in going through the locks. Most of day spend in doing nothing but loafing. So far there was no detail for me until later in PM and I was given Police Officer again – Jesus, but I was mad! Of all the officers on the boat, they draw me as the goat. Met Lt. Col. Peca who asked me about transferring rust – could not talk of it at that moment.

Some time trying to get the AA crew next to the guns – McPheeters almost driven crazy. Capt. Cantill was the "spanker" – had to move AA crews and boat detail up from various decks to the Promenade section so that they would be available to stations. Worked detail again at midnight.

November 28, 1942 – Job is not so bad. Had a good time – there are quite a few boats in convoy. I have counted as many as 24 and understand that we will have 32 or more. 4,069 USA from 32 units (1 RAFwoler an American) on board – also a Lt. Col. Dashwood, British Liaison Officer, on board. Capt. Moore is Captain of Boat – he commanded the *Duchess of Atholl*, a sister ship of the *Duchess of Bedford*, which was sunk – says proudly "She went down like a lady." This is a good boat – rides very evenly – but gear in a mess – it all needs cleaning. Boat drill was much better – I am broke and borrowed 10s from Capt. Theodore, "Self-Propelled" Dastale (Lowellville, Ohio) – he is busy as a one legged-chicken – trying to get majors to all officer's sections – he tries to please them all. Sunset was beautiful. Silhouette of the convoys showed up very plainly –

light signals smoke from additional boats coming to join convoy.

Figure 4-1   Convoy on way to North Africa

Inspected the boat this AM and section included the nurse's quarters. Took a couple of pictures of the convoy by hiding camera under the combat jacket. We dress for dinner. Have changed places with Capt. Vincent D'Antone for a 2nd setting at table #43 – Hickox, D'Antoli, Hughes, Broders, Wilder on table – a good lunch. Col. Peca has the 103rd and McPheeters says that it is a National Guard outfit. The nurses are getting quite a play from the officers – but they just get in my hair. Passed the Donegal Mountains going south at one time today.

Trying to recall my impressions of Northern Ireland and England – the Irish were easier to know and get along with but the English were more like us – even to the point of trying to overcharge us for food and drinks. Thinking of money – Lt. Eddie Jacques of Cleveland, Ohio has a wife who is a real philanthropist. She is a very attractive and beautiful lady (model at times) and one of girls where she works is in a family way by a G.I. whom she doesn't know and so what does Mrs. Jacques do but let her have $200.00 for expenses. I gave Jacques Betty's address to give to his wife. This is being written in officer's lounge of the Bedford and the gang is all about the table and the old boat is starting to real and rock – at last I think that we are getting into the open and among the big ones.

At the evening meal tonight, Broders left our table and ate at the nurses table. An impromptu show by Red Cross and men was really good – especially the colored singers.

<u>November 29, 1942</u> – This trip is much better or my part of it is better organized. At least I am not getting ying-yanged about so much. Looks like the 103rd detail is not going to work. At inspection today, several of the officers were sick with a touch of flu or had the old seasickness. Took a picture of Buck on deck and he knew nothing of it. Saw the prow and water and sunset. Boat drill was better. Several from South Carolina are on board – sighted a plane at 1600 hours but too far away to get a shot at it. Water was off and I shaved and bathed with one glass of water. Lt. Adams from Maine is sitting on our talk as guest of Capt Broders. McElhenny has taken up with a nurse and is trying to rate Harry Ty out of his room. Spent quite a bit of time on boat deck – boats are swerving out and are double tiered. This boat is built to handle about 1200 and wobbles like a "drunken duchess." Sister ships are *Duchess of Atholl, Duchess of Richmond,* and *Duchess of York.*

Waiter on new table is quite a card – has a fast line of chatter all of the time. Boat is armed with new mine throwing AA guns on each side that send up rockets. Had a dance on "A" deck at foyer near main stairs and Chaplain Martin ying-yanged his body about like a two-year-old. The General took Buck and I on a tour of astronomy on the boat deck – the stars were very bright. The wake of the ship stewed up quite a bit of phosphorescence.

November 30, 1942 – Had the problem of getting a shower place for the 50 or 60 Negro troops aboard. Finally solved it. We are to land at Oran. Are all set to dock on land by beach if necessary. Had a good talk with the Chief Engineer – there are boats from French, Polish, Dutch, English, Canadian, and American merchant marines in this convoy. The Monarch of Bermuda is here and several from the South African trade are in the convoy. There are 10 destroyers guarding the 32 or so ships in this group. Played Black Jack today and won my money back. All money turned in today to be redeemed in occupation. It will sure be good to see American money again! Changed my inspection area again and have hospital and lower decks aft – just over the propellers. Another amateur show. This is really a good trip. I've everything so organized that there is nothing to do.

December 1, 1942 – Started day with a look-see at the flotilla's commander's boat breaking loose. It almost hit several of the other ships. Afternoon meal saw them work out their AA gun equipment. Stationary pillboxes amid ship that fired stat rockets up and moving pillboxes fore, aft, port, and starboard that fired several at one time. Am afraid that it is not too effective except to some hill out of the pilot. There are also some rockets fore and aft to carry wire up. Plenty of MG and Oerlikons – a damn good gun of 20mm. Played rummy with Chuck and Rice – an AP War Correspondent who is a hell of a good egg. Played bridge in afternoon with Buck, Cecil, and Hickox. Several destroyers took out after a strange ship at 3:00pm and have not returned.

They have returned our money in overprinted V8 dollars – thank god! Drew my sun goggles, mosquito salve, and water tablets. "Half Crown," the Hqrs. and Service Company pet is aboard and having one hell of a time. Food on this boat is excellent. Beyond a doubt this is going to be a most interesting trip. General Ward said that the African Campaign was planned in its entirety in Washington. At least 18 months – two years ago. Oran and Algeria were determined because it had port facilities and would extend the German line and hinted that Italy would be next – be revolution and invasion. Also predicted that Roosevelt had promised to deal with Admiral Darlan if he could bring the fleet (French) over – it apparently could not be done and so French fleet was scuttled at Taylor and Marsailles and Roosevelt repudiated deal of U.S. troops with Darlan. He also told of meeting DeVabia in Dublin and said that D. was like Abe Lincoln – would resist invasion by anyone – could muster 250,000 men but had no arms. If invaded by Germans he would welcome U.S. troops – seemed to be a sincere man. A very interesting talk with General Ward – who by the way, is a plenty smart monkey. Raised hell about the ventilation in C-2-3's, D-2-3, E-2-3 with the ship's officers and they promised to speed up fans. General Ward also hazarded a thought: All of our naval power was centered in Mediterranean for the Campaign and therefore the Solomons were lacking in sufficient strength to resist the Japs. He also noted to Rice that the Rangers had a good publicity man – the 1st Armored Division (1st AD) made the assault at Oran and Tunis and the propers gave the Rangers credit – St. Gilmore shown in the pictures as a Ranger and was Supply Officer of the 13th AR. There was no excuse for this and Rangers are of no value unless used as such. I can see that this will make a real story when we get back. Played bridge with Lt. Col. Peter Pica (103 CAE), Lt. Col. Grubbs, McPheeters, and Tyson. Lt. Col. Grubbs is a good egg and good bridge player. Lt. Col. Ginn ("Gov" & "Doc") was sick that day with flu.

December 2, 1942 – Sunrise was beautiful after an awful night – quite a storm and a near collision. Nothing could have been prettier than the convoy and destroyers and the white tops in the sunrise. Worked with a sun compass today and it seems to be very simple. Capt. Moore, the ship's commander is called

"T-5" by Buck and myself. The General gave us a pamphlet on North Africa the other day – I hope to save one copy for the kids – it is very interesting. Has quite a bit about what we can and cannot do and see. Sun stayed out all day and I really soaked it up. Sat with Chuck and a nurse on the starboard side all AM – in the PM slept on #4 hatch until T-5 changed course and put it in the shade. Everyone is skipping rope on the deck. Mac Brown (G-2) took some pictures. I dropped my camera and the General almost saw it but don't think that he would have given a damn. Hoped to catch one of the General on board but was unable to do it. The various ships changed positions in the convoy several times. T-5 Moore was telling me that on the return trip there is no convoy and everyone high-tails it like a stupid ape – this gives the U-boats a chance and they got one in our position out of the last group. 400 Northwest of Gibraltar – we expect to pass through the Straits tomorrow night and dock at Oran on the 5th, but I doubt if all boats can be docked at same place. Capt. Hughes took the boys at poker last night. Played bridge with Tyson, Grubbs, and Buck – studied stars with Cecil and Buck afterwards. General and Ham Howze came up on boat deck to check stars.

<u>December 3, 1942</u> – Cloudy day – got a real Prussian Haircut – no hair on my head longer than 3-8" – Betty would get quite a kick out of it. Inspected nurse's quarters again – they are very clean – talked to the troops on the pamphlet about North Africa. It is a damn good booklet. Orders are changed and we go to Algiers instead of Oran – looks like we will get the Division again together after all. The real joke of the trip – we have about 30 America Nurse's Corps aboard and the boys are still talking about the Irish Collans and how easy. The 2nd night out a condom was found on the boat deck – so it seems that the American girls are available after all. Another joke: No need to send troops over for the next war – just leave the equipment and there will be enough Irish-American bastards to handle the

equipment – what an army! No sign of Christmas anywhere – have thoughts of the kids and Betty an awful lot and sure miss them.

Got a book on astronomy from Chauncy and drew charts of the stars all day long – it may come in handy. McElhenny and Chuck and myself got hold of some alcohol and we all pitched a real drunk – Chuck and Rice (the War Correspondent) really got a snoot full. One of the nurses was from Charlotte, N.C. It is really and truly a small world after all. Broders, McElhenny, and Capt. Clay (Signal Co) are certainly squiring their nurses about – at all times and all places. Doc Ginn is having one damn good time kidding Lt. Jones who is the C.O. of the ANC Detachment.

December 4, 1942 – Still no sign of Christmas. The British certainly put the Old Man in the hole – we have several tons of maps aboard – all of Casablanca, Oran, and points between – we land at Algiers and no maps are available better than 1 inch – 4 miles. Too small for any operations. We lost 18 hours due to weather and so we dallied outside of the Rock for six hours in order to go through the Straits at the proper scheduled time – this convoy has several code names – D+X and Xt27 and Bluff. McElhenny talks too much for the good of the General. He was talking of all this to an officer in front of the crew. Had to reassign some areas to the units at inspection today. The B deck aft where trash is thrown overboard twice a day was very dirty. One hold was poorly ventilated. The nurses came over to England on the same boat that Betty's friend sailed for Honolulu while we were in California – *Mariposa*. One thing to remember – the troops were taking exercise and 10 of the British RAF aboard came over to work out with them – all were damn clean-cut fellows and had excellent posture.

The weather was very poor this afternoon. General had his generals down to talk about protection in the bivouac about Algiers. At last I have money – Lt. Jacques paid up what he owed me – I now have over $30.00. Jumping rope is quite the craze at the present time – the General is getting to see us get good at it – can change step and hands and not miss a beat. Funny, but when I was a kid it was considered sissy to jump rope.

This boat was made to carry British refugee children to the US and to Canada – in appreciation the parents had a drawing made of the ship – it is framed and is on the main foyer on "A." It is signed by parents and children alike. The lettering under the drawing of the ship –

"The Prussians say 'Breath of my life, light of my eyes, soul of my soul.' So were the hundreds of children entrusted to your keeping in their journey from the Old World to the new. The anguish of the Mothers facing the unknown with their children has turned to comfort and gratitude on board the Duchess of Bedford with her gallant Master, her wonderful crew, her tireless Stewardess and Stewards.

It is this gratitude that we wish to express, but unable to find adequate words, we simply say: Thank you! Thank you all so much for the children."

This was covered with kid's signatures – Bab, Yvonne, William, Bill, etc. One Martha, three Tony's, about 25 Elizabeth's, and Betty, 5 or 6 Anne's, 3 Kay's, etc. and at least a hundred X's. It is a wonderful thank-you note and a good piece of English composition. It almost brought a pang to my own heart. Am glad Betty and the kids did not and I hope they never will need to go through that experience.

Adams, our waiter is quite a character – told us about the peacetime trips – this one carried 1,300 3rd class on its maiden voyage – immigrants and harvest workers to Canada.

Entered the Straits of Gibraltar at 8:30 and cleared them in about two hours. Not a sign of a light and in perfect formation – a real exhibition of seamanship if there ever was one. My hat is off to these people. The channel is fairly well defined but mines are numerous and are marked with a pole light – they are remote controlled mines. Passed several small fishing smacks on the way in and one of them yelled to us in Spanish. He had two flares going. On the European side, there was a tour before the Rock and one after and several search lights. On the African side, there was one before and a large one opposite the Rock. Two planes came over – British? It was dark as hell, a slight mist, could just make out the Rock. Closer to Africa than to Europe. Contrary to belief – the Rock is on the Mediterranean. We are now within easy bombing distance of both Italian and German bombers. Everyone is keeping their fingers crossed and hoping that it all comes out okay. One of the most dramatic nights that we have had yet. It was really a sight to behold and a tribute to the British Navy. Adams, our waiter, also said that this boat took some from Singapore on the last batch. The officers say that it is scraped about once a year (others one in six months) due to the fact that it is cleaned by traveling in fresh water of the St. Lawrence. It is a seven day trip from Montreal to Liverpool and eight days from New York.

December 5, 1942 – Inspection plans had to be re-arranged as the Captain's deck was dirty. After I got it straight went up and saw the sea – the Mediterranean Sea is really a place to reflect – as still as a small pond – very blue and sky was very colorful and convoy looked beautiful. We are going slow and sweeping some mines as we go – tried to take some pictures but the decks were too crowded. Our boys are the hairy-breasted poker players of the boat – they have the money and the other passengers have the experience. About 2:30pm, the General called all unit commanders in and told them that we land at Algiers, no transportation available, will live in the fields and will leave the baggage. This will be quite an experience to most of these officers as I am not so sure that they have ever lived off the country. The British Debarkation Officer is calling for all petrol stoves to be made ready for immediate use. Then we had an "Actions Stations" at the sight of a couple of planes – but it was only a practice and the ship did okay – Father martin, as usual, directed traffic, supervised the operation of making a nuisance of himself. The wags were busy today. Doc Ginn said that the new camp would be called "The Garden of Allah" – Chuck called it "Repent at Leisure." Tyson is writing a book "The 1st Armored on Three Continents." After we came through Gibraltar, it continued with land on both sides and we stuck to the Spanish Coast for some time – it goes directly east from some 50 or 100 miles. Then we picked up the African Coast and followed it for some time. Saw where Col. Robinette and General Oliver landed – Oran at about two hours before dark. The shoreline is mountainous along this stretch and the terrain looks hilly. At night, we went up on the deck (Buck, Hatfield and I) to see stars – dark and some clouds. The water is phosphorous – the ship's wake stands out and the water seems to spark as well as glow. Buck is a good guy. McElhenny has been playing one of the nurses and had her in room last night. Some man. A new insight into his powers that I did not know existed before. We are getting out a pamphlet for the natives on how to behave towards us – one of the cracks: "If you see two soldiers staggering down the street they are not queer – just drunk." In the pamphlet issued to us is a similar one: "If you see two natives walking down the street holding hands – they are not queer." The 9:00pm news tonight stated that enemy air action is reported over Algiers. Met a Clemson man tonight – will try to see him again – finished in 1926. Am packing tonight to get rushed off tomorrow AM. Very nice and warm – can see why Mediterranean cruise is a winter luxury.

Number of boats times 200 questions.

Chapter 5

Landing in Algeria

December 6, 1942 (Sunday) – Saw several porpoises between Oran and Algiers. Got up and ate early – had boat cleaned and inspected same. Arrived at the Algiers Roadstead at 9:00am. A very large harbor and anchorage. Saw a most beautiful sunrise while boats came into the harbor slowly. Howze commented that we came in under the force of osmosis or capillary action. Sky and water was a pastel pink and blue. The Kasbah showed up very clearly. The city is in two sections: native and European. It is built on the side of a hill with homes mostly two stories and over and is a nice looking city. I took some pictures of Algiers Harbor and several on deck. Rick Yahner, our AP correspondent, was in one of them. The General and CC Benson have a good one:

> *If in danger,*
> *If in doubt,*
> *Run in circles,*
> *Scream and shout!*

This was one reported as the motto of the 45th Inf. Coming into the breakwater, we passed several schools of jellyfish. They are very large here. A U.S. Navy PT boat came by and the cheering of the boys almost got me. It was the first time in a long while that I had seen the Flag. Our ship blew its whistle for it. Many British warships are in the harbor. One, a tender, had a very large hole in it. One U.S. boat was beached with a large hole in it also. The France Union V and VI are alongside. The V is full of water and both are rusty.

Many French boats in harbor are rusting from non-use. They are not war painted. The *San Lalfor*, an oil tanker, was alongside with two British destroyers tied onto her. It is a sight to see them "pipe" the commands onboard. Barrage balloons are over the city. Some from ships (our ship could send up five.) Several seaplanes with noisy motors are here. One, an amphibian, took off and landed near our anchorage. The British are real seamen and seem to be able to do everything in teamwork. One of the destroyers had been hit several times by small cannon fire. One had several torpedo tubes and much armament. They were busy as hell blinking messages. There were aprons over the lower guns to keep blast from upper guns from the gun crew. Dastoli says that he lost $3.00 in poker. Church services were held for Protestant and Catholic on the forward deck. Inspected the Oerlikon AA guns on ship and they were not so hot. Our dual .50 cal. seem to be okay. Dastoli had to make maps in the middle of the ocean.

December 7, 1942 – Up an hour earlier to get a start on disembarking. Waited around until they told us to clear out. We were supposed to land at Oran – another hurry up and wait snafu. The British War Office and Admiralty got mixed up. Our sealed orders said Oran and the Captain's (called "God" by all seamen) said Algiers. While waiting in the harbor, there was a great deal of swapping of oranges, lemons, limes, and candy for our cigarettes. Some fall short and hit the water. They were fished out with buckets, brooms, etc. One man reached out a porthole and got quite a few while the top deck washed his head with water and hit him with anything loose and he tied up buckets, bins, etc. The whole thing was very funny and like a carnival. He was called "Porthole." One named "Jack" could really pitch to us.

We left Algiers at 4:00pm. We took aboard the German Consul's wife, two kids and a maid. Seemed to be very nice people. Had a drink and a bull session before mess. Our group has cleaned the ship. We are a tough poker crowd!

December 8, 1942 – Arrived at Oran at 8:30am and docked at 11:00am. Col. Dashwood, the British officer on board and Col. Robert V. Maraist try to see who the biggest liar is. Dashwood is a blowhard of the old school lie type.

A small sailing ship with red sails came about us. Quest from the 27th came aboard and reported on the Oran affair. One incident: The 16th Inf. was held up and reported that they could make no headway so Col. Robinette sent one platoon of mediums and it opened the way easily. The 1st Armored Division seems to have given a good account of themselves.

Had a nice talk to the German Consul's wife. Gave her a knife to give to the kid who is about the same age as Tone. The daughter is Anne's age. Their names were Hans and Marie Thresa. Both very cute. Showed Marie Anne's picture and she said "Bebe-Bebe!" Mrs. was very much like Helen K. back home. Had nice clothes and well-tailored – a good advocate for Germany. Raids reported on the way every day, but none so far. I go ashore at Mers el-Kébir to check the transportation for the General and the staff. We leave by truck and trailer for a field 16 miles from ship.

Oran dirty with Spanish type buildings. The Arab children beset Dastoli and take him for a carton of cigarettes and some candy. Women are veiled and wear dirty clothes. No need for a paper to our soldiers to leave the women alone.

Signs are Spanish and French. The weather is poor with rain, rain, rain. We are fed "C" rations and borrow tents, cots, and blankets. A poor, cold, and wet night. Chuck to Oran.

December 9, 1942 – We are eating with the 47th Medics. Smitty a great deal of help. Everything wet as hell. Bozoane telling of Oran job – pretty much of a fight. Several Distinguished Service Crosses were won. Robinette now a Brigadier General and won one and a Cross de Lorraine. Alger, a Major General and Jake Shapiro, a Major and a DSC (won with light tanks.) I go on a reconnaissance with Maraid, Ginn, Buttelph, Gruble, Price, and Percy Brown. Saw many Arabs and much of the country. It is like western Kansas, Montana, New Mexico, and Arizona all in one place. Water is the problem and the land is poor – scrubby palm and palmettos all over the place. French Algeria troops in Sidi Barton and St. Clouid were very interesting. Their officer was very intelligent. Bought some tangerines and they were like sugar. Ran out of gas on way back and got very dirty. Our bedrolls came and could have had a good night's rest except there was too much on top of roll. Am in a squad tent with Hughes, Buttoff, Cantils, Hickox, Wilder, Hight, and Long. Crowded, but all in good shape. I am still getting the camp in shape with no tools.

Chuck to Oran.

December 10, 1942 – Equipment starting to arrive. Chuck is sure worried on account of no promotion – it is really getting his goat.

OP6 and Nettie all set up and functioning.

One soldier up and playing with the Arab women woke up to find his testicles were sewed up in his mouth – a rare sense of humor! These people seem to have a cruel streak in them.

Sun came out and felt very good.

Taught Buck how to ride a motorcycle today.

December 11, 1942 – We started the AM walks again. Walked about ½ way up Eben Ben Kar, a large mountain in good view of our bivouac. Talked to some natives about ½ way up. They were wood cutters and very friendly. I gave them some cigarettes. Chuck went out and got a bath and changed $10.00 into francs for me. I have 750 francs. The rate in England was 1L = 4.035. So far, I have had no use for money. The native's need clothes more than money and would rather swap. A mattress cover is worth 800 francs when they can be bought. Buck is doing well on the cycle. The General and some of the boys got to talking after a band concert from the 13th FA Brigade. Its seems that some of the paratroopers landed in Spanish Morocco and very little good was done by them as they were too scattered.

The officer in charge of the Oran affair would not send a crane and a wrecker in the same boat and of consequence much of our bridge equipment was lost. The *Caribou* was beached in 14 feet of water! It looks as if Pershing's mistakes were repeated.

I've heard that Red Hagood is S-3 of the 13th FA Brigade.

I now have four scout cars at my disposal.

December 12, 1942 – At the walk this AM, Cochran, Clay, Dittemore. I got lost and walked until 9:00am – no breakfast. The General turned left and we turned right. Took a motorcycle to St. Cloud and St. Denis du Sig to see new bivouac area. Rained like hell and had to reverse raincoat to keep water out. I saw a real extravagant home near St. Denis. Tennis courts, swimming pool, etc. Talked to some Arabs – they wanted to know if war was still on and whether the French were on our side and whether the Algerians were on our side. When I said yes (ie "oui"), they said we will win sure as hell. One G.I. trying out his high school French and the Arab finally said: "What in the hell are you trying to say?"

The natives seem friendly and shout and wave to us even though we shot the hell out of their towns. Passed through one village, on G.I. stood up in jeep, took off his helmet and shouted: "Hello you filthy, dirty, stinking Arabs! How are you?" and they waved and shouted back! I take several out to the new area. My half-track blew a radiator plug and engine got hot as hell.

Still on "C" and British rations. British rations are better: better jam, chocolate candy, crackers, meat, and pudding – but it all tastes like mutton. Spent evening in the tent with McPheters and Chuck.

December 13, 1942 – Moved the division to a mountain top near St. Denis du Sig and south of a salt lake. We are loaded to the gills with baggage. By Wednesday, we expect to move again and leave some of the equipment. The bombers passed over in droves all day. They are sure pasting someone. We have our AA guns alerted but they leave us alone. A dog, "C-Ration", took up with us and is very friendly. Showered today. When I get back, I will live with the hogs for a month in order to gradually become accustomed to cleanliness!

Figure 5-1 Captain Lumpkin (center) among a group of officers and soldiers somewhere in Algeria

There is a desert owl in the area somewhere and we are near its nest. It flies out now and then. Ate lunch at 3:00pm today. Cal Martin had church at the old bivouac area "The Garden of Allah." The radio is full of Algerian jabber. After the bivouac was set up we have taken it easy and everything seems to be okay. The Arabs are trying to sell either one or two eggs for 15 francs. Nick gave them hell in three languages. Cal Burke came back from CCB. The Germans are giving and taking plenty. Our gunners are much better. The B occupies places that we seize and have trouble in handling our tank units. CCB has over 900 hours on their tanks and have had no time for the 100-hour check. Planes going out every day.

December 14, 1942 – Write Betty a Christmas letter. It is to be delivered on Christmas Day. The weather is warm and at times hot. Arabs are a problem in the camp – bringing in wine. Rode to St. Dens with Buck. The town is full of Arab and French soldiers. Several small children are about and dash across the street. Hughes lost his bedroll and almost had a fit. They are sure yanking Hqrs. Co. about. No one seems to be able to decide and stick with a decision.

Doc Ginn has a good one: "Gold help the patient whose Dr. has had one patient." This is about CCB. Doc really has a rare sense of humor.

These items still come up: the British did not follow in the 1st Army (CCB and 1st Div.) after Oran. We are being pushed back because no air support and this hurts all vehicles except tanks. Buck did not go with Jake and is back with us now. We have two trucks and cannot move until they are furnished – which will be when we are alerted. Everyone has too much baggage and we must streamline. Doc and Buck came over and we talked for all hours.

December 15, 1942 – Had $16.00 changed to francs – now have a roll of bills that would choke a horse! The smallest bill is

5 francs. The Arabs have no use for money but will swap and wager a wagonload of tangerines for a full set of G.I. underwear.

Raining like hell today. McPheeters and I got lost in the rat race and only came in cross country when we heard the bell. This walking is something. We walk from 7am to 8am. When we return at 8am, it is just getting light.

The portable radio is a real joy these days. It tends to keep the old balance wheel turning for us.

It is reported one battalion of the 6th Infantry and the 27th Field Artillery were to cross a bridge held by tanks when shelling started. Lt. Col. McGinness (6th Inf.) turned off and went upstream and lost all transportation and guns but four of the guns. The 27th lost 14 guns. McGinness is being reclassified and to be tried by a court martial.

What a life. Buss is an old G.I. – 30 years old from Ohio – from private to lieutenant colonel in 8 years! He says to keep in condition and study minor tactics.

Stukas only bother the thin-skinned vehicles.

Chuck to Oran and back at midnight with a real toot on.

December 16, 1942 – Bugler made a mess of the AM calls – reveille sounded at all hours. We packed up on a rat race and it was a snafu – radio did not work and we had no control of the column. Everyone is getting on each other's nerves. The General and the C/S & G-3 are working us over. We re-packed car and gave away a whole lot of our equipment. The Arabs wear anything in any manner: a barracks back for britches – a set of G.I. underwear is full dress – mattress covers, sheets, etc.

One G.I. said while driving through the rain and mud "Some bastard ought to call of this problem."

December 17, 1942 – Shot craps last night and lost 1,000 francs to Buck and the Hqrs. Co. officers. Lots of wine and a good time though.

Buck, Cecil and I went to Bou Hanifia and got a real hot soapy bath. It was a very picturesque place like Hot Springs, Ark. though the beggars were in force and so were the Arabs! In a very pretty valley, we bought tangerines at 9 francs per kilo. Not many trees, but a colorful country – farms on the sides of hills and the soil does not erode.

<u>December 18, 1942</u> – In evening shot craps with Ulmer, Datoti, Buck, Eddy and the Rover Boys (Price and Combs). Was hot and won between four and five thousand francs. Left game with a snoot full and fell in a slit trench! It rains like hell all of the time.

<u>December 19, 1942</u> – I turned in the last of my good U.S. money. We rearranged plan of the camp. Shot craps with Eddy in the PM. Got all set for CCA and rest of Service Co. to come in.

<u>December 20, 1942</u> – A break. We went to Oran with Buck to pick up Bruss. Left at 9:15am. Bruss said to pick up at 4:00pm so we roamed the streets. Recall Martial Foch Square, gold plated statue of Jeanne d'Arc and a Jewish synagogue. Talked to an old man – a Parisian – and several Moroccan soldiers who really wanted cigarettes. He had been to Berlin and was very interesting. Lots of beggars and shoe shines. In a park, we talked to two kids. Pierre Danan, 6 Paris St. Oran, Africa and his brother-in-law. He was very smart -13 years old and from a good family. Their father is an engineer. A Gendarme chased him off and we tried to rescue him. Almost made him cry. It seems that the Gendarme did not want any natives to associate with us. He had a regular tailored suit.

Remember the perfume of the natives and the general smell of the natives. They eat too much mutton. Also remember the mess at the Continental Hotel and how we had to bribe our way in and its Chamber de Counvettes on the 2nd floor. The drunk soldiers "rolling out the barrel" with song and wine while driving a cart and dating one of the hooded affairs! (not sure what this meant)

We came back by La Sevia Airport – it was really wrecked. I am amazed at the nice shops with nothing in them to buy. Canvas shoes were 130 francs ($2.60) and a child's cotton dress was 980 francs ($9.60.)

Food is scarce and gum unheard of.

December 21, 1942 – Have certainly seen the Army in a poor spot today. The rest of the Division was due in and they were allotted areas in the bivouac. Transportation is nil and they brought them off the boat all night long and dumped them on the ground in the dark. There was no traffic control requested and no one was told where each unit was to go. Yet, there was enough officers present to take each unit into its area. Then, the Arabs swarmed over the road selling oranges, tangerines, and wine. Chuck and I went out and swarmed over them. Chuck fired a pistol and I shouted "Danger de mort!" They are afraid of us now. Chuck is in the Marechal de Gendarmes. In the meantime, scout cars, half-tracks, and 2½-ton trucks are clogging the road and sliding into the ditch – some scene.

December 22, 1942 – Went to Bou Hanifia? for a bath and stopped by Mascara and talked to a small boy, Jean, about the same age as my son Tone. Bought much wine and had a good time but almost froze to death coming back. Champagne is 150 francs, wine from 40 to 100 francs. Talked a long time to a Gendarme who was born in Alsace. He had been in the army for three years and now a policeman. Natives swarmed about the jeep. My French is improving and am trying to talk to Arabs as much as possible. General McQuillan and CCA are really learning to soldier. Mac is a bull-slinger and took up most of officer's call repeating what had been said before by other officers. The Division has certainly lost its transportation. CCB is outposted 450 miles up the coast and we cannot move up there. Only one battalion of mediums is left up there with the British in a blade force. We are bombing the hell out of Bizerte.

After this is over, I will have to re-learn how to spell and write.

December 23, 1942 – Rains all the time. Mud is everywhere. We are in a tent with a Coleman stove. Bruss stays with us quite a bit. Have tried to wire Betty several times but no luck. If thought waves could span the distance, she will have known than I am okay and thinking about her. No mail and it looks as if some will never get here. One ship was lost in the last convoy. The other day, 4,800 sacks of mail was lost just off Oran. I yanked 300 francs from Ray Cochran the other day. My hands are cold as hell but must quit and write the folks more later on today.

December 24, 1942 – Went to St. Dennis de Sig to the Royal Café and bought wine and champagne for Christmas. I was with Captain Myron Davis and we had some time – bought 1,955 francs worth! Much mail came for everyone. Had a haircut in the mud, lost at craps with Eddy in the mud. About 6:30pm, alert came from II Corps as Darlan had been shot. I am not sure whether we are lucky in this or not. Bruss came over and we shot the breeze until 1:00am. The G-3 sure stirred up a rat race and had us going head over heels in all directions. Have thought of the kids during the last few days a lot. Hope that they have a good Christmas. We are giving "C" rations to the natives. Rains <u>all the time</u>.

December 25, 1942 – Christmas. Slept until 9:00am. Started in with wine and more wine at 10:00am. Col. Burke, Bruss, Cochran, Brown, Ginn, etc. all came over. We took several pictures using Stribling's Christmas card as a background. Sobered up and cleaned shoes in the sun during the PM. The party was going all day long and into the night. Stribling's Christmas card hit the spot and was used in may pictures. Bruss bought several chickens and we had a feast. The chicken was so tough that we called them Rommel's Armored Recon Pigeons. It was a good party.

December 26, 1942 – Have a mild case of diarrhea that I hope will soon go. Reorganized the bivouac. The Arab merchants left our area when it was reported that the French Gendarme was coming to inspect licenses.

In the PM, Bruss, Donado, and I went to St. D. to buy some onions to have with some chicken that we had caught. Bruss is a fine fellow. He still has some of the bribe money used with the invasion. The chickens were tough. The General returned from the front. There are lots of conflicting reports. We are in a hell of a mess for transportation. Hopkins issued a "Hopkinese" order: "Shoot at everything larger than a goose regardless of markings."

Rearranged the CP and some of the boys are screaming.

December 27, 1942 – Have a cough and a sore throat. McPheeters and I get a kick out of kidding each other on whether we are "mice or men."

Noticed are the effects of promotion on certain types of men: some take it gracefully (Haines, Cohran, and others), some arrogantly, and those who don't get it are frustrated.

Talked with McGinness a long while. He just had tough luck with the transportation. He seems to be okay and just had tough luck.

Chuck's feet are bothering him again. Bruss came by and we talked during the night.

December 28, 1942 – By direction of the C/S, we took the CP out on a march, less the tanks and infantry platoon. Better on distance and packing, but poor as hell on radio procedure.

Wrote letters in the PM. Cory of Shreveport came in. Col. Maraist tried to give me a boost to take the Headquarters

Commandant job but I still want combat. However, it seems that there is no use trying to get out of this niche.

<u>December 29, 1942</u> – It rains all of the time! Went to Oran with Buck Hatfield to check our baggage at the docks. There wasn't any. So we really hung one on at the American Bar and the place was full. We met a naval lieutenant from Charleston, South Carolina who went to school under Betty Pringle and had a long talk with him. Buck had a friend that he had met earlier. Madame Rosette at 5 Rue Bayer. Lots of cognac and then to the Florida Club where I met "Andre" who ran the joint. He insisted that we have a good time. Met up with some Naval officers of the *Marabou* and took them to the boat. We went aboard and had some scotch. It was a real night! Buck and I can really whirl nicely together. Nick had a bad time with the General's blouse and we were too drunk. We fell all over the bivouac and had mud from head to toe.

<u>December 30, 1942</u> – What a headache! Met reveille and back to bed. Mud everywhere. Had a hell of a time trying to get heater fixed and B's jeep working. At a meeting called by G-4, we had the dope given to us. We will fight as a Corps and wind this up. Ward to command the Corps. So secret that I dare not write it down here or anywhere else. We move to an assembly point near a large town, regroup and smack hell out of them.

<u>December 31, 1942</u> – Rained all day. Mud! The whole area is a swamp. However, there is bedrock of shale about 2 feet down and no vehicles have been lost. "Half-Crown" came in this AM and was tossed out. Washed face and hands for big party at Davis's tent with hot dogs and wine.

Wrote Betty and Gus. Sent some coins to the kids and an Oran paper to Betty.

<u>January 1, 1943</u> – New Year's Day and the sun is really shining. Doc Ginn had a party at his tent and we talked for some time. He told me of a friend of some 20 years who was still

waiting for him. The whole thing was really beautiful. Made a stove for the tent from old meat and gas cans. We are getting ready to send the rest of the Division up by water, rail and over land. Burke was left behind for drinking. He was a good egg and a real soldier and I was sorry to see it happen to him.

Had two eggs for breakfast and turkey for dinner and then steak for supper. They are fattening us up for the hill.

Buck stopped by for a talk. A tanker was blown up in Oran Harbor. It had 100-octane gas in its holds and made quite a smoke and scared the hell out of some of the boys who are bringing equipment via water. Two German Ju 88's made a reconnaissance flyover yesterday, but all else is quiet.

Lt. Col. "Daddy Rabbit" Todd was killed. He had a Battalion of light tanks at Oran. I liked him an awful lot during the short time that I knew him.

January 2, 1943 – Boiled clothes and scraped mud. General McQuillan says that Constantine is the assembly area (out loud and no secret) for the attack. The date and place are too secret to put down.

They now ship us U.S. oranges and grow them over here. Col. Maraist and Col. Benson are squabbling over their seniority – all over the issue of field glasses. Beyond a doubt, the army is full of too many rank-conscious officers. The G.I.'s are okay and will win this war in spite of us. They have already demonstrated that they can take it.

Chuck into Oran for his feet again. They seem to give him a lot of problems.

Our stove is a dinger – it gets so hot that it actually carburets the gas and keeps the flame out of the tent.

Am trying to write Betty each day.

January 3, 1943 – Nick was NCS and almost blew a top.

Got a card from Dorsey Barnes and Mr. Hart. Got a haircut in the field with the wind blowing about. CCB has lost 1-3 of its officers and seems to be hard hit. More trucks are in and have to be reissued to Maintenance Battalion for repair. We are shot of equipment. Hope to get into Oran and get pictures developed before we leave. Sent $300 home. Hope that Betty gets it okay. Went to St. Cloud with Doc Ginn's rum jug and Chuck. Met some medics from Charlotte.

January 4, 1943 – West to Oran with Davis and Dastoli. Had a roll of film left to be developed and some shoes to be repaired. A good time. Talked to a French lad who helped me find the shoe shop which was located in the Kasbah. Talked with a very attractive lady in the photo shop. Went with Tyson to his friend's house and they were out. Met "Helen", the bartender at the American Bar. She lived in Cairo and spoke good English. We all have Cognac on Rue Boyer. The bartender there, a woman who went by "Madame Collect", is a very interesting character but spoke poor English. "Helen" made a remark that is worth repeating: "We can be poor, but at least we can be clean." I am certainly of the opinion that the French women are much more neat and clean than the Irish or English, but they have a poor sense of humor.

We seem to be selling ourselves to the people better – i.e. the sailor telling the native to quit the double talk.

January 5, 1943 – Word came that Devers and a lot of generals are coming. Policed area and got everything in shape. They arrived amidst sedans and pomp.

We are to move out tomorrow. Wrote the march order and got set. A fire broke out in the CWS section and was reported as the ration section by mistake. Turned out everyone with shovels. Starting to rain again. Wrote and read until midnight.

January 6, 1943 – Up early and packed out at 0800 hours. We still carry too much. OP6 still with us. The sky and mountains are beautiful on the way up and after leaving the mud hole the weather got much better. Bivouacked at

Orléansville and the Arabs gathered about. Talked with a local banker, his wife and daughter. Ate noon meal on the road and I gave an order over the radio: "Kitchen trucks remain in position and officers eat in cars."

Chuck is on the edge. Burke started with us and was called back. Bruss has conned me out of a blanket – He is still a G.I.

Took a picture of Arabs outside of Ferris (sic?) Remember the truck column trying to double ours.

Talked with McPheeters a long time at night. Several cyclists fell in mud. Saved in cold water and almost froze to death doing so. Arabs "sit" mules funny – on sideways and beat them with both heels. The French police are rough on Arabs.

January 7, 1943 – At Larba, just outside of Alger. One of the towns passed through was full of kids shouting "Ho Kay" and "Toom." The Americans have sure made friends quickly. Country here is better with some pretty homes. Cemeteries are full of mausoleums and fine iron filigree work for wire flower stands. At night, 12 of us (McElhenny, McPheeters, Chuck, Dasti, Syd Combs, Current, Price, Green, Cochran, Tyson, and me) went into Alger and saw Leigh Hunt. Two air raid alarms while in the city. A very large convoy is in the harbor and they are expecting it. Blackout is good except for officers in cars. Ate at officer's club, the "Alexandria." Alger is a beautiful city. We saw some bathers and skiers walking side by side. Visited the Sphinx for cognac. Saw the 1,000 mirrors and heard the natives say "gawrd dammmn." Had champagne at 100 francs a bottle – very cheap. Climate is warm.

A new signal officer replacing the one captured is with us and bunked in our tent. He is from Georgia and seems to be okay. Gave same "Blue Devils" some cigarettes. Their spirit is good but their equipment is lacking.

January 8, 1943 – Column left at 0800 under British control. Passed through some very pretty mountains, much like

Shoshone Canyon in Wyoming with waterfalls of some 150 feet. Railroad tunnels on one side and road on the other. Snow on the mountaintops. Elevation up about 3,500 feet at bivouac in an open field near a town of two buildings. The British are on one side all lit up and lighted convoy, but we are blacked out. At a halt in the AM, an olive merchant gave us oranges. He complained of taxes and the Germans taking everything. He also said the Americans gave and he was glad to see us. Gave away lots of cigarettes today. Some to the farmers where we bivouacked tonight. He was set to scream at us and I quieted him down by telling him that I was a farmer also! His friends helped me sell him. British have some clever signs: "Slow down – you have been warned"; "Fast drivers take it slow for a change"; "Slow down all cars, Army and RAF."

Bought some eggs at 5 francs each.

Some units were alerted <u>before</u> Darlan's death.

Nick, Irvin and Good are in our car. After mess, Maraist called all officers and gave them hell for letting us do all of the work. A damn good radio program is coming in while I am writing this at 9:15pm on a cold, open plain surrounded by snow-capped mountains.

Cochran is doing a good job as C/S. He has a fine mind and will use it. There are only two roads and one railroad into Constantine and they are plenty overloaded. Some notes on the country: Haystacks are packed together and covered with mud, grape vines are trimmed and branches are used for fuel, irrigation is extensive, some native huts have no chimneys, plows are wooden and generally pulled by two oxen and one horse, plenty of tandem hitches of animals, they drive donkeys by poking them in the neck or buttocks, people ride in inflated-tired buggies and carry spares and pulled by mules or horses!

<u>**January 9, 1943**</u> – Left bivouac before sunrise and almost passed a British column of heavy artillery. Radio for Eddie's traffic control went out. Country here is bare like Wyoming.

Went into bivouac about 2:30pm just west of Constanople. Area is crowded and vehicles are too close together. There is a lot of air corps about. Saw the wreck of one of our transports. Hope the picture is okay. Cold as hell. CG, G-1, G-2, G-3, and G-4 are in Constantine with II Corps and 12th Service Command and a mess of miscellaneous U.S. stuff. Also, 1st Division and 1st British Army. Doc Brown says that Germans are being reinforced and it does not look so hot. We are out posted by tanks from the 1st Armored Division and they seem to be okay – about 1,500 to 2,000 yards out. We are aside a small brook with Service on one side and Headquarters and Signal on the other. We are almost ready – all equipment except half-tracks for Signal Co. and tanks for Headquarters Co. are in. Rumor has it less than a week – wonder where and what will be written here later?

January 10, 1943 – Got more dispersion by rearranging the C.P. Sunday services held at the 68th Field Artillery. Chuck goes to Maraist's tent and returned late. He said that he was going up to take a battalion and I was to take his place. This AM he and Eddy take out amidst much preparation to go on a reconnaissance to find roads to take the Division up to the front. Red Williams is back and started to raise hell with his outfit right away. The officers sent back for a truck. Played chess with Nick and helped CCA get into bivouac. Mailed some letters home and a card to Kay Kelly.

January 11, 1943 – Reveille at 0730 and mess at 0830. Got a cycle and tried to locate some straw for the men to sleep upon but found that the Arabs were stealing and selling it to the soldiers for 20 francs a mattress cover full. Repacked my bags to store them in Constantine. Doc Ginn came by. The General just made three towns off bounds after 6:00pm because of prostitution. General Mac also said that there was no need to put MP's out and all should remain in bivouac area to keep up training. So, 81st Recon is posting those towns and no one is allowed to leave the bivouac area. Chuck and Eddy are back and figuring out this problem of guides. McPheeters and I went to Quad Artheminea to check the casualty lists of a British hospital. Several of our boys and three POWs who were members of the Luftwaffe were also there. They were young and rather intelligent. Chuck says that he is going to a tank battalion and I get his job. Ham is going up and Davis will eventually be the headquarters commandant.

January 12, 1943 – Had a time getting into C. – G-3 crossed me by not assigning me the men for patrols. Finally got away at 4:15 with McPheeters and Helsel. Took a bath in a public bathhouse. It was real hot water but a dirty place on the side of a canyon (very deep) with a beautiful arch bridge. Had a snootful of vin blanc at the casino and at upstairs. Went for a walk and ended up in a native café. Talked with a man and his "friend" whom I thought was his wife (from Paris.) Helped my French a lot. Going back, I passed a photo shop and saw some pictures of officers of the Luftwaffe. People are helpful in aiding you in all circumstances here. Natives do not like the French. We store our bags tomorrow. The dope: March two days and two nights and then attack and destroy!

January 13, 1943 – Caught a rabbit in our tent. Seemed so tame that we gave it to a French farmer on whose farm we are bivouacked. He and family posed for a picture and they showed us their rabbits and pigeons. Gave them some candy and gum. Hard time trying to get to Constantine. McPheeters forgot to pick me up. Went in with Chuck and bought six bracelets, two leather bags, a belt, and napkin rings. Ran into the same native café and some vino blanc again. Almost a fight about the price – three bottles 20 francs and the fourth bottle was 65 francs. Coming out, I buddied up with a policeman and he took me to the Kasbah to buy the bracelets. Saw quite a bit of the city – bridges, tunnels, and the Kasbah. A British M.P. driving a jeep. The natives don't like the French and the French don't like the British. Came back to casino and picked up "Johnny" Otto Kemerling of the 81st and he and I did another section of the Kasbah. Some fun and no harm. French is getting better and I can be understood now. Cantil, of the G-2 section, read in the *Stars and Stripes* newspaper that he has a new daughter!

I am struck with the engineering ability of the French with their bridges, tunnels, irrigation, etc. Recall the canals, arches, aqueducts, viaducts, and the old mill with the 500 pigeons flying about. Also the road coming up to C.

January 15, 1943 – We have six planes in the Company now. All are Piper Cubs for artillery observation. The morning was used in getting all luminous buttons together for use in moving the Division unit up. The plans are being changed again. The best to date – a letter to a manager of a French photo shop in Oran to send film and shoes. Sent many cards home.

January 16, 1943 – Still collecting buttons. A B-25 ran into a P-38 at Thélepte Airport and bombs exploded and destroyed both planes. General Ward, at officer's call, asked all unit commanders to be on their toes. Some of his remarks: "Sun at our backs worth 25% more tanks. Take care of transportation. 32 trucks could carry a battalion of infantry; the end justifies the means, sometimes a violation of principle will fool the enemy – use dispersion and be smart."

Chuck, Freddie Hughes, and I go to Telergma and saw "Dee II" – General Doolittle's plane. Many P-38s and B-25s shot up. Also lots of Spitfires and some B-17 Flying Fortresses just came into Aine Mlina.

Group at Battalion was really bedded down. There was a Roman inscription on the stone fence in the yard. Cold as hell.

A camel caravan was down the road. They go at a faster pace than you would think.

We are now at Oued Seguin. One of the cyclists smashed his cycle and I have to investigate it.

January 17, 1943 – McQ read the order of march and we are third group. I went to Constantine with Hay to get additional data and to arrange about picking up General and C/S. Saw a large camel caravan. People here, like those in Ireland, dress up and parade about on Sunday. At night, we went over to airport at Telergma and bought some dates and a bar of candy. It is reported that the Arabs are digging up the battalion's dead to get clothes. The jokers are really in rags.

January 18, 1943 – Walked to a nearby farmhouse to talk with the French family there. They are Madam and Monsieur Magota, Oued-Seguin, Department de Constantine, Ageria. While there, I saw the rabbit which I game them, their other rabbits, the pigeons, a turkey, and some guineas, one of which was pure white. The Arabs are digging up the trash and refuge that we bury! Too bad as they scatter it to the four winds. We are moving up and our tanks, half-tracks, and scout cars sure make a sweet sound at night. General Mac came over and raised hell about fires in my area. Then he called later and raised hell about all fires. While chasing fires, the British warmed up their guns and the tracers looked pretty in the sky – so "Mac" raised hell again. Finally got disgruntled and went to bed.

January 19, 1943 – Morning used in getting ready to go. Sent trucks in to pick up C-A, etc. and bring them out. After much checking of the times – we have one time and the British have another – we finally leave at dark to push up to Aine Bedia to bivouac. Some 80 miles in a total blackout. I was in full charge of our column. Chauncey said "Tony, I am a passenger." Picked up several "strays" along the way – everything from a cycle to a medium tank. Word was passed around that paratroops had landed near and their rifles were all cocked. Bivouacked at 0330 with an assortment of cycles and tanks as strays. I'm dead tired, but we lost no vehicles. Too tired to pitch a tent and so I slept under a tree.

January 20, 1943 – Woke up at 0600 and started to plan the movement of the Hq. CP by infiltration. Sent them up in groups of 8-10 vehicles. I take up the second group. Chauncey is one hell of a good egg and has a fine sense of humor and real powers of leadership. Saw a herd of camels grazing outside of Tébessa. A lot of guns there. Arrived at Bou Chebka at 4:00pm and started to rearrange the bivouac to suit the vehicles. Everything came in okay – even the planes which landed in the road and were wheeled into the woods.

January 21, 1943 – Everyone was on edge waiting for something. Checked all camouflage and of course "OP6 and Nettie." In the PM, I tried a man for opening his "C" rations without authority. Fined him $5.00 per can so as to establish a policy. Then Chauncy sent me out to straighten out a matter of one of our road blocks. The 6th Infantry had come across a road being mined by the French. I arranged to have the mines removed during the day and replaced at night. The French officer was Captaine Bodiot, Genie Divisionnaise, Divisionnaise de Marche de Constantine. He was quite a talker. He has a family like mine (no boy) and all are older. Lived in Paris and was a building engineer. He had been a POW, but was released by the Germans because he was a veteran of the last war. Said that Weygand's Army disbanded for lack of equipment and was depending on mules. He was very easy to cooperate with and ended up eating supper with us.

II Corps has rifled the General again. CCA was called up and he was left out of the picture – someone is gunning for him at the expense of lives. Politics has really entered this theater. He knew that Roosevelt knew that this war was coming about three years ago – so he is on the outside and will be kept there I am afraid. McQ is making the effort and Robinette is in support of him. General Ward just knows too damn much for Eisenhower, Clark, Fredendall (who will be in command of II Corps), and Porter. Where the hell is Oliver? I am sorry for the old man as he has worked hard to get this Division here and properly equipped and trained.

A jeep just turned over on the main road and injured four soldiers. Had news today that Walker, one of our cyclists, missing for the past few days has been found dead. A good kid ("Porky") even if he did let a British guard pass into the bivouac without a challenge. The whole CP is down in spirit tonight on account of the General not getting his chance.

January 22, 1943 – Still checking the camouflage and OP6 in the AM. In the PM, fired my Garand and my pistol. The rifle really shoots well. Took a bath (whole body) in a gallon of water in a small can. It was probably a sight and wish that I could have had a picture. Later, Chuck and I got tight with the rest of the scotch bought in Telergma. Maraist and the French liaison officer, Colonel Bruze, came by for the end of the bottle. Chuck really gave me a boost and told the Mariscal off. Later, Chuck went out on a cycle and scared the hell out of me.

I forgot to tell of the old Roman ruins that were in our minefields. As near as I can see, they were custom houses for the old site of Carthage. Everyone is really on an edge about the deal the General is getting.

A funny report is back to us: A Sergeant of CC "A" who was sent to an aircraft recognition school and is an expert on aircraft identification, broke his leg diving in a slit trench when of our P-38s came over!

January 23, 1943 – Our M-3 came in and is in good shape. The issue of command is in doubt: there is a radio silence and we cannot talk with our reconnaissance or them with us. This

Figure 5-2   Roman ruins

will needlessly cost many lives but II Corps will not give us the okay to lift our radio silence.

This PM mail came and the German reconnaissance planes were up very high – we can only see their plumes! They are probably taking a few snapshots of our positions and I am sure they have spotted our CP. So, the slit trenches go deeper.

CCA, gone only one day, has already lost three officers and some enlisted sent out in jeeps on reconnaissance.

Chuck and I go to Thélepte and saw airport and some ruins – four columns of an old temple.

I opened my sample "K rations" which were very good.

Stacks' 6th Infantry left at dark to kick hell out of the Krauts. Chauncey came by and made Chuck the Provost Marshall and me the Headquarters Commandant.

<u>*January 24, 1943*</u> – We kicked hell out of the Italians and the Germans. Stack is headed for Sfax but was called back by II Corps. Their order was funny: "Send part of force to 'H'." No

objective, no number, and no mention of what part of force. We are still too close in bivouac. Our artillery lifted its fire today to allow the Germans to attend to their wounded and bury their dead. A pilot tells an interesting thing: An Italian pilot, shot down in his bomber, cursing the Germans and got out maps and told where their airfields were. He was mad because they had assured him that no Allied planes were in the area.

Chuck and I had chicken in the mess truck tonight.

A rabbit is playing about in the bivouac – black and white with some tan. He is making the General's tent his headquarters. Mail today.

January 25, 1943 – Rained and very cold. An Arab was brought up speaking fluent Italian and turned out to be the undercover man for the French police. We captured 150 men and lost two medium tanks. Some Italians captured offered to take arms against the Germans.

January 26, 1943 – Saw several snapshots and other personal effects of the prisoners captured by Stack's force. Some had been in Norway, Denmark, France, and Italy. The preponderance of those captured were Jaguars (tank destroyers.) Stack said that he got out just in time as roads and mud would have caught him there and possibly caused him some trouble. As it was, he had to have some MPs get his stragglers back. Kelly reports that the M-3 has "Missouri Military Academy" painted on its side and is ready for a picture. The tent is full tonight – Percy Brown, Ray Cochran, "Swiss" Pritchard, Doc Ginn, Chuck Miller, Eddy and myself – all trying to get warm or write letters.

Chapter 6

Success against Italians

January 27, 1943 – Took some pictures of our M-3, "Missouri Military Academy" with Colonel Dittemore, Ray, Chuck, Buck and other tank crews. Hope that they turn out okay.

The General called a meeting and asked that reports be accurate, check up on orders, take care of transportation as we had lost many half-tracks and tanks in the mud (6th McGinness) and we had no removal vehicles present. Leave a man with each vehicle!

Checked camouflage most of the morning. Wrote letters at night. Another Arab brought in with a U.S. Message Book. Turned him over to the French who handle all Arabs very roughly. G-4 had a laugh on him… all captured vehicles go through his section and Stack's outfit brought in a bicycle which was listed as enemy transportation. Chuck's MPs are getting a workout these days taking the column forward.

Chapter 6 – Success against Italians 97

Figure 6-1 M3 medium tank dubbed "Missouri Military Academy"

Top: Chuck Miller, Detroit, MI, Gunner: T-4 Harold V. Richardson, Orleans, IN, Left to Right: T-5 Irvin A. Miller, St. Paul, MN, Sgt. William L. Ranerie, Chicago, IL, Capt. Ernest C. Hatfield, Malone, NY, Lt. Col. H.P. Dittemore, St. Joseph, MO, Lt. Col. Ray L. Cochran, Joplin, MO, Pvt. Edward Miller, Cleveland, OH, Lt. Lee Kelly, Oden, AR, Sgt. Charles H. Sutherland, Sturgis, KY

January 28, 1943 – This morning I go in search of a larger bivouac and find none. I saw a native Arab *sans* a stitch of clothes. Also saw some old ruins.

Pete Haines came in with a plan to tear hell out of Rommel and it set the staff to work.

General Fredenall and General Anderson came up to see General Ward. Fredenall seems to be a very pleasant person and considerate of all of those under him. Colonel Pritchard was supposed to take me on a rail to help with tank salvage, but at the last minute, it was decided that we wouldn't go.

One of the artillery battalions sure blasted the Wops at dinner. Heard third shot registered and then they put 18 in for effect.

Send some rolls of film to Constantine to be developed. The General's rabbit is still about. Wayne Smart came in about the time we were getting ready for bed. He is certainly a whiz – very witty and full of life. He has a very good sense of humor and is good at handling people. He was S-4 of CCB. He said CCB was on the way.

January 29, 1943 – Some of the tanks were coming in at breakfast. The General was out at the junction saluting them in. Went over and checked the tank platoon and found some dirt and oil in the engine compartments. Got Signal Company to develop the roll of film of the MMA tank exposures. Went with Lt. Col. Dittemore to see new area and to inspect Jake's battalion. A new idea of burying the front of vehicles – very good to protect tires and engine. An Arab family was wiped out by our artillery practice and is being investigated.

Stack's raid for tonight called off. He is really a damn good officer and is excellent on these raids.

General Robinette is here now and General Ward has gone back. Towards Thélepte, there are many ruins of old cities and towns. Some are very large. One still has its pillars standing with the stones on top. The French soldiers are to be pitied. They have no guns, supplies, or transportation.

January 30, 1943 – In the AM, tried to get to Kasserine Pass, but CG says no. About 1:30pm, a staff meeting was held and we were informed that at last the division would attack as a unit. Our mission: We are to reestablish the French at the Faid Pass; to take Maknassy and be prepared for action either on the coast or to the south; to cut off Gafsa-Gareees road and bottle up and destroy the enemy in the vicinity of El Guettar. We also are to take precaution against enemy action in vicinity of Fondouk-Pichon. Hay had recon, McQ, CCA, Stack CCG, Maraist, CCP, Inskeep division reserves, Robinette CCB. We were to leave for Gafsa at 8:45pm but didn't get away until 10:30pm. Delay due to 168th Infantry which our staff forgot to furnish gas. The General was mad as hell and I didn't blame him. Column in a complete blackout. On the way up, I picked up at least 20 or 25 trucks, jeeps, etc. who were out of gas or lost or out of water. Just had them join the tail of column. Got in about 0400 – almost lost some.

Bivouacked out on the desert out of Gafsa. Everyone satisfied except for Col. Williams – you can't please them all.

January 31, 1943 – About 0900 and again about noon, German recon planes came over and were engaged with our AA. Several camel caravans passed through the bivouac area which is a sand desert between barren hills. The 81st came in all busted up. Stukas and artillery and mortars. The infantry with Maraist were bombed and strafed and their morale was hurt. Howze is ready to expand bivouac distances.

February 1, 1943 – Spread out farther. Several German planes came over and were driven off. At last, II Corps, now a part of the British 1st Army, gave the General the go-ahead signal. We pulled out at "2nd dark" and went to Sbeitla, a trip of 89 miles. Complete blackout and darker than hell. All vehicles came through okay.

Things to remember: two extra roadblocks outside of Sbeitla; the mess up over our radio especially when Ray "Cork" asked "Who in the hell was officer one!" and "What is my read Dutch!" and the General replies "Roger, slow down Colonel as Fox 5 is lost and he was behind me." Also funny was Nick's "Fox 27 to all of the little foxes."

We pushed a busload of French soldiers to the side and pushed part of the 6th Inf. ahead of us but ran into part of the 13th which was the tail of CCB. Good speed until 1200 and then slow after that. Pulled in at 0300 into an ammunition dump east of town upon the recommendation of Col. Bouley and decided by the C/S, Col. Benson. The General thought that I had disobeyed him about where to bivouac until I explained that the C/S had ordered it.

February 2, 1943 – Spread camp out farther and found a new bivouac area. No sleep last night and little rest today. Destroyed a demolition grenade found in the camp by rifle fire. A Ju 88 came over and set the guns in the area popping.

Got hold of some oranges at 150 francs and five gallons of vino rouge at 16¢ a gallon. Had some party in tent. Ray Cochran came over and talked of mice and men.

February 3, 1943 – Got CP responsibility divided according to groups. C/S decided to change bivouac and selected a patch of cactus as the CP! Col. Williams came out and we set the signal center up. Two air raids today.

The tent caught on fire and burned Chuck's combat jacket and field jacket. A lieutenant of the 81st was in there and kicked over the gas stove. He told of a scout car and crew that were caught in the wadi and they were captured by the Italians. They asked for cigarettes and got none. Then were searched with force and received a cursing from one of our soldiers. One Italian pulled a pistol out and shot him in the stomach. The others were lined up and set to be machine-gunned when a Spitfire dove and scattered the Italians. Two of our soldiers escaped and they murdered the other two. It seems the 81st is not going to take any Italian prisoners!

February 4, 1943 – Moved the CP by infiltration into the cactus patch. Dug fox hole and slit trenches and spread nets. The Stukas came over and gave us a working over three times in the afternoon. They also gave the CO a going over. Some ran and dove for the slit trenches and some manned the guns. We lost a CP tent, a half-track and some holes are in the ambulance. One man injured. We also lost one of our Piper Cubs and two men at the airport. The craters of today's bombs are four to six feet deep.

We have an arch (possibly old Roman) nearby and the Italians were holding a victory march in it until the 701 arrived and ran them out. Everyone is trigger-conscious and will fire at all sounds and planes. We have two AA guns and the crew of one left theirs during an attack, as the gun was not working.

Irwin, my driver, stood by, fed the ammunition, and was a real help. Hope that I can always stand up and fire back.

Freddie Hughes is missing. He took a column to Col. Maraist and did not come back. He's still gone and I hate to lose him.

February 5, 1943 – Buck got a letter from a kid who wrote: "My friend received a letter from another soldier in your Division named Orlando Ward who is a general. Do you know him?"

A Ju 88 Stuka came over today but no raid.

A box of films (18) came in today from Betty.

Colonel Boule, our French officer, told of his experiences before Oran. He was jailed and sentenced when our outfit rolled into Alger. We have lots of magazines now – three *Saturday Evening Posts*, and four *Lifes*! No Freddie Hughes yet. He led a battery into German patrols and is still missing.

February 6, 1943 – Did practically nothing all day long except get mail (boxes for Haynes and Oliver) and send the MMA picture home. "Chief Wahoo" died in his slit trench last night and was buried today. Thompson was also killed by planes yesterday. Hughes and Steiner are definitely missing. Four in three days is very fast.

Maraist captured the headquarters of an Italian general.

February 7, 1943 – Cold as hell and not much to do. Buried extra gasoline bins to keep down fire hazard. Twenty planes came over and gave the boys a scare but they worked on Sbeitla instead. There was not too much to do so I took T-5 Nikolin to

Figure 6-2   T-5 Steiner and Capt. Frederick Hughes (both later captured)

see the ruins. They are definitely Roman. Chipped tile floors and heavy rock from the Atlas Mountains. The French were bivouacked there today. A very beautiful arched bridge crossed one part of the stream. There was a ruin along the banks further down. My thought – the building was put up to impress the Arabic and Phoenician chief. The city housed about eight to ten thousand people at one time.

Cut on the stones:

> *NIONINOPO*
> *MP·CA—AVRELI COMMODI*
> *LVG*
> *PTT·FF10CIS PATRI*

February 8, 1943 – Took some pictures of Eddy, Nick and White. Three Ju 88s came over and got a pasting from our AA – we even threw up the spare sink! Tanks and material are getting hard to get. We are using some stuff left from England.

Rearranged my files in a different box. Tried to get some combat clothes for some general in the 34th. They are all wanting our zuit suites.

Took a bath in the French barracks at Sbeitla. It was full of G.I.s, Moroccans, French, etc. Water was a trickle, but got a bath.

On air alarm today – "Snow White" was finally shot down by some 90mm AA in town. We had gotten quite fond of him.

February 9, 1943 – Two alarms today but the AA boys are keeping them up ahead of us. We are credited with three planes – i.e. – the battalion is credited with three kills. We are putting braces in front of the jeeps to ward off piano wire. Got some letters today but did not write any as I worked on some napkin rings and a flower vase for Betty and the kids made from a shell that shot down a Stuka. Tools are very poor and job may be rather jerry built. We are well hidden in a cactus grove. Food is "C" and Compote and plain but there is no grumbling yet. It looks as if we will park here until the push starts.

February 10, 1943 – I am certainly amazed by the thoughts of the officers in the headquarters. We were sent over here to fight a war and many hold back and think only of getting home. Eddy, McElhenny, Chuck and I are sitting in the tent doing nothing but discussing who and when certain officers will be sent back to the U.S. Eddy possibly has a reason as he has a new son that he has never seen, but the rest of us are here because we're sent here to fight a war and now we talk of getting home. Hell, we should be talking of taking the offensive and kicking the hell out of the krauts. As they say: "It beats the hell out of me."

Ernie Pyle, the columnist, came by and we talked and talked in the tent at night. Has some canned coffee and crackers. Told him about Nick and how he was a smart boy and also about the Missouri Military Academy. He talked as if he might put us in his column.

February 11, 1943 – Up early. Col. Bouley was one of the plotters in turning over Algiers to us. He had been imprisoned and sentenced to be shot for his help when we took the city. He is accompanied by a 3rd Lt. who spent some time in Milwaukee and spoke English and acts as an interpreter.

Figure 6-3 Famed WWII correspondent Ernie Pyle

Another thing: The Germans send over Stukas three or four at a time – never over six while we send over 12 at a time. Which makes most sense?

Rommel reported down to 50 tanks moving and about 100 stopped for no oil or gasoline. Col. Maraist came over to help us drink a bottle of scotch that Chuck had dug up. We hear of the battle of Sened Station where he had a combat team. Quite a battle, but the talk is beginning to become stale as this was the 4th time that we had heard it. All in all, I draw on conclusion – one battle (the first) is like a football game – there are Saturday quarterbacks, heroes, and goats! General Eisenhower is now in charge of the 1st, the 8th and II Corps – watch for the popping now!

February 12, 1943 – These cactus needles are the nuts! If one sticks you near a joint of the body, then the joint will tighten up and be sore as hell. Pictures from Constantine came in with Gen. Fauwich. "Doc" Ginn, in the regular Army for 16 or 17 years, is planning to receive his uniform allowance! I hope that he does, but it all adds up to no sense. I already received $100.00 for the balance of my uniform allowance. The 5th Co. of the 7th Panzer Regiment is now equipped with our light tanks. The krauts have much of our equipment – radio crystals, jeeps, 2½-ton trucks, etc. They are using them often and it confuses us to no end. G-2 has warned us all of this several times.

February 13, 1943 – Dug in our canvas tent and our vehicles. We are now underground to get out of the bitter cold wind and safety from the bomb fragments. Snow drifts three and four feet thick are reported north of here.

Lt. Col. Williams is now C/S and Chauncey takes over the 13th AR. Had to file the papers on my 1st court martial. A G.I. who opened his "C" rations.

"Chuck" is sure down; he thinks that he is a "has been" and it is too bad as he does have a lot on the ball but they pass over him too often. Eddy sure wants to get home to see his son and it bothered him a bit today.

Forgot to mention about a visit to Sbeitla yesterday. The most impressive thing in a very torn up and deserted town was the Catholic Church. The statues were very good and very beautiful. Dust had settled over everything, but it was easy to see that this had been one of the better-kept buildings. There is a mosque in the town surrounded by a wall and we (Capt. Davis and I) could not enter the court. Another sight to recall: a painting of about three or four silver popular trees (like those in the paintings of Picard or Normandy) and an almond tree in bloom. Not a leaf on the almond tree and covered by a white blossom with a background of African blue sky and a few spots of cumulous clouds.

By the way, the skies and sunsets are beautiful here – spots of clouds but too windy for dive bombing. One or two formations looked as if they were in the center of a whirlwind.

Chapter 7

Krauts Break Through

February 14, 1943 – Looked for a new area this AM as the krauts had broken through. Cochran and I found a spot at Kasserine – an open field. Went with Cochran and Eager on a dusty, but uneventful trip.

Stukas came over at 3:50pm and 4:15pm. We definitely got one and he fell kerplunk in the olive grove. They came in and shot at the crossroads and hit a jeep with three soldiers. Everything was demolished. Some money and letters were torn to shreds. Only the engine block remained recognizable. Our gun jammed during the first raid, but we got in on the second one. I sure thought that they had gotten Service Company as three bombs hit in that area. One hit about 25 yards to our rear, cut a telephone pole in two, and tangled up the phone wires. The crater was 4 ½ ft. deep and about 15 ft. across.

A Bible was torn up in the jeep mentioned above and Nick brought in a few verses and read Acts 16-9 – quite a sermon about the second front.

Figure 7-1 Remains of downed German Ju-88 Stuka

A funny thing: two lieutenants from the 13th came in to ask for something and were griping that Headquarters Company was sitting around doing nothing while they fought the war. They had just beaten everyone to the slit trenches (one of which we had condemned because it was too deep.)

Ernie Pyle came and I helped him pitch his shelter tent. Nick has been of great assistance in fixing up the tent and stove. Tex Hightower came by in the shank of the evening. The krauts are much closer and have moved to Sidi bou Zid and have occupied it. The firing is louder. II Corps has left – the French have left and our 90mm AA crews have left. They are all getting the jitters. The staff calls every half-hour to ask who is on the road and passing the bivouac.

<u>*February 15, 1943*</u> – The British have doubled the column and we are left high and dry. Four observation planes came over about breakfast and we gave them a hot reception. Our

group shot at a flock of our own coming in very low and hard to see. No one was hurt. Gave most of the men a chance to get some sleep this AM to make up for last night. We organized a combat command and sent them on towards Sidi bou Zid but no contact had been made with the enemy. Nick and Eddy had quite a discussion as whether to fire on dangerous aircraft or not. It is an almost endless task to determine when to and when not to open fire. So far, we have had four refugees from Sidi bou Zid, a couple with two kids. We fed them and sent them on their way. The situation is bad. Rommel is about six or eight miles up the road. Chuck starts out in the armored car to bring back part of the 168th that had been trapped but was held up by a German road block and had to return. We had all on duty again at night. A German patrol in an American jeep was reported. Chuck left at 0500 to try to bring back part of the 168th and succeeded. It turned out to be a very wise move and saved a lot of trucks and men.

February 16, 1943 – G-3 sent us on a rat race this AM. About two or three miles south of us several strange vehicles stirred up the dust so we were ordered to have our tank engines warmed up. Then, the order was to find out who they were so Chuck and I started out. Right away, our M-3 threw its track so only four could go out and did go.[1] About five or six miles out, we observed both groups from some high ground. In the meantime, a Piper Cub had been dispatched to check also. It turned out to be Crosby's battalion and no one knew where he was. It was strange that neither G-2, G-3, or G-4 did not know this.

One rumor is that Alger's battalion cannot be contacted. I hope it is false. Division kept telling him via radio to push on so

---

[1] This would be the end for the M3 tank dubbed "Missouri Military Academy." It was never recovered and was most likely captured by the Germans.

much that he finally called in and told them that he was turning his command over to his executive officer. Now they cannot find him.

We lost 53 tanks there. Lt. Col. Williams sent for me. It seems that the 47th Medical sent an ambulance full of prisoners into the CP. Everyone crowded around after an MP let them through the gate. He was sore as hell and I don't blame him. But later, he sent for Capt. Davis and Lt. Ulmer and we waited 40 minutes outside his tent for him to tell us that he wanted hot trays sent to those who worked thorough the meal hours. It really beat the hell out of me. Griping about cold food when hot food could be obtained by walking to the kitchen 500 yards away? We had just lost a battalion of tanks and men! This from the same guy who didn't know where Crosby's battalion was and had just lost as much equipment as we had in Ireland. They just can't get into their heads that this is a war and is a discomfort to all. We will win – the G.I.'s will do it in spite of us officers...

Maj. Auttman, from Oklahoma, lost all of his equipment and had to return on foot as did several of them.

An air raid again today, but turned out to be just a questionable plane flying rather high.

The shelling and artillery fire can be plainly heard all evening and at dusk.

Ernie Pyle has just turned up again with Cole of the V.P. and we invited them in to get warm. The Rec. was almost taken out of the picture by Maraist at Station Sened. Later, Lt. Current called to report that tomorrow may tell the tale as there are some 155mm cannons being dug in by the Germans just out of Sbeitla. We will be registered on more than likely.

Looks bad. Shelling is in plain sight and German tanks are reported near us. They started burning the fuel and ammo dumps at about 9:00pm and it continued until the wee hours. Tracers made a pretty picture at night – except when coming at us! There were lots of flares also. We organized a combat team to try to hold Sbeitla. We have our artillery emplaced in the ruins.

February 17, 1943 – Shelling continued all night and increased starting about 0400. The ammunition dump and town were blazing at dawn. We could also see that the airport at Thélepte also was ablaze.

We had a French soldier die in our hands and we buried him in the cactus. There was lots of talk with Doc Steinberg about burying him without permission.

At noon, the road was filled with French stragglers and our 168th Infantry. We were strafed in the AM but had a good air cover most of the time that was worth a great deal. By 2:00pm, our artillery occupied part of our bivouac area about 100-200 yards up the road. Corps told us to withdraw at 11:00am and then at 3:00pm asked us to hold ½ hour longer. The General gave them hell for vacilating so much and told them that holding would sacrifice a battalion of infantry and the blood bath would be on their hands.

The road in front of the bivouac area was being bombed when the 6th Infantry comes piling through the cactus in their half-tracks and debouched on the plains. Then the 27th Field Artillery comes streaming through the cactus and takes position near the General's CP so he says we had better move out. When I get started, he says to withdraw to an area in the cactus about three miles back. There, we pull up and reorganize the column amid some confusion and some bombing and strafing. We pull through the Kasserine Pass and bivouac in another cactus patch for the night. McElhenny sure worried at 11:00am. He said, "The Old Man has gone crazy – we should have left at dawn!"

"Whitey" White pulled his stakes, disconnected his phone, and left without permission. We were all scared as hell but not bad enough to do anything like that.

February 18, 1943 – Howze called Chuck and I about 3 or 4am and said that we would move. I was to send an officer to recon a route cross country to get on the west road to Tébessa. Lt. Stargel went out and reported no road so I set out and try to find one over a deep wadi (valley) and a ford crossing. After reporting back, they decide to use my route. In the meantime, Lt. Eddy and G-3 traffic MPs had gone on to post the road through Thala. No MPs were available for me, so I borrowed a jeep from G-3 and lead them out cross-country. We halted on the other side of the wadi and reform the group. Then, I borrow a jeep from the artillery and head out. I ran into RJ and find that there is no road in the mountain pass. So I grab a bulldozer that was handy and made a lucky guess on which way to go. Then the C/S, Lt. Col. Williams, calls me back and very excitedly tells me that the column is to be moved off the road and be straightened out. It took about three hours and proved nothing to me except the C/S knew nothing of columns. All during this time, the C/S was screaming and shouting "If in danger, if in doubt…!" It was a real show and a lesson to me. I was doing too much: operating the radio, the column, finding the correct road (even making part of it), and just sweating it out in general while he was screaming. I was mad enough to be tied. Finally, we pulled through and bivouacked on a plain south of Tébessa. I was dead tired and ready to hit the hay.

Things to recall: the team of infantry and artillery in the Sbeitla bivouac, the destruction of the phone poles by the tank platoon, the route across the plains to the 2nd cactus patch, the burning of Sbeitla, the dive bombers on the road attacking the column, the shells whooshing past your ears, the tracers at night, the burial of the French soldier.

February 19, 1943 – Slept late and then got up and spread the bivouac. II Corps has moved from Tébessa and we are reinforced by more medium tanks. It is rumored that Rommel will try to defeat the British 1st before the 8th can make contact.

We are part of the 1st Armored and will try to hold him as well as we can. Our losses have been high in vehicles, but we have taken some of their vehicles also. Alger is gone completely.

February 20, 1943 – The C/S sent me out to recon another road out of this location to Tébessa past the pass. I found a fair outlet that cut through some country that was very much like the Ozarks. Tébessa is a very interesting city – an old walled city with tunnels, etc. I bought some bread and the owner would take no money so I paid him with cigarettes. I wish I had more time to see the city. There were two white Spitz dogs herding goats. There is snow in the mountain passes coming back and it is cold as hell.

Mail from Betty and Stribling.

February 21, 1943 – What a day. They decided to move CP over the pass into an area next to ammo dump and I vetoed the location. It was too rough and near our ammo dump. Williams ("War Horse") screamed. He loses his temper too easily. We ended up putting it in the "Ozark" area with perfect cover – one of the best locations yet. Lt. Current, leader of the 3rd group, lost his group and turned to column in the wrong direction and headed down the pass. After lots of screaming and shouting, we finally got the CP in and bedded down.

February 22, 1943 – After all the planning yesterday, we are to move near Haidi (pronounced Hydia). So we move out down the pass with "War Horse" screaming at trucks, etc. who were entering the column. Trip was okay, but the C/S doesn't know a damn thing about leading a column.

We had a bad road and kept speed at 15 mph. We pulled in during daylight and everything was okay except the parking lot was disorganized. We will whip this CP yet! Had a hectic night checking the guards and the outpost, billeting the officers for 1st AD, putting in the AA, and alerting the guards for Maj. Gen. Harmon who is a big shot.

February 23, 1943 – Checked bivouac and sighted machine guns all day long and tired as hell. A good letter from Betty about the Christmas at home. Also a good letter from Kelly. Some POWs, one German officer and eight enlisted, were brought into the bivouac last night. A big artillery shell hit near us and shook us all up. We are well hidden and they were using fire as reconnaissance. The C/S is satisfied with this bivouac area.

February 24, 1943 – Our losses have been large but have been replaced somewhat. About 0230, I was called to the CG's tent. We are to occupy and defend the Kasserine Pass. Our bivouac is to be near there and I am sending Lt. Helsel forward to find billet for the CO.

A Sgt. of the 81st Recon had quite a story: His company was wiped out at Sidi bou Zid and he and 17 others start cross country on foot. Sixteen of them were captured and he and one other escaped. Arabs with U.S. guns and ammunition took their clothes. They hit his buddy over the head with a rifle when he resisted and left him in the gully. They took their clothes and he walked back last night stark naked and cold as hell. He was picked up by a British officer who outfitted him with a British uniform. He then made his way to the supply dump and met Colonel Dittemore.

I saw a covey of large quail or small pheasants in the "Ozark" area where the engineers bivouacked south of Tébessa. We stand by all day to move and then do not go anywhere.

February 25, 1943 – We are definitely chasing the Africa Korps from the Kasserine Pass and beating the hell out of them. General Ward has gone forward to CCB to help direct the work of clearing them out. Stragglers are drifting in – some walking as much as eight days with no food or water. We are shooting at all Arabs as they are giving our positions away by fires to sheep flocks. They are also stealing anything they can and digging up our garbage pits. One of my sentries got one in the leg last night and Sterling fixed him up and turned him into the 47th Medical Bn. The tide has turned to favor the British for their conduct in this war and away from II Corps which has fettered away our Armored Division. We have the Guards Armed Division, the Derbyshire Yeomanry, and the Constantine Division de Marche all in this area. We chased the Germans out of the Pass. The British on the left and we were on the right. The Germans are decent fighters. They bury the dead, tend the wounded and are more or less considerate of POWs – more than I can say of the French or Italians.

February 26, 1943 – Have reorganized the column and the CP is set up. Reviewed the transportation of the CP and made recommendation to the C/S to cut down our 125 vehicles. At noon, I received an order to move the CP to the same place where we just came from after 2:00pm (later changed to 1:30pm.) We really hustled. It started to rain and everything looked snafu – a real mess. Right away, Ray Cochran lost his new jeep against the culvert. Road bad – lots of slipping and very wet. One mile out of Tébessa, my recon reported a bridge out just before the pass so we halt the column. C/S gives me okay to go forward and check. A 2½-ton truck broke through a bridge and blocked the road. After a one hour delay, we detour around and come in over an old trail to the "Ozark" woods area. About one mile out of the bivouac area, the vehicles start to slide off and stick. We yank them out with the wrecker and a light tank. To place it all with a laugh, Bouly, in a touring car, gets across the road and slides off. He will not let the column go through until I get there. His 3rd lieutenant, the interpreter, passes out in a fit and – there I was – mad enough at the French to be tied. We finally got everything into bivouac.

February 27, 1943 – Checked the bivouac. Bouley's driver, a wealthy Algerian wine maker, gave me a drink of wine. Took a German sight apart and sent the prisms home. Shot craps with Davis and lost some 1,000 francs. Had a real feast on jam, cheese and crackers.

February 28, 1943 – Tony Dantoni came up and reorganized the pay for all. It looks as if we will rest for two weeks. Maj. Gen. Walter "Beetle" Bedell Smith and Col. Bradley of Eisenhower's staff are to visit with us tonight. I borrowed a cot and bedding for them. Buck Hatfield came over and we talked for a long while. He had some good dope:
- Recon should be slow and deliberate – especially ground recon. The Germans try to suck you in.
- Heavy artillery is effective on 88's and tanks at long range.
- Artillery should be utilized rather than tanks for shelling.
- Expect a counter attack at dark.
- They attack when they outnumber us.
- At night we use coaxial guns to aim gun sights on targets too dark to see.
- The Germans use wide and double envelopment and dig in and wait for target to approach before opening fire.
- We should open up when they start using anti-personnel shells or stop firing altogether.
- Immediate air support could have saved Sbeitla.
- Before attack they send out a recon plane and will not fight tank to tank.

March 1, 1943 – Pictures came in and I gave a set to Chuck and Buck. Most of day spent trying to see Cochran. Again, Maj. McElhenny said that I should be given a chance at artillery. We are well hidden in woods, but the camouflage is an ever-ceaseless job.

Figure 7-2 Capts. Venerie and Ernest "Buck" Hatfield outside Oran in the back of General Ward's half-track

Prio R promised us something today, but I did not hear it. Packed napkin rings, flower pot, four glasses, two pieces of chipped marble and sent them home. "Fats Freddie" came over and says nothing. Again, I am promised a promotion and a transfer but doubt if it goes through.

<u>March 2, 1943</u> – Getting ready to fire Headquarters Bn. range ammunition. Had the men police up with washing, shaving, etc.

Snow White over again.

<u>March 3, 1943</u> – All morning on the range. Some of the boys are developing to be good shots. I was hitting at 200 yards with a pistol!

The "Fairy Queen" over again and it took some pictures.

In the afternoon, all unit commanders assembled in a pass about 20 miles south to discuss how to defend an area and refuse entrance to enemy tanks. They decided that all positions could be outflanked. It looks like the 25th and 3 (B-F-US) at once! Chuck and I saw a monastery coming back about five miles south and I will look it up one of these days.

II Corps (Fredendall) does not trust the old man[2]. They even picked every single one of his positions for the Kasserine Pass defense.

"Otto" of Constantine is missing according to Haywood. He was a good egg and I will never forget his screaming "Tony!" in the Kasbah of Constantine!

Losses are great: About 1 tank regiment, ½ artillery battalion, 1 infantry battalion, and 1 engineer company. However, we are ready to go and I am trying to get permission to reorganize but permission has not been okayed.

General Robinette seems to be the fair-haired boy of II Corps. He wears his Croix de Guerre on his coveralls. He will be watching.

From POWs, it appears that these units opposed us:
5th Panzer Division
10th Panzer Division
Herman Goering Regiment
334th Infantry Division
86th Panzer Regiment
90th Jaguars
288th Panzer Regiment (Afrika Korps)
334th Schneller Abt (AT)
580th Recon Battalion
190th Feldgendarmerie
5th Bersaglien
132nd Contracelli

---

[2] Presumably referring to General Orlando Ward.

Quite a bunch.

The gang came over and played poker last night.

March 4, 1943 – Took our new gun, a 20mm, out and fired it. The barrel is from a Spitfire and it sits on a home-made frame with home-made sights and all. It fires a tracer, an anti-personnel shell, and an explosive shell that is super-sensitive. This gun is great and should be manufactured as a real gun for our use. Chuck, Dittemore and I fired at a tree at 300 yards and tore it up. The sights were wobbly so we took it to the Maintenance Battalion and arranged to get some ammunition from the British in Tébessa. While there, I met a Captain Browning and he seemed to be a good egg. On the return from Tébessa, I find that there is an all out to get the boys on a line (in formation) in dress and cleanliness. All after I just got my trousers muddy. We have a huge ammunition dump at Tébessa and one of the poorest roads down the pass. Tex Hightower has quite a write-up in the *Stars and Stripes*.

March 5, 1943 – Took a bath in a 5 gallon can with 1 ½ gallons of water. Checked with headquarters for proper uniform and markings of vehicles. Attended a class in the evening at Sail Five-Seven-Six-Seven east and south of Tébessa Pass on the Bou Chebka Road. Broke my horn-rimmed glasses and now use my G.I. ones from Belfast. At the class: keep tank companies together, put artillery on less mobile side and back, infantry can be used for recon. I was impressed that Howze is not favorably looked upon by the unit commanders. Stack is still best at infantry, Maraist at artillery, Chauncey at tanks. Robinette is one smart monkey. Brigadier General Bradley is visiting us from the British 8th Army. He is here to give advice and talk with any and all of us.

March 6, 1943 – War is hell. From Sbeitla, we hear that dogs are eating the dead in burnt tanks and fresh graves. These same dogs are held in great respect by the Arabs who think that they are people reincarnated. Arabs are more or less patriotic, but are fatalist and disregard gun fire on the battlefield.

Went to Tébessa to see how the 20mm gun was coming along and stopped by the airport to get a cleaning rod and brush.

When I got back, the news broke that "Blood & Guts" Patton is now the II Corps Commander and that Fredenall had been sent back to the States. Right away, everyone put on steel helmets and black ties. Just watch the fur fly now!

A platoon of the 81st captured 100 prisoners around Gafsa today.

I saw a small child playing and running about Tébessa.

March 7, 1943 – "Blood & Guts" Patton is certainly making his presence felt. We had to change the bivouac about in order to get 75 yards between vehicles – even though we were perfectly camouflaged in a forest of pines. By the way, the trees have a very thick bark for the size of the tree – indication of a poor growing season.

My new driver, Buck H. Gibson from Jenkins, Kentucky is doing okay. He is learning the new radio procedures. Our radio operator, Bob Conigan, seems to be okay also. In the afternoon, we went on another tactical walk. Patton was there cussing up one side and down the other – "We don't want anyone to die for our country! We want the g—d------ bastard Germans to die for theirs!" I was not impressed with his style of leadership.

General Ward is certainly a good leader and will shine with the passing years.

An anecdote – Gen. Ward and Col. Williams went up to see "Blood & Guts" at II Corps. There were several British officers present. Patton held his nose and smelled a stink and would not talk to them for four or five minutes. He may be the "hot stuff", but I must see it first. Robinette presented his arguments on tactics at the walk very aptly today.

We sent back to Constantine to get trains and baggage today. The road at the bottom of the Tébessa Pass is sure a mess. Col. Martin held a confession and a mass today.

<u>March 8, 1943</u> – What a day! G-3 called and requested that I go forward to select areas for the Division near the Kasserine Pass with Lt. Current. We are to leave at 8:14am. We finally get away at 9:55am and drive like hell. We have dinner with a company of the 16th Infantry and locate the CP, CCA, and Division Res. The roads and lines on the map do not agree and we have a hell of a time crossing a wadi and a mountain ridge. Even the jeep gets stuck! Finally, we get into the valley and see the wreckage of the battle. Graves of German and Italians. One German grave labeled "Frederic Ritter" and one Italian one labeled "Mario Consumo." We also found a Stuka down near the mouth of the valley. It starts to rain and we had to fight and slide our way back. It was one hell of a time. Each time a truck passed, we would get drenched with mud and water. We get back at 9:30pm and I am so tired and hungry that I can't even get into bed.

<u>March 9, 1943</u> – In the morning, I sweat out trucks to pick up the gas cans and salvage from the Kasserine Pass and tell Signal Company about the phone connections. In the afternoon, I go to Tébessa to get the ammunition and see about my AA gun. I got a new barrel and gun from a British ordinance company at the airport. It was a very muddy ride back.

Mail from Helen, Kay, Kelly, and Betty.

The baggage is back from Constantine. Mine is okay, but someone from the warehouse opened the General's, Colonel Dittemore and Colonel Benson's bag and stole articles or everything. Col. Williams is really ready to raise hell.

Figure 7-3 The new "Jeep" negotiating terrain

March 10, 1943 – General Montgomery and General Patton visited us today. I remember his red hot band and the plated pistols of Patton's. I had a brush with Col. Williams about requisitions for the MP's and I was not at fault since it did not come through me. There seems to be many booby traps. We lost a warrant officer by a booby trap in the olive grove at Sbeitla. An Arab was brought in our outpost clad in an almost full U.S. uniform. He said he bought everything in Tébessa. We turned him over to the French.

March 11, 1943 – A funny thing: prostitution is licensed by and only permitted to be used by the French Army.

An MP picked up an Alabama Negro in an Arab costume – complete with a turban! He hung his head in shame.

Took Elsel forward to see new CP area and formed a mess. There was a gully through the area that was completely hidden from view when we reconnoitered it today. So we'll need to find another location and I came back to tell Col. Williams that the one selected was not okay and I would go out again in the morning.

I got a letter from my son Tone and wrote a reply.

<u>March 12, 1943</u> – I went forward again and selected a new bivouac in the Kasserine Valley. I took a picture of a baby camel and was almost bitten by its mother. Tired as hell.

<u>March 13, 1943</u> – We moved by infiltration – seven echelons of 20-25 vehicles. We lost a water can off of a car. Several vehicles got stuck in the corner of the bivouac but we pulled them out with our M-5 of which we have two.

<u>March 14, 1943</u> – It rained like hell and the place is full of water and mud. I am kidded quite a bit and earn the nickname "Noah" Lumpkin. Everyone seems to be taking the wet conditions in good spirits and are rather nice about it as a whole.

Ray's scout car is stuck and I dubbed it the "Normandie."

Col. Williams came up in a tank and screamed about the arrangement of the tanks.

<u>March 15, 1943</u> – Checked tanks and C/S promised me that I could go to a combat unit after this campaign. We had a good talk and I am commencing to understand him better.

Lt. Fitzgibbons ("Fitz") is being cited for work as an MP straggle duties. Chuck went to the rear echelon. I am busy as hell.

<u>March 16, 1943</u> – I heard a good one from Fitz – "as slow as a heard of turtles."

We are moving up today. We were supposed to leave at 4:30pm, but didn't until the next day at noon. The Kasserine Pass is almost a road of mud. Everything is being winched through or pulled through by a bulldozer.

I had a long talk with Davis. He is quite a philosopher. He says that C/Ss come and go. We either promote them or they get sick. The C/S and CG are at odds over a T-4 Varney, the CG's driver, who is reduced by order of the C/S to the grade of private. Varney, seeing Shackleford, Percy Brown's driver, stuck in the mud, had offered to help pull him out. So they hooked up and were tugging away when the C/S saw them and reduced them on the spot without listening to their side of the tale. Shackleford knew that he shouldn't have tried to move and he was guilty as hell. Varney had McElhemeyer's permission and did not know that he was not to move any vehicles. McElhemeyer tried to see the C/S and take the blame and the C/S would not listen. Therefore, I try to get a word in edgeways with the C/S in Varney's behalf and he would not listen. The CG says that justice was not done. One of his remarks was particularly good: "I have lost all faith in human nature – it is something to see what levels a person will stoop in order to get a promotion. This may cost him. If he is this way in some things, he will be the same way in others." The CG is a rather smart man. He will have to wait until after this campaign and then make an issue of it.

Some time! All night long, we waited to follow the war guard of CCA but everything was late clearing their IP's and the pass was terrible – mud holes with bypasses over 400 yards wide, etc. Chuck and his MPs are out on the job steadily.

March 17, 1943 – Some day – from 1am on we were expecting to leave in an hour or and hour and a half. Had Stangel establish liaison with CCA and he kept me informed of the situation. We ate a hurried breakfast. The kitchens had moved up closer to the road during the night and had new slit trenches already dug! I have offered to have several new exits made in the kitchen trucks to expedite their getting out during an air raid.

Finally, at 11:45am, we pulled out. The CG, G-2, G-3, and G-3 (air) had gone ahead to set up an advanced command post. We got past the Kasserine Pass and streaked out to Thélepte to give the road to the 60CT. We talked at Thélepte by the C/S in order to have some trucks of the Supply Bn. get on the Velivert Road (cross-country) ahead of us. The C/S screamed for the number of vehicles and I said about 100. "About nothing, exactly how many" he replied. Therefore, I get on the scout car and head back up the column. It turns out to be 92 here and some not yet caught up. So I start out cross-country and pull in after dark. Helsel had already set up everything and I thought that he had done a fair job of it. Supper was at 10pm. I checked over the bivouac and started to bed about 11:30pm when the C/S sent for me and then had me get Helsel. He raised hell because of a road and the CP not living up to his plan. He threatened to court-martial Helsel and have me re-classified. I took him up on it! He said that the road should be one way and Helsel had set it up another way. I thought it should be yet another way altogether. He cussed about and raged at Helsel in front of enlisted men. He even warned Helsel that anything he said could be used against him. All this time, it was raining. The whole thing died out with Helsel relieved as Billeting Officer and the C-P refusing to let me go to bed. He said to me, "Hell, I haven't slept for 36 hours myself." Later, I found out that he slept at the advanced message center in the Kasserine Pass and had left word for no one to disturb him except in an emergency. Finally, I go back and he phones me at 1am to move my tent across the road from the MP station.

<u>March 18, 1943</u> – I get to bed at 2am after moving my tent in a pouring rain. One end of the tent falls, but I sleep on. After thinking it over, I get madder and madder about last night. From now on, Grant T. Williams, Signal Corps, will be called "eg" for egotistical.

A pen study of the man that I hope is an injustice: He is the Chief of Staff. He is never wrong. He will be supported or he will not be the Chief of Staff. His main weakness is a minor one – he loses his temper and talks without listening to a word and with not much forethought to his statements. He is a good person to study. I am afraid that he is just too spoiled and an only child. He has traveled quite a bit and went to the U.S. Naval Academy for a few years.

Some things to recall:
- Sending a volunteer 40 year old MP to the 6th Infantry because he did not halt a Lt. Colonel in a jeep crossing a parking line. Broke Varney for trying to help out a fellow driver and save vehicle for the CP.
- Got mad because food was cold after an aluminum tray had been carried ¼ mile in the cold.
- With a shortage of gasoline, sent a heavy scout car 16 miles to see the exact number of vehicles in the column.
- Wants camouflage, but burns a wood fire for himself.
- Wants "yes", "no", or "Maybe" and no other dialog.
- Loses his temper over the smallest and most trivial thing and ignores much larger matters.
- Lied about sleeping.
- Got mad as hell when he had to stand to eat.

This is all good ammunition for the Honorable Clarence Cannon and some of his debates in Congress relative to the War Dept. Someday I may tell Clarence of all of this.

Lt. Col. Howze told me of the plan last night. We are to draw as much of the German Reserve against us in order to relieve Alexander at the Mareth Line. It will be a real fight as the Germans are always looking to go on the offensive.

Davis, Ulmer, and Helsel were parked in a wadi and are about flooded out. Helsel thanked me for taking his side last night. It is the consensus of opinion that we will all be transferred out to the infantry one of these days. G-3 just corrected Eddy. He was getting ready to post guides beyond our outpost! The G-3 section has a time trying to keep all of its details strait.

<u>**March 19, 1943**</u> – One oddity that I have not mentioned before: The ground over here is covered by snail shells. They cover everything and, in some spots, the crunch of breaking the shells while walking is very audible. The ground does not absorb a great deal of water. After a hard rain, you can find dust dirt ½ to 1 inch down.

Chuck returned last night rather late and I was glad to see him back. It is certainly lonesome in a CP tent by yourself. The job of C/S is finally getting old "eg" down. He was sick all day and stayed in until later afternoon.

"Blood & Guts" Patton due to arrive today. We checked the camp, camouflage, motor park, etc. When he arrived, he broke all rules of camouflage and drove right through the CP to the General's tent. I think that someday he should be called on it.

Coming into this area, the main section picked up an Italian motorcycle and repaired it so that it could run. We are having lots of fun riding it behind the tanks and letting its funny sounding engine run. Davis claims that it will hasten the breakdown of the C/S. "eg" is sure burning up the boys. He has raised hell with everyone – even the "Phantom" units of General Alexander on our side! Also gave hell to the Derbyshire Yeomanry officer parking in the wrong area. "eg" just gives them all hell.

We shot down a Me-109 fighter this morning. The pilot landed safely with only his eyebrows singed. He was a very pleasant type of kid. His was Sgt. Tony Ulnur from Nuremburg. He was a civil pilot from Tempelhof and had been flying for five years despite being only 23 years old. He was unmarried. His father, a seed merchant, is old, 72 years, and his mother was 69. He has already lost two brothers in Russia. He came from Russia on Christmas day. He said Russia was "very cold." He has one sister and her husband is in the army. His brothers were in the artillery and infantry. He was sure that Germany would win in Russia, but not so sure about beating the Americans in

Africa. He said, "Joseph Stalin was not good for any of us." He does not want to fight, however he did try to escape. His attitude and demeanor was a very good advertisement for the Third Reich. His intelligence was above normal. His hands were beautiful and nails were well kept. His clothes were cotton and he said he kept warm from the heat of the engine! He enjoyed our cigarettes and gum. He also tried to return a pair of our no-glare goggles that he had found somewhere. Any German would have been proud of him. He was trying to clean his uniform even though a prisoner of war. His plane was burned into two parts and was a complete loss. Someday I would like to see this young man again after the war. You could not help but like him and wonder why we are fighting the Germans when they seem to be so clean and more of our type. When asked if he thought that Germany was right, he replied: "I am a soldier. I do what I'm told. I don't make policies." He definitely did not want to be turned over to the French. The French do not treat the Germans too kindly. So much on him in this diary, but he was impressive in a very great way and sold his country in a way that is hard to put on pages.

We also had some Arabs going towards the German lines. The Arabs are so treacherous and hate everyone so they cannot be trusted. Therefore, we put them to work digging slit trenches. One was a very old blind man and I felt very sorry for him. Another claims that he has a family and three kids and is going to buy some wheat nearby. Poor devils. Another one had some German Marks, some U.S. money, and some Banque of France notes. What can be believed in these days? As a whole, they were awkward with a short-handled shovel. The Germans are parked in plain sight on a ridge about 10-12 miles away. They are setting up a battery of large caliber gun positions within range of our assembly area. But so far, we have no indication that we have held out large reserves of Rommel's force from the attaché by Alexander.

March 20, 1943 – This morning I go with Chuck to see CCA and establish collecting points for prisoners. After one of the hardest rides in a jeep yet, we get to Gafsa. The buildings are still there in fair shape, but the power station is a shambles and most of the wires are cut down. We retook the town by firing a few shells and the Italians marched out – even though the papers said that we stormed it under the eyes of Patton, Eisenhower, and Alexander.

Spring is here and the trees are all budded out. The Germans and Italians have mined the roads and fields about Gafsa very densely. You really must stay on the land and not get off! The enemy signs for a mine field is orange, white and black squares set within one another. Ray Cochran was with us and he was scared to death of mines.

We leave Gafsa and go the Station ZANNOUCH, where CCA was parked temporarily on an open field. General McQuillan was there and he really seems to be a good egg. The more that I see of him, the more that I like that man. He grows on you. He offered some "C" rations to us but we declined. Later, we found out that they were running short.

The Italians are about 2,000 yards away and McPheeters and his 91st is blazing the hell out of the hills to bring them out. We inspect the railroad station and it was a shambles and fires had been started in all rooms. However, there was a water tower there that might have some value. Both sides had been there many times. There was German, Italian, French, and U.S. newspapers. There was a row of poplars near the station that were very beautiful. From Gafsa to Zened there were blanket fields of desert flowers that had a pungent smell and a herd of about 250 camels grazing about. Four of them were coal black and the others were from white to light tan to dark brown. They all looked like snakes and are not the romantic "ships of the desert" that I had been left to believe. We come back to the same route and go to the Supply Bn. and had coffee and the best cherry preserves and crackers with "Puttie Put." He had been flooded out with the heavy rains of the past week or so. We came by the ration dump. Here we found prisoners, food, MP's, mail, gas, oil, and even a body of a soldier recently brought in from Gafsa. He was a victim of a Tellermine which, when they are tripped, they jump from the ground and explode in the air just like shrapnel shells. Puttie Put says that the shells we heard yesterday at the dump were the detonation of mines by the engineers and there were 70,000 gallons of gas less than 100 yards away.

After getting back to the bivouac, I meet a new guest. He was a tall (6'6") Scotsman from the British 8th Army who is here to help with the G-3 Section. He had been a leather merchant in London before the war. He described how the 8th crossed one of the numerous salt marshes on their dash to the west. They used the stones from a native village to build the road. McElhemeyer tipped me off that we would have quite a delegation from the Turkish Army with us about the 3rd of April. It looks as if we are to honey them up. My letter to Oran regarding the roll of film is getting results. Davis received a money order for $3.50 as change from the shoe-roll of film deal. Better sounds tonight the medium tanks are rolling on the road just outside of the bivouac.

Betty writes that Tone and Anne are kite-conscious and are having a real time with the ones that I made last spring.

I've tried to fill these latest sheets with my impressions and any other notes that I could recall on this country or any people that I might have contact with. Perhaps the most interesting character about this section is "Nick" – a gentleman, a scholar, and a man of work.

William Milo Nikolin, 30 years old.

He is great on argument and debate. He has studied:

    Kindergarten   Innsbruck, Austria

Grammar School	Zemum, Autro-Hungary
High Schools	Belgrad, Servia
	New York City
	Elizabeth, NJ
Colleges	Columbia (1yr)
	Rutgers (1 semester)
	Butler (2 ½ years)
	Sorbonne (1 year)
	Rome (2 ½ years)
	Belgrade (1 ½ years)
	Pittsburg (1 semester)
U.S. Army	(2 ½ years as of this date)

Speaks the following languages:
  English
  French
  German
  Russian
  Some Slovakian

<u>**March 21, 1943**</u> – We captured 109 Italian prisoners. About 7:30am, HQ called me to look for a new bivouac near station Sened! Roads poor and drove like hell and back at noon – Lts. Ulmer, Helsel, and Jacobson (sig? Co.) were with me. Saw the 6th Infantry put on a real show: they came across the valley in ag? cal.? And the 68th Field Artillery was ahead firing when a plane came over – each infantry man had no place to go and kept head down until it was pronounced friendly. Recall going ahead of the guns to all the new positions. We leave at 2:10pm and start trailing the advance guard of CCB? A mean trip – at the end four Stukas came over and disorganized our column somewhat but all came through safely. Tired and sore from riding a rough jeep so much.

Figure 7-4   T-5 William Nikolin "Nicky"

March 22, 1943 – About 12:30 or 1:00am the C/S called and sent me, Ulmer & Eager (Sig. Co.) on a chase for another command post. It was difficult on account of no light – back about 6:15 or 6:30am. C/S asleep so I tell the General – he said that there would be no move until later. So I catch breakfast and get some snooze. Lt. Eddy was wounded in the shoulder by the planes yesterday at Zannouch Station – not serious but painful. About 5:00pm they decide to move after dark and so I yank them out and sit them down. We are beating the hell out of the Axis here now. Many prisoners – a funny one – an Italian Sergeant, in charge of a gun crew, after seeing one of his shells bounce off our Mark IV said "Boys let's be reasonable" and they surrendered.

<u>March 23, 1943</u> – CS let me go up and we find about 30 Italians ready in our enclosure at Sened. One was about 32, nice looking, and a Professor of Contemporary Literature at the University of Tunisia, married, and studied in London. He said: "Our union with Germany is not good." I go and find Col. Dittemore in charge – there are 250-260 prisoners already and so I am taking them back "en Quantro"? when the C/S sends for me. I take Ulmer and Sig Co. forward, select a CP in an olive orchard south of Maknassy and send back for the CP to come forward. It was a rush job and very dusty – report of 120 Italians just over the ridge has alerted some of the boys. We are ahead of everything and all set to kick hell out of the Afrika Korps. About 9:00pm, I get several jobs for Chuck and work them out as he is not back. Enemy planes came over, (?) and some bombs nearby and some strafing. We do not return fire.

I am tired as hell. General Williad II Corps stops by and I had the maintenance section repair his car.

<u>March 24, 1943</u> – Patton called on Ward to attach with tanks last night and Ward settled for this. At 7:00am, 3rd Battalion, 60th Infantry did not take their objective and it is holding up the plans. Duck says that Patton may relieve Ward if attack does not move okay. Ward went up this AM to lead them on – he is certainly one damn fine able officer and if relieved then we deserve to lose.[3]

Bombs falling about this AM but we are not firing as it looks as if we are well hidden in this olive grove south of farmer Louy's house. Bombing keeps up most of the day. A refugee

---

[3] General Ward was indeed later relieved of his command by General Patton. He would be the only general relieved by Patton throughout the entire war. Many scholars believe that political factors played a significant part in Ward's relief.

with several in family was dumped on my hands. Their house had top blown off. Two old parents, two young parents, and three small children. Germans are sneaking around to the south of us and infiltrating through the passes in the ridge – seen by (?) C.P. and substantiated by G-3.

I put everyone on guard – and enemy plane with us most of the night. Stopped by the farmhouse of Loury – he has some real horses and several small colts – all race horses. I gave his son some sugar and coffee for showing me the stables. They seem to be rather wealthy – barns and stables were large and well kept – farm was 10 by 20 kilometers.

We shot down one of our own planes during fracas late in the PM – so an order came out for no firing in any way shape or form unless attacked. There was a mix up by the 81st Recon. And it is not certain what we have on the flank. Reported that 350 infantrymen were through the passes and ready to swoop down on us at 8:30pm. Col. Rose left his rifle, a carbine, in his car – and no one with it. It was stolen and he rained all kinds of hell about it – rather dumb – a G.I. would be tried for the same offense.

March 25, 1943 – The circling plane has finally dropped its bomb at daybreak and there were several guns firing at him – am really up against it trying to catch the culprit. In the afternoon searched for Mr. Loury's Farm with Maj. Clay – is a sincere Fighting French and dead out against the Italians. Raises racing horses and has a real up-to-date farm with lots of US machinery and good buildings. Had hidden Zanshine? from the Germans.

Picked up quite a few of the gas cans and some grenades from the battlefield. Children in Tunis – raises almonds, feed, olives, citrus. Fed locust to horses to prop them up. The Germans are coming over every three hours and giving us a pasting. General Patton ordered General Ward to lead the infantry assault of the hill north of Maknassy in person. He received a slight wound in the eye. Patton stayed in Firyanah and talks big fight all of the time.

<u>March 26, 1943</u> – Had an easy day – camouflaged the paths, wrote letters, and listened to the cannon all day. We sure spanked them today. However, at night, the C/S called and raised hell about his light being out. He ordered the jeep removed that we had placed there for his lights so we put a storage battery in its place and since he used a 110v light, the battery gave out at 1:00am and he cried – threatened to reduce Davis and Mann and transfer them to the 6th Inf. to an assault platoon and threatened me with a court martial. All in all, I am fed up with him. He has good ideas but cannot handle people.

<u>March 27, 1943</u> – C/S hits the ceiling because a jeep is parked out of place. He wants to reduce the MP and send him to the 6th Inf. - told me to tell Cochran to write 6th a letter about Mann and put him in assault platoon. I finally put the cards on the table with Cochran. We are trying our best and cannot out him. Of all the people that I've met in this war, he (Williams) has stooped to the lowest tricks in order to get his way.

<u>March 28, 1943</u> – C/S had his half-track come in and it is a daisy. Completely modified and equipped with an extension tent. Chuck came in with a Purple Heart for a wound in his eye. He has been turned down for rotation and will not be sent back. I am sorry for him as we are really in the same boat and he has been booted about. We have been ordered to withdraw again – just as the Mareth Line is breaking – and there is only one hill of Germans between us and the Mediterranean Sea. This is certainly a funny war. Something stinks in the upper crust. We are 25-35 miles for the coast.

<u>March 29, 1943</u> – Shelling started early and we are just about to be registered upon as I write this in the AM! Was sent to Gafsa with Curtis to set up a new C.P. Left at 0800 and arrived and 1030 – waited 5 ½ hours on the desert for Curtis to return.

Finally tapped a telephone line and located him at "Speedy" – raining and a very raw late evening. Finally, we found our location in an olive grove south of Gafsa. Then there is doubt as to whether we will go there as the situation has changed. Area is small and crisscrossed with irrigation ditches. At dark, I start back and Roberts is scared to death of planes and mines. Promised the boys that I would send rations and bed rolls back to them, but C/S would not let me go. So to bed.

March 30, 1943 – About 0300 two planes came over with flares and plenty of bombs. Dropped flares and then bombs. They are now dropping a breadbasket type of bomb – many (40) small bombs (anti-personnel) in a large container with a burst radius of about 150 yards. I was too tired to even get out of bed roll. Some earth shaking! Am working on a new AA defense and a split up of the C.P. so it will be smaller and more mobile. A fair day and a chance to get some rest.

Figure 7-5 Captain Lumpkin's volunteer patrol in a pass outside of Maknassy, Tunisia with their "home-made" gun fashioned from a 20mm canon from a scrapped British Spitfire aïrplane

March 31, 1943 – Took gun to pass and take a few shots at passing vehicles. Can account for one definitely and one probable. I am to take a patrol down the pass tomorrow.

April 1, 1943 – Take Sgt. John T. McG and four others and start down the pass. Everything was okay until I hit the mouth and all hell broke loose. Two machine guns and a platoon of infantry boxed us in just as we had held at a rally point. Got two of them before they took us hands down. Two officers and about 25 men – all very young and clean looking kids – but wild as hell. Took us to their C.P. in the pass and rounded up the rest of the patrol. No one seriously injured but took a bullet to my hand and a hell of a lot of near misses. Left there at dark and was taken to the battalion C.P. Met Colonel Lang. All in all, I am very impressed with the condition of the German officers that I've met. They seem to be very nice, courteous, efficient, and no browbeating. Remember Col. Maraist – Ward – Patton. Spent the night on the ground with six men and one blanket.

Chapter 8

Captured Yesterday

April 2, 1943 (Captured yesterday) – Was taken to Sfax about noon and wrote this in a pup tent. I was captured by an outfit whose emblem was a tiger. Left Sfax in two boxcars with 53 others for Tunis. Cars were small – hot as the devil. A German non-commissioned officer finally opened the window. One corner of the boxcar was used for a latrine. Not much sleep. Much singing by the British of the "Cow Gun."

<u>April 3, 1943</u> – All day in cars with a long halt at Sousse and one other town whose name I could not catch. British are still singing like a bunch of college kids. One Arab and two French officers in the same car. I am suspicious of the Frenchman as he stated that any Frenchman wearing the Cross of Lorraine should be avoided, as they are Vichy French.

<u>April 4, 1943</u> – Nearing Tunis. Poor train ride. Have been fed once on this trip, but we can probably stand it. We are taken to an old schoolhouse on the outskirts of Tunis and are given a meal by the Red Cross of Tunis. Lt. Warren Curtis of Freemont, Ohio, and Lt. Russell (Russ) Ford from East Orange, New Jersey are brought in. A Frenchman tried to give us some bread and a French woman tried to give us some oranges. Both were

knocked down by the German guards. We are deloused. Lt. Col. Walter Oakes is also here.[1]

On the wall of the schoolhouse is the name "Anthony Jablonski of Cleveland, Ohio." It is a small world, as this man is a good friend and a football teammate of Dick Rowdon of the Missouri Military Academy ("MMA").

The Tunisian Red Cross fed us and gave us two cigarettes. For money you can buy almost anything within reason. Much discussion all day long. Oakes says to defend topographical crests rather than military crests. We are in room 10 of the schoolhouse. About the only thing good is that we can stretch completely out in a horizontal position on the stones. I shave the next day for the first time. We carve forks and spoons from wood taken from a school desk. I am somewhat suspicious of the Germans because of the displayed lack of hostility towards Americans. They try to be affable, and by repeating things over and over they hope to make the statement true. We are paraded through the streets of Tunis and there was much squawking about this, as I firmly believe that this was done only to impress the Arabs. Some Arabs are wearing the Star of David on their arms.

<u>April 5, 1943</u> – Oakes and two officers left to plane to Germany. We are marched two miles south and are given an opportunity to take a bath. Upon getting back I am called before the German Intelligence for questioning. Much argument over saying nothing but name, rank and serial number. German claims to have master's degree from Cambridge. He can be upset by asking him a question rather than attempting to answer his questions. Oakes and the other two officers return, as there was an air raid this morning which left a time bomb on the runway.

---

[1] Lt. Col. Maynard W. Files – Oakes, Spicer & I were together. Oakes was interrogated and stole some razor blades.

April 6, 1943 – A couple of air raids in the morning and more questioning. They brought in an Arab barber and we all had haircuts. The menu is: coffee in the morning, camel stew at noon, and bread at night. Have changed all of my money into francs and invested some in cigarettes and food. Cigarettes are 140 francs per pack. Our room is getting organized so that each and every man will say exactly the same thing to the interrogator and we share everything equally. Last night we even cadged some wine.[2] The guards act as if they would like to help us, but are very attentive to their duty in keeping us in the compound. Oakes overhears a conversation that we will leave in the morning before 7:00am. The latrines are very dirty and flies are plentiful. Hope I can keep my hands and face clean.

Everyone has an attitude of contempt for the Italians – not only by the Americans but also by the Germans. Germans seem to be very much afraid of an air-land-sea attack with paratroopers, and have an attitude of "how long can we last?"

April 7, 1943 – We are awakened by the guard at 6:00am, to leave at 7:10am. It looks as if the airport is working again. We march out and wait around all day. Had an excellent plan to escape, as the guards were thin during an air raid. Could have made it, but for two German screwballs who merely flattened out where they could observe us.

Returned to camp and found that we were able to cadge up another bottle of wine.

Spent the last of my money.

The "man" in the men is starting to creep out. We finally insist on everyone pitching in, getting the latrines cleaned and the debris swept in the yard. We are told that we will leave by plane or boat tomorrow, for sure. We pass the time by heckling the Italians and the Arabs, with the result that a fight broke out

---

[2] Lt. Col. Maynard W. Files – Willy Endlain from Astoria, Long Island, got us eggs and wine.

between an Arab and a French boy. The Germans immediately clobbered the Arab.

April 8, 1943 – Very cool last night – almost uncomfortable. Three British officers brought in: Lt. Walter Lees and Lt. Hervy Robinson – Argyles Highlanders of the 8th Army – and a major from the 1st. Robinson is from Ceylon, a planter of tea and rubber, and the other is just a man about town. Both men hard and tough and will add to our room. Lt. Edward Berlinski, from the 13th, also brought in, and gave us the news which is good.[3]

The Red Cross gave us some jam and stale cakes. One of our guards, Fritz, has a wife in Brooklyn, and would like to join up with us, but not wishing strong enough to get us out.

The three British officers left by boat for Naples. Remember Lees when he said good-bye. Lt. Curtis knew Julius Wilde, one of my former students. Fritz came by at night and talked. The guards seem to be O.K. as long as we are not making an effort to escape.

April 9, 1943 – We cleaned up the house, sat about and talked. Red Cross gave us a can of orange jam which was delicious. American Army reported in Sfax but the line is somewhat fluid. Wish there was some way I could tell Betty that I am O.K. Berlinski brought in a deck of cards and we have been playing Hearts all afternoon. Everyone cheats.

More prisoners from the 8th Army come in. A reconnaissance patrol captured 15 miles this side of Sfax. This is one of the famous phantom patrols put out by the 8th Army. Good night for bombing, but no bombs fell.

April 10, 1943 – Oakes, Spicer and Files were alerted at 10:00am to leave for Germany via Naples. Spicer very sick; has a piece of shrapnel in his leg and they do not seem able to get it out. Food makes him very bilious. Curtis wants us all to go and

---

[3] Lt. Col. Maynard W. Files – Berlinski was sent out to effect liaison with Files (E Company 16th). Finally made it.

be together. I argue that we should delay as much as possible and sweat it out. Maybe the 8th or the 1st will get here first. They did not leave, after all, as the planes were to be used for those going on furlough and for the wounded. Some material being flown out by the Luftwaffe.

Questioned again about our ROTC and the attitude of mind towards the Germans. Lt. Stewart Cameroons, 8th Army, brought in. He is from Edinborough. Told how they broke the Mareth Line. An average of one gun every 40 yards and 500 rounds for gun. Fired on the German lines all night and rolled the barrage in the morning. The infantry advanced one minute and rested two minutes. Lt. Ford is taking Spicer's place on the plane in the morning.

April 11, 1943 – Oakes, Ford and Files left at 4:00am but returned later in the day. A British captain, Strange, came in from the 8th. The 8th Army is now at Sfax and the Germans are demolishing Sousse. He was captured two days ago. A German Lieutenant came in and we had quite an argument about the Jews, *Lord Haw Haw*, Germany, US, Russia, and who would win the war. Captain Strange, whose mother came from Luxembourg, argued our side very convincingly. There was an air raid at noon and the bombing was apparently successful as there was much smoke in the distance near the dock area. We just might be able to sweat this out yet. Through the barbed wire we could see a soccer game between two Arabic teams from Oran and from Tunis.

Oakes related his story of his ship being torpedoed off Algiers, and his description was really rare and salty. "I hate pancakes and anyone who likes them." Oakes apparently steered the landing craft ashore by use of a G.I. compass. He has no use for the Canadian Navy.

Feel very sorry for Spicer, with his wound which will not heal, his upset stomach, and on top of everything else his wife is expecting.

April 12, 1943 – At 10:00am we are all called up to go. Lt. Curtis stays back on account of his foot having a blister. We march out eastward about 15 miles to a small seaport and find that the boat has already gone. We march back about 4 or 5 miles, and the guard finally gets us all on trucks. At the seaport several French women came out and tried to give us fruit and bread, but the guard would not let them. The only eating we had for this march was one cup of coffee each.

The straw apparently has some type of parasite in it, as I am chafed raw from my ankles to my stomach. I take a shower and sleep each night with my clothes very loose.

April 13, 1943 – Extremely sore in the thighs. Not much sleep. The German lieutenant reminds me of J. B. Robinson of Mexico, Missouri. Berlinski has been very generous with his money. Fortunately, he was captured with his musette bag and had some cash on him. There was an air raid on all night long. The docks and the airport are being plastered. I find an American canteen and latch onto it. The Tunisian Red Cross deserves a letter of commendation and a donation from me if I ever make it back.

April 14, 1943 – No way to get word to Betty that I am okay. Hope that I can escape before she gets official news. Four officers and one warrant officer of the 1st Army brought in. The 8th Army is on this side of Sousse, and the 1st is about 8 or 10 miles west of here. No news of the 5th Army. In the morning we fill everything with water, as we expect the water to be cut off sometime today. The guards have been told that they will not be evacuated from Tunis. Looks like we may make it after all. POW life certainly impresses on one that the greatest pleasures in life are the simple things. This is a truth that I never fully understood until now.

Have borrowed some books from a French medic and these have been passed around and around. Captain Files is really a master at wrestling up extras. Our ration consists of coffee in the morning, stew at noon and bread and sometimes cheese in tin tubes at night. The stew was better today, as it did not have such a smell of camel in it. The Red Cross gave us a meal at 4:00pm and also some tobacco. The Germans give us three cigarettes per day. Germans are very conservative with gasoline. One truck pulls another, or often three trucks are being pulled by one prime mover. No truck ever passes a walking German soldier without offering him a ride.

Chapter 9

Tunisia to Poland

April 15, 1943 – Awakened at 4:00am and went to the airport. They have some very large transports with six motors, ten wheels.[1] The plane takes off and lands first at Sicily in a small, crowded, bowl-shaped *Flugplatz*. Unable to see anything out of the plane. At one time thought the plane was leaking oil. We are stored in the luggage compartment with two guards. Plane takes off for Palermo, where it is refueled. We are not allowed to leave the plane. We land at Naples in the midst of an air raid. Mount Vesuvius was smoking in the distance. There are lots of ruins about the airport. The fields are very green. There is no waste of tillable soil. Lots of wheat and something that looks like alfalfa. Grape vines grow up into the trees, with leaves from tree to tree.

We are taken by truck to a camp at Capua. We insist on being treated as officers, in accordance with our rank. At Capua we get tea, bread and butter and jam, some straw mattresses and two blankets. I am now with Col. Oakes and Lt. Ford.[2] A German sergeant was the pilot of the transport. Another sergeant tried to have us carry his bags, and we raised

---

[1] Probably referring to a Me 323D German transport plane.
[2] Lt. Col. Maynard W. Files – (Files, Curtis, and Berlinski also).

particular hell about it, as no officers do that. I notice that our bombs cut a wide but not a very deep swath when they hit. There was an air raid at Naples and Capua that night.

April 16, 1943 – The doctor painted my legs and wound with a yellow solution. I walked about camp with no clothes in order to absorb all of the sun possible. The latrine is a slab of concrete with holes cut in the slab. I am issued a British Red Cross box which was delicious. American cook is preparing a meal of spaghetti and vegetable soup and tea for the evening.

April 17, 1943 – Had a <u>HOT</u> shower. A G.I. from the 168th gave me a half-cake of soap. The German doctor repaints my body with a yellow solution. The skin is better and the wound is closing up. There is a mix-up over the food at noon. We have been eating with the wrong group, apparently. We are short of bread — one roll per day and it is about the size of a biscuit. Blankets are very thin and I sleep very cold at night. The Vatican has a representative who visits the camp. Lt. Ford takes his last slice of bread and burns it to remind him of his wife! Oakes is very clever in getting small things done. Five of us are shaving with the same razor blade. The French POWs are apparently not prisoners, as they are freed when they get to Germany, and seem to draw a heavier ration. Living in close quarters makes one be on guard not to lose temper or take offense at any small incident.

April 18, 1943 – This is Palm Sunday. Remember Sherman and McDowell. Made a new spoon out of a broken aluminum cup. Made a bag out of an old Italian pup tent and yarn from a G.I. glove. The German bread seems to have quite a bit of nutrition, although I doubt if it is made from grain. The wrapper on one of the loaves indicated that it had been baked in 1929. It had been wrapped in wax paper, tin foil and cellophane, and has some type of syrup in it to keep it fresh. It is black and very hard. The Italian bread is like our brown bread, and is more palatable.

I have started to make a pair of shorts from some canvas taken from the Italian pup tent.

<u>April 19, 1943</u> – Still working on the shorts. Made a tobacco pouch out of canvas. I am hungry as hell and really tried to catch a dog that is running about the camp. Oakes and I are ready to eat the dog raw. Luckily we received an individual Red Cross parcel and split it four ways. Tasted milk for the first time since leaving the States. Lt. Ford has a very sore throat. In civilian life he is a singer at Grace Episcopal Church in New York City and has a hell of a good voice. He has studied music and has a real knowledge of it, especially the choral side. Oakes is devoted to his wife and seems to be a good egg. British are quartered next door. One of them was shot yesterday, trying to escape.

<u>April 20, 1943</u> – Completed the drawers, and even put buttons on them. Sgt. McEwin came in last night. He and the gang had been in Reggio and had a very rough time there, as they had to move quite a bit of ammunition. It is rumored that Tunis has fallen. Certainly they have flown the krauts out by the planeloads.

We make a jam out of dates, raisins – very good! The cook takes our can of meat and makes some delicious meatballs for supper.

Ford taken to the Lazarette on account of tonsillitis. We trade our cake of soap for some cigarette papers. This gives us an opportunity to smoke any cigarette butts. Flies are terrible in this camp. I would certainly like to get the hell out of here. The French soldiers and one officer eat separately but sing together almost all the time. I wonder why there is such a great collection of the passports of all soldiers. The German doctor in the Lazarette gave me a small bottle of gasoline for our lighter. I start studying the German language, but there is no book or dictionary and it is very difficult. One G.I. in the camp has his father living near Naples and they are allowed to talk through the fence. This camp has a permanent detail to operate it as a quarantine camp, to be sure that no diseases are brought into Germany. It is very easy to get depressed with so much time on our hands and an almost futile chance to escape.

April 21, 1943 – Salvaged a pencil, took out the lead, and thus made a stem for a pipe. The bowl is made of tin. Sgt. Harrison is the cook responsible for the noon slum. Throat better, but having a bad case of diarrhea. Time sure hangs on hands. Very hot in the afternoon. The church or cathedral at Capua can be heard in the late afternoon. The bells and chimes, with the French soldiers singing their peasant Catholic songs, it is very impressive.

Two British Naval officers off a sub have joined us. Their sub was lost by a depth bomb off the coast of Capri, in action with a German destroyer. One of the British officers had been taken to Greece. The German destroyer was equipped with the best *ASDIC*, etc. They told us that the sub had been lost at 185 feet, which information they hoped to get back to the Admiralty. They report that Tunis is still held by the Germans, but the British still have control of the Mediterranean. Both officers are regular navy and are from Scotland. They got quite a kick out of our tale of the work at Reggio. (This refers to Sgt. McEwin loosening the heads of the ammunition while working on their dump at Reggio.)

One of the German non-commissioned officers has furnished me with a German grammar book and now I can keep mentally busy.

April 22, 1943 – Oakes and I split one Scottish Red Cross box, and studied German grammar all day. Ford has diphtheria and they have taken him to an Italian hospital.

Lack of sufficient food definitely gives one the cramps – diarrhea still bad.

The German priest, Father Marius, has plenty of guts. He has taken out our names and the Pope will broadcast them to the States via the Vatican radio. Father Marius brought some nuts and oranges to us for Sunday. The German non-commissioned officer says that we will be here for some time. He left an orange and an extra blanket when I promised that I would study my German.

<u>April 23, 1943</u> – Forgot to mention that when I was interrogated in North Africa immediately after being captured, it was done by a Col. Lang. He was a good friend of Hans Hauser. I must remember to tell this story to Bob White, as Hauser was a good friend of Bob White's.

We moved our quarters today and I am in a corner southeast room. We are suspicious of the French soldiers. They get a German newspaper every day, and are apparently in cahoots with the Germans. Everyone in the camp is attempting to take a 20-franc piece and make it into a ring. This is done by tapping the edge of the silver piece in order to broaden same. However, my ring started to split.

Mount Vesuvius can be seen in the distance. There are mountains to the North and sea to the south. Our boys lost some warheads (?). The German non-com, brought over some dates, and Spicer, Berlinski, Oakes and I sat up and shot the breeze.

<u>April 24, 1943</u> – Father Marius brought us 5 oranges, 28 nuts, and, above all, a razor with 10 blades, tooth paste and a tooth brush. Brushed my teeth for the first time in over six weeks. Certainly feels good. Still have a touch of diarrhea and the boys give me an extra orange and I donate some of my portion of the nuts. Father Marius is certainly nice to us.

The Germans appear to be faster on the pick-up than the Italians. A lieutenant in charge of the outpost, who picked me up, looks exactly like Frank Pearl at home, and accused me of using explosive bullets. I am certain that I killed two and wounded one, as the bodies were laid out.

Oakes and Curtis are attempting to play an accordion and it almost drove the rest of us mad. My guess is that Vesuvius is about 18 miles away. Diarrhea is better. Naples got a real plastering last night during the air raid. Shook up our building and got the entire camp awakened. The Italian soldiers wish to trade bread for anything we might have, such as fountain pens, watches, rings, tea, soap and jam from the Red Cross packages. The best trick we have pulled was to trade them a British cigarette carton filled with straw for a loaf of bread. Did they raise hell!! Another one was that we had some tealeaves which had been boiled 20 or more times. These were dried, then put back into the container and traded for 8 loaves of bread. Needless to say, the German guards were protecting us at this moment rather than keeping us contained. The Italians are truly jerks.

April 25, 1943 **(Easter Sunday)** – The Italian sentries outside of the Lazarette beefed all day because they were on duty. They are the worst soldiers I have ever seen. They walk past in the most unmilitary manner, with blankets, mess kits, rifles, slung in any and all fashions. At the changing of the guard they argued with their officers continuously. It may be that drawing guard duty is against their principles. Was a bit bilious at noon. Am still studying German.

Speaking of soldiers, I cannot say too much for the French either, as some new French prisoners were brought in and they will scavenge around in the dirt for anything left in a food can, for cigarette butts, orange peelings, paper, etc. I understand the French are taken from here to France and are demobilized. I suspect that most of them will return to the line soon after. They are certainly peculiar, and have peculiar ways. Oakes and I worked out a fairly good solution for the macaroni drawn at noon. We eat one plate and save the other plate for the evening meal. The tea is all gone, and we get German coffee, which is boiling water poured over parched barley.[3]

<u>April 26, 1943</u> – Drew a British hospital Red Cross parcel and it was delicious. Did some trading; traded a can of meat loaf for some sugar. Thus far I have been able to store up one or two items that might come in, should we make it to the other side of the fence. Listened a long time to a French prisoner, Lt Roger Penes, 16 Chemin Dames, Constantine, Algeria. Before the war he was a salesman for dental supplies. Another officer joined us who had been the gym instructor at Constantine. Cannot help but be suspicious of them because they state in case we get to France beware of anyone displaying the Cross of Lorraine, which I knew was DeGaulle's personal flag. These characters are just turncoats.

<u>April 27, 1943</u> – Lt. Muehlbar, of the 47th Infantry, was brought in. He had been captured because a sentry went to sleep and the whole outpost was caught. Two British officers came over and we had a long discussion of the political set-up of Europe and the United States.

<u>April 28, 1943</u> – Holy Joe! The Germans issue us bread, jam and cheese in the morning. No one understands why. Later on I found out that we had been drawing Italian rations, and the Germans were taking over. I suspect this is to impress us as to how much better their food supply is. We have organized the Red Cross parcels and the tea is taken from all boxes and prepared for everyone. This raised such a squawk that later we had to change it and everyone went back to brewing his own individual pot The meat of the German ration, what little there is, is thrown into the spaghetti.

---

[3] Lt. Col. Maynard W. Files – Naples bombed last night. Germans tried to get us to clean up but all of us refused.

There were a couple of civilians in the compound today, questioning the enlisted men. I was unable to get their names.

One man taken to the hospital in Naples, as it appears that he had spinal meningitis and could be the forerunner of an epidemic.

Father Marius gave us an Italian deck of cards and we made a cribbage board.

<u>April 29, 1943</u> – One man shot trying to escape, and the German sentry actually shot an Italian soldier, so we were even up.

There is much trading of commodities from the parcels, and the prices are in cigarettes. Chocolate is 35 cigarettes, a tin of cocoa is 30 cigarettes, a package of cheese, 10 cigarettes. Washed my socks, drawers and shirt with cake soap I found in the hospital ward. We have had several air raids in the last several days.

<u>April 30, 1943</u> – Borrowed some ink from the German non-com. Made a towel from an old piece of cloth. Talked a long while to a British G.I. in charge of the British camp. He has been a POW 15 months; captured in Tripoli. Spent 5 days in the hold of an Italian boat. The Italians do not treat their prisoners well.

We tore up a blanket to obtain some thread for sewing. The Germans say that we are going to a good camp near Munich. The Italians attempted to run in a marine officer from the Italian Intelligence. My estimate has been revised: the British is up, the French is down. The British criticize the French and I say that most of their remarks are true. The French are dirty, sloppy, undisciplined soldiers, and use the latrine in a most dirty manner. Furthermore, they will attempt to steal your ration if they think they can get by.

<u>May 1, 1943</u> – Have been captured a month, and it seems like a year. Diarrhea bad. The names of the two naval officers

are McGeough and Berkwell. McGeogh's eye is badly injured and the Germans are moving him to a German hospital.

<u>May 2, 1943</u> **(Sunday)** – Berkwell came over and we talked about maps and things.

<u>May 3, 1943</u> – We form at 6:00am and are taken to the railroad station. The train left at 11:00, one guard in the compartment and another just outside the door. There were four guards in the compartment ahead and four guards in the compartment behind us.[4] The outside door was locked and the windows welded down. The country towards Rome is very flat and is farmed extensively. An old aqueduct paralleled our tracks. Rome seemed to be very interesting, but could not get out to see any of it. That night, in the marshaling yards, an Italian kept us in stitches laughing at his screaming for his friend Benito. This section of the country seems to be very air-minded, with airports all over the place. North from Rome we pass through several tunnels, many of them several miles long. Sleeping is a crammed affair: one man in the luggage rack, one on the floor and five on the seats. All in all, a very rugged day. We got 5 loaves and 2 cans of meat for the 7 officers in our group. The French, as usual, got better rations and were allowed to leave the train at stops.

<u>May 4, 1943</u> – All mileage is in kilometers, and placed on the nearest building, post, tree, etc. that is available. We pass through Verona, Trento, and the Brenner Pass, to Innsbruck. The Brenner is heavily fortified, with plenty of rails and dies to repair all damage. The highways are clearly marked for all dangerous curves and railroad crossings. Roads in the Alps appear to be maintained in good order. People in this area are electric-power minded, and seem to have plenty of electricity.

---

[4] Lt. Col. Maynard W. Files – We were in second-class cars.

At Copperno an Italian girl smiled at Berlinski. The wop officer who was with her tried to make her quit. Needless to say, we kept the racket going and finally the German sentries ran the wop down the block.

The Italian Red Cross came aboard and gave us some dried figs and some hot spiced tea which was really good.

Houses do not look so good. Houses in the Alps are of the chalet type as compared to the cement-asphalt homes in the low flat country. Many churches about, and several crucifixes are set along the highway. Trees are plentiful on the German side, and the sights are really beautiful. Mountains are half-hidden by clouds, and many are now snow-capped. Vineyards are in good shape, and are plentiful, all vines being supported 5 to 6 feet above ground. Many water wells. We follow a river to the Brenner but there were no boats on the river. Many beautiful flowers and fields so green. Roads are curbed. We go on to Munich under the home guard and find that we have been cheated out of our rations by the old guards. A German captain insisted that we draw a loaf from the German sentries. (The Italian Red Cross gal had the same type of face and features as Mrs. DeRosa whom I later met in the Dairy Queen business at Wallingford, Connecticut. In talking to Mrs. DeRosa I found that all of her folks came from the same mountain area in Italy. There is no doubt in my mind that it was some of her kinfolks.)

May 6, 1943 – Most of the early morning and day spent in the marshaling yards at Munich. They shift cars here with a skid, and it is interesting to watch them place a flying skid, dodging the train wheels.

We finally get to Moosbürg. There are many kinds of prisoners here: Russian, French, English, Greek, and even some Chinese. The guards sang many Tyrolean songs on the trip, which were very pretty. The guards are just kids who should be in some school. At the camp we were thoroughly searched, allowed to take a bath, and our clothing deloused. We are put in camp with the British, who are real people. They took us in, split their rations with us, and saw that we got a part of a Red Cross box. My box put me in the running again, and I feel much better.

They have many tales to tell. Dr. Skol, a world-famed chiropodist in Munich, and his family were all thrown in the concentration camp because his daughter pulled down the Nazi flag. They also tell of playing an imitation game of cricket with no bats nor balls, and it seems to completely confound the Germans.

Was propositioned by a German looking for someone to administer a school. I told him to go to hell.

In passing through Nürnberg we were taken by the guards to a Red Cross counter in the station. Here we were given a bowl of hot soup and some German coffee. For the first time I heard that some Germans were not sure that they were winning, and the lady in charge told me, in perfect English, "We are not all happy with what the *Führer* has done in getting America into war with Germany. It looks like we are going to repeat the same mistake we made in 1918."

Another funny thing which happened and it illustrates the German mentality: We were counted each hour on the train trip through the Brenner. Immediately after passing through Copperno, I asked the guard to let me go to the toilet. Here I noticed that the window was movable and was almost out the window when the train started to slow down. I was immediately apprehended, having been loose only some 40 minutes. The Germans were very efficient! A good example of their stupidity would be: On one of the hourly inspections we were so tangled up in the compartment that they were able to count only 6 men. They awakened Oakes and asked him where the seventh man was. Oakes pointed to the floor where a helmet was sitting and said, "Oh, he is under the helmet." Believe it or not, the officer actually picked up the helmet to see if the American could be hiding there!

May 7, 1943 – Shot the breeze with the British POWs. Most of them had been captured in Crete and had some tall tales to tell. Some Serbians in camp. Thus far the British and the Yugoslavs seem to be cleaner than the others. The British are truly a scream. They imitate various athletic contests without the use of bats, balls, rings, etc., and this absolutely maddens the Germans. This camp is used by the Germans as a source of workers. I can assure anyone that the British are artists on slow-down work.

I am able to draw some new shoes, underwear, trousers, and two handkerchiefs. Believe that we are the envy of the Germans, who cannot get such quality material.

Two British G.I.'s brought back who tried to get through the Brenner Pass to Switzerland. Interior discipline of the camp is excellent. Present order is that no one will try to get away until this last incident dies down. I do not believe that the Bavarians are very much sold on Hitler. A German cat wanders around the compound, and I will swear that it thoroughly understands English, French, and Polish.

May 8, 1943 **(Friday)** – Repacked all of my gear, rested, talked to the British, and got ready to leave for a new camp at 5:15am tomorrow morning.

May 9, 1943 – Lost the remainder of my money at a search in Moosbürg. Believe it or not, I got a receipt from the German guard, and I swear he signed Hitler's name to the receipt. Two guards accompany us to the new camp. They are real characters, and with half a chance we should be able to get away. At one time both fell asleep, but the train was completely filled with German soldiers. Stopped in Munich and the guards bought us a bottle of beer. While in the railway station one guard relieved himself in full sight of everyone, against a wall.

Such manners! One of the Americans gave a small girl on the train a bit of his chocolate. This immediately called for a thorough search and lots of disturbance. I was searched very thoroughly at the new camp. They punched holes in all of our cans of food, or we had the choice of storing them. I took some raisins into the new place for the evening meal. At this camp they confiscated my canteen and my helmet.

The name of the new camp is "7B" and is in a valley just out of Eichstädt. The scenery is very pretty and the evergreen in the hills of a beautiful dark green. Everyone very nice to us. I am assigned to a mess of British officers. We were able to obtain oatmeal, cigarettes, soap, a checkered sheet, towels, and toothpaste. All of the British officers seem to try to outdo themselves in getting us settled. I am invited out to eat with Lt. Burkhart and his block.

Col. Waters and Col. Alger are here and they apparently identified me. They are in good health and O.K. Morale here very high. Slept soundly that night, for the first time.

May 10, 1943 – Rained and was disagreeable almost all of the day. Had an invitation out to eat. No food, but plenty of conversation. Heard the canary sing very sweetly. (This camp has a radio hidden from the Germans, and are able to get the BBC news each night. After it has been received it is then distributed through several "editors" to the various buildings by word of mouth.)

Jeff got me a ticket to a lecture by a Captain Peters of Australia. It was very good. Wrote a letter to Betty. Talked a long while to a Canadian who had been in the Dieppe raid. All prisoners captured at Dieppe are having to wear handcuffs. This is because when they landed and took some Germans prisoners they had no way to contain them except by hand and leg cuffs. By way of punishment the Germans have each of the

Dieppe prisoners wear handcuffs all of the time.[5] However, the handcuffs are quite a joke, as each man can pick his lock in less than five seconds, and most of the time they just carry the cuffs in their pockets. Jeff was born and raised in India, and is an expert in (painting roses?).

<u>May 11, 1943</u> – I am getting to be a regular Kriege. Drew one-half Red Cross parcel and had all cans opened. The Germans trust no one here! There seems to be a guard of about 250 men present in or around this camp at all times. The camp has a ditch dug around its perimeter to prevent tunneling out. Still, the British are able to get out now and then, but the figure is extremely small. The news reports that the German casualties have been very large in Africa.

I forgot to report that on the trip through Nuremberg there was a group of SS troops guarding some beat-up political prisoners. These people were in chains and could hardly move one foot in front of another. I understood from talking to the German guard that these were special troops used to guard special prisoners. For the love of me, I do not see how any one of them could have walked away, even if there had been no guard present. At the tunnel in Innsbruck, I noticed that the entrance and exit were guarded by soldiers of the Hermann Goering Division.

We drew another blanket today. Morale is high, as Tunis has fallen, with a large number of prisoners taken. I understand from the British that basically the Germans realize they are losing the war and are much more humane in their treatment of prisoners now than they were back at the time of Dunkirk. A large number of the prisoners in my block were veterans of Dunkirk. Talked to Lt. Ken Young, of Australia. About a year ago he had been shot in the leg for touching the trip wire. The

---

[5] Gen. John K. Waters – The Germans also captured an order directing prisoners to be handcuffed if necessary.

Germans left him in the "no man's" area until they could get the senior British officer to come up and identify him. He received practically no hospitalization, and will probably keep his limp for the remainder of his life.

We had an extra roll call tonight, as one of our men failed to get out to the formation on time. The British Red Cross gave me a new shirt which was perfect. We definitely have word from the canary that Tunis has fallen.

<u>May 12, 1943</u> – Sat around most of the day and read. Believe it or not, they have library facilities and quite a large number of books, although most of them are very old.

Col. Oakes can certainly use some juicy language. He went to the library to obtain a book. The library is operated by an Oxford graduate, and as I understand it he taught in one of the colleges at Oxford. He is a true scholar; reminds me very much of Major Lamm, our principal at MMA. Oakes goes up to him and says, "In what section will I find the *&*^% books?" The librarian almost had a duck fit, as he rarely heard the word used, and I doubt whether he understood the meaning.

<u>May 13, 1943</u> – I am in bloc 7 in a mess of English officers who were captured at Dunkirk:

John B. (Dickie) Dixon
High Oak Lodge
Warehertz, England

R.H.C. (Ronnie Eastman)
Royal Masonic School
London Road
Bushy Hertz, England

A.B. (Art) Walker
The White Horse
Chatham Hill
Chatham,
Kent, England

G.G.C. (Geoffrey) Cowen
15 Lime Tree Grove
Shirley,
Surrey, England

M.R.M. (Robin) Steele-Mortimer
Golden Grante Llanasa
Hollywell
Flintshire, North Wales

B. L. S. (Bryan) Rich
c/o Barlay's Bank
103 Queensway
London W2

J. A. B. (Johnny Mumford)
Lydford Road
Willesden Green
London N2

R. D. (Tiny) Waters
Spanden Forest Row
Sussex, England

R. J. (Jimmie) Fitch
Park Lands
Esher Place
Esher
Surrey, England

All of these men are excellent examples of the British Army at its best I was indeed fortunate to be thrown into this mess.

May 14, 1943 – Wrote Betty another card. Was finger printed by the Germans and had quite an argument as the protest was made that this was done only to criminals. I have been assigned to the parcels division of this camp for my work. Col. Drake was influential in getting me this position. This camp is highly organized and administered by the British. There is a senior British officer, and under him are several committees: a security committee, both for internal security and counter intelligence; a parcels division having charge of all incoming parcels/cooking; tailor shop.

The security group is further organized so that they can duplicate passports and documents, dig tunnels, and keep the Germans under constant surveillance. This latter is done by a series of so-called bird watchers who give every intention of watching birds in the surrounding country but are actually noting the whereabouts of each German at all times.

Two Germans are fishing in a nearby stream. (I cannot recall what I meant by this sentence.)

May 15, 1943 – Talked with the officers in my mess most of the day. They were very much interested in our school system. Johnny went to a similar school (Forest) in England.

Tiny is quite a character. Remember his fuel store (I cannot recall exactly how it was worked but I know that Tiny had some way of stealing fuel from the Germans.)

All formations here are conducted in a very lazy manner. The Germans sound the signal for an *appell* and we take our sweet time in going to tine formation.

Remember the lack of answers to questions (cannot recall); the two hour-*appell* that did not occur (cannot recall); parade tonight at usual time (cannot recall).

We had an incident today that was comical and illustrates the way in which these Germans can be handled. For some reason the Germans decided to take one blanket from each POW. There was a great deal of squawking, hollering and beefing. We also had some blankets which were "security blankets". These, when washed in cold water, would give the design for making a sport coat for escape purposes. There was quite a bit of beefing and hollering back and forth between the Germans and the British until it was decided that each bloc would line up and every man would bring two blankets to the truck, throw one in and keep one. This operation took several hours, as each man argued with the Germans as he gave up his blanket. During this argument there was an organized detail that was stealing the same blankets back out of the truck, and finally it was worked around so that one blanket was cut into three parts. A third of the blanket was turned in, taken from the truck, and turned in again and again and again. The truck left with just a bunch of rags.

May 16, 1943 – Too late for the Canadian talk.

Most of the Kriegies have put in gardens. Read a book, "Prisoner's Progress" by Lt. L. C. Hunt. This book is about Dunkirk and the soldiers who were taken prisoner. Dickie has a part in the play. (By this I refer to the fact that the British were digging a tunnel, and Dickie was involved in some part of this tunneling project.) The Germans take on a sweating and a worrying (do not recall). Several shots fired tonight by German guards. (Do not recall why, etc.)

<u>May 17, 1943</u> – This is some place!! There are bookies here who will cover all types and kinds of bets. Some are in lagermarks and one is in English pounds.

Went to see "The Frightened Lady," which was a production put on by the Little Theater group. Two of the German guards came in during the show. One of the guards had been born and raised in England.

I am now learning how the parcel hut operates.

Bombs fell near here last night.

<u>May 18, 1943</u> – Remember the German lieutenant in the tobacco section of the parcel hut, and the string (cannot recall). Job in the parcel store is starting to be a real job. Packages come in from all over the world, even Italy. I believe that I am gradually being accepted, and I am learning one hell of a lot about the make-up of this place. (This refers to the fact that the parcel hut received contraband material which we were able to smuggle out.)[6]

<u>May 19, 1943</u> – Parcel store is most fascinating. Wrote Betty a full letter. I am learning *draughts* and getting to be quite English.

<u>May 20, 1943</u> – Spent the entire day reading and re-reading the correspondence of the International Red Cross with Lieutenant Clay.

---

[6] Gen. John K. Waters – Suggest this be deleted. I believe this info should not be revealed.

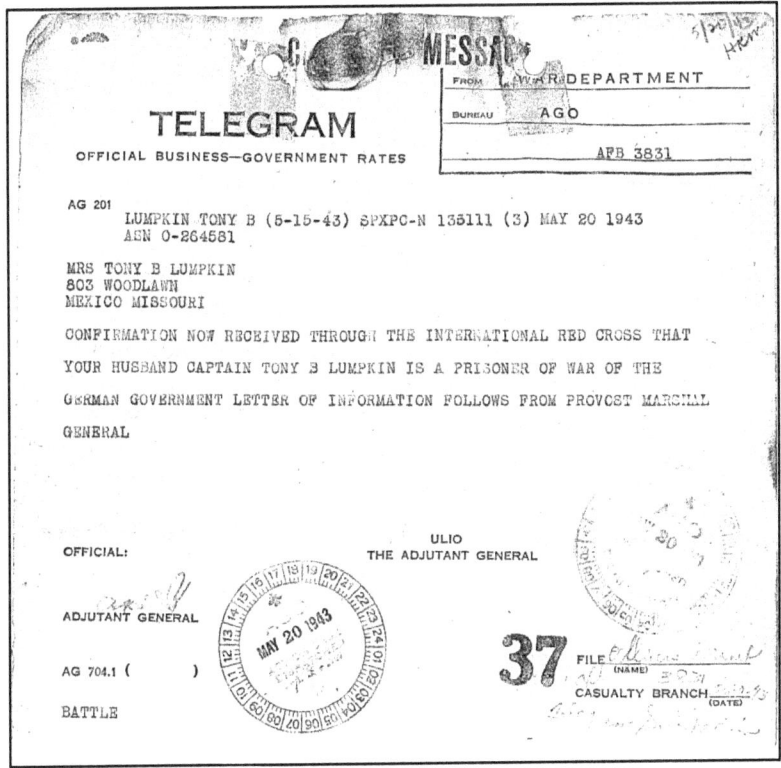

Figure 9-1 Telegram received by Capt. Lumpkin's wife almost two full months after his capture

May 21, 1943 – Got a haircut by appointment and another long session at the parcel store. Johnny is really a scream, and will start an argument with any German that comes within hearing his voice. He is a very large man and I really believe that the Germans are afraid of him. He certainly is absolutely fearless in attacking them on any question.

May 22, 1943 – A mild touch of diarrhea. Lt. Burkhart, of the tank destroyer battalion, was yanked up by one of the guards for laughing at him. The Germans have no sense of humor. The New Zealand contingent brought me a ticket to the show tonight. The British are great on tea at 11:00 and 4:00, and with visiting with each other.

Paid 30 lagermarks. (Cannot recall why.)

<u>May 23, 1943</u> – My mess invited Spicer and Curtis over for 11:00 o'clock tea and everyone got quite a kick out of them. Read another book, and studied the geography of England, particularly the names of the counties. Wish I could get the hell out of here.

<u>May 24, 1943</u> – Cleaned up my equipment and repaired it, in preparation so that I could move fast if the opportunity presents itself. The Germans are making another attempt to inspect blankets, and this calls for a great deal of re-shuffling of the rags. The Germans take my picture, and are not satisfied as I am distorting my face when they snap the camera.

<u>May 25, 1943</u> – The Germans are nervous over something. The *appell* lasted 1 ½ hours. They changed the occupants of one of the huts. Tiny has quite a time baiting the Germans, and he is a past master at it. He has stolen another board off a vehicle which the Germans have brought to camp. (Could this be the source of fuel?) Played bridge most of the day.

<u>May 26, 1943</u> – Everyone in the mess got mail except me. Tiny stole some more boards. I was invited out to eat in block 3 which was celebrating three years of a Kriegie life. Still cold and wet. Tiny always addresses the Germans as the members of The Third and Last Reich.

<u>May 27, 1943</u> – Captain Files comes in from Moosbürg and looks very thin. I am trying to sign up to take an extension course from the University of London which is being offered through the Red Cross.

<u>May 28, 1943</u> – Sent some fuel of sawdust, coal, and tar. (Do not understand unless it is a description of the German coal). In talking to the British I find that *"The British Grenadiers,"* a song sung by my children, Tony and Anne, is the regimental march

of the Grenadier Guards and the Honorable Artillery Company. The words are:

> Some sing of Alexander
> and some of Hercules
> of Hector and Lysander
> and such great names as these.
> But of all the world''s great heroes,
> there is none that can compare
> with the rat-ta-ta-tat-ta-ta-ta-tat
> ta-ta-ta-tat-ta-ta-ta-tat
> of the British Grenadiers.

The Honorable Artillery Company was founded in 1537, and the Grenadier Guards about 1590.

Col. Drake, the senior American officer, asked me to prepare a paper on the United States. This, with my work in the parcel hut, and the study of accounting, keeps me busy. One learns that this is very important in POW life, and it is also important that you learn to eat any and everything.

<u>May 30, 1943</u> – Studied most of the day, and visited at 4:00 o'clock with other American officers.

Met the son of the Prime Minister of India.[7] I understand that Sir Stafford Cripps' son is in this camp also.

Went to play tonight with Johnny.

<u>June 1, 1943</u> – Spent most of the day working on paper and in the parcel store.

<u>June 2, 1943</u> – Just got news that we leave in two days. Talked to Col. Drake. He wants me to see that everything is packed up ready to leave at 2:00pm tomorrow. Visited with a number of people and got their addresses. "Jeff" – from India: E.F. H. Jeffery F. A., Lloyds, #6 Pall Mall, London. Had a cup of tea with Hugh C. Mundy, Chalgrave, Ralle Road, Barkhurst,

---

[7] Gen. John K. Waters – This refers to Charles Hopetown.

Exmouth, Devon, England. The two men in the parcel room: R. B. Sleeman, Vulands, Painswick, Gloucester, England, and "Chas.", who had connections in New York – C. J. Clay, c/o Anthony Gibbs & Sons, 22 Bishopsgate, London. The bankers (?) of Mundy: Glgh Mills & Co., Kirksland House, Whitehall, London.

My mess gave me a real meal tonight as a going-away party. The "vampire" came by and gave me some cigarettes. The "vampire" refers to the German interpreter who questioned many of us at the schoolhouse in Tunis. By some hook or crook he got back to Eichstädt, and had me come out for additional questioning. He was thrown into absolute confusion when I warned him, "Be careful what you say, as I understand all of these rooms are wired for sound and I certainly would not want you to tell me now the same comments you told me in North Africa." Believe it or not, this completely befuddled him, as he was not sure just what comment I might drag out which hidden microphones had picked up as if such had been present in the *Kommandanture*. Again, this is a good illustration of how the Germans simply will not trust each other. I am thoroughly convinced that if it had happened on the American side no one would have paid a bit of attention to the rantings of a German POW under the same circumstances.

The meal had fish, meat, dessert and coffee, in very small amounts, and I certainly did appreciate this British hospitality.

An American officer came in, who had been wounded.[8]

June 3, 1943 (Wednesday) – Worked on getting parcels on the train and all O.K'd by the Germans. Had a slight mix-up on checking the parcels. The "Baron" came over after parade. This

---

[8] Lt. Col. Maynard W. Files – Yes, it was Lt. Robert Young – P38F pilot badly wounded in left arm and shoulder. Came from Ohio.

was the Camp *Kommandant*. The British gave him the full treatment as to military courtesy.

The British had a retreat in celebration of the King's birthday. Many German officers came in to view it. The Scots were dressed in their kilts and had bagpipes and drums... a most impressive scene. The British Army selects a day of each year to celebrate the present monarch's birthday. It has no relationship to the King's actual birthday.

Had a hard time telling my mess good-bye. I wrote Betty, exchanged addresses with many people, and many of them promised to see that my wife was notified that I had gotten this far.

By the way the "Baron" was almost a psycho when it came to matters of the military. After the evening *appell*, or sometimes during the evening *appell*, one could see him up on the hillside outside of the barbed wire, with his hand in his great coat, like Napoleon, overlooking the parade ground and the prisoners assembled for counting. I never did learn his name, but understood that his family was a very old Prussian family and that he had spent many years in the German Army.

The British paid very close attention to giving the full military courtesy treatment to all superior officers. This policy, I am quite certain, paid good dividends, in that the ranking officers always thought that the POWs were well disciplined, and they had no reason to believe otherwise since all of the arguments were conducted between officers of about equal rank. I was told on several occasions never to argue with a senior ranking German, but argue all you want to with one of equal rank, and, above all, never be convinced by a German of lower rank.

We were going to a camp location in the Polish Corridor, somewhere south of Bromberg. One scene to remember – and it is quite possible that it is an index to use in handling the Germans: While we were loading the baggage and the German

Kommandant came in and every man, German or British, as well as myself, froze to a ramrod position of attention. The British have advised that the Germans respect this type of treatment, particularly if you are talking to a member of the regular army. It is something that I will have to remember. I have also observed, as well as having been advised by the British, that you must always speak down to a German if he is of lower rank, but adhere very closely to all military etiquette in speaking to a German of equal or higher rank.

June 4, 1943 – We are up at 3:30am to leave. The old dome in the city had been constructed in 1300 (I believe this refers to either the castle or the cathedral. I was never sure just what that building housed.) This building had many busts and full size statues on the outside. Eichstädt at one time ranked very high, as it was the home of the Bishop. The rail cars are definitely Victorian and are rather dilapidated. The ventilating systems work on the same principle as a spark arrester does in our commercial chimneys. On the way to Nuremberg the train passed a very old castle, which I am told by the German non-com was part of the old Roman defenses. At Nuremberg the Red Cross gave us a real meal – bean soup and coffee. While in Nuremberg saw another batch of political prisoners, handcuffed, in chains, and barely able to move. They appeared to be very feeble.

A troop train passed through Nuremberg, headed east. At one of the windows I saw a German colonel whom I believe was the man who questioned me at Makanessay.

Bamburg and the country is flat with a slight roll. Towns all look very much alike. Passed through Kronach. There were some mountains around Steinbach am Wald. There was a *"Schokolade"* factory at Saalfeld, where the German Red Cross gave us some millet soup and coffee. Got into quite an argument with a German who was an interpreter. I do not believe he is as sold on the Nazi Party as many other Germans.

June 5, 1943 – June 6, 1943 – We passed through Lampue (Sp.?), through Halle (Saale). There were a couple of windmills used for power. The country is very flat. Passed through Kyhna and Delitzsch where I see the first onion roof on some of the buildings. This is the first evidence of western influence on architecture. Falkenburg very flat, and is grain country.

At Cottbus, we had a bowl of good hot bean soup, and saw two trains of German wounded on the way back from the Russian front. Country has some roll near Culun and Cuien (Sp.?). Many houses have vegetable gardens, and two of them had what looked like excellent tennis courts. We passed through Tullicov, which seems to be a fairly large town. There was a number of prisoners working in this area – both men and women prisoners – and are required to do much hard work. Saw three women attempting to drag a rail car up a siding.

The train had a long wait outside of Bentschen (Zbaszynek, Poland), where there was much evidence of shelter-trenches and hangers. For some reason the Germans had five locomotives attached to a train of only two cars. About a half-hour after midnight we were awakened and a check-up was made. At Sid, Lt. Thal, Duckworth, Spalding and Frank Aiten had jumped the train and had spent the night at Posen. They had been picked up immediately. The Germans served us soup which was very hot. The train is apparently ahead of schedule.[9]

The country is still very flat and has many buildings which look like grain elevators. Also noticed a peat bog in this area. We finally get to Altburgund (Schubin, Poland), where we

---

[9] Lt. Col. Maynard W. Files – When we went through Posen we saw the Jewish people being transported to the Ghetto outside of Posen chained front to rear and side to side. They were butt stroked because they waved to us. Remember?
Thal was run down by a horse ridden by a Hitler *Jügend* and remarked that the *Jügend* were worse than the soldiers. He came back and then in hospital for a few days.

started a new camp – 21B. There was a group of Russian G.I.'s as POWs here. Tonight they sang, and their singing was very good. We are quartered in a large building that must have been a school at one time, as there are barracks rooms on the ends and administrative cubicles between the large rooms.

Chapter 10

A New POW Camp: *Oflag 64*

June 7, 1943 – Up and going at 8:10. Very poor tea, as it was barely colored. Found all of the packages except two boxes belonging to Col. Drake. We issue boxes to everyone and get the parcel storeroom settled and organized. I am in a large room. Everyone tried to be of help to each other. The Russians sing again, and I must say they sound very well.

<u>June 8, 1943</u> – Diarrhea started again, but not enough to complain about. Changed rooms and am now in with Files, Jacobs and Smith. Three of the four at Posen and are returning. Changed mess. We are expecting 150 new POWs. Played ball tonight, but just did not have the energy for it. I am attempting to learn Russian from the Russian G.I.s. Dr. Jacobs says all of it sounds like, "You take Monday and I will take Tuesday off."

<u>June 9, 1943</u> **(Wednesday)** – About 150 officers from Rotenburg came in at 9:00 in the morning. Amon Carter Jr. and several others that I knew were among the group. All of these men were not cleared up by inspection and had to remain in the barracks. I move again, to room 21. Jacobs is moved to the hospital. Col. Drake is having a hell of a hard time as SAO. Files is doing well as a group commander.

June 10, 1943 – Remainder of the officers came through. "Otto," whom I had met in Constantine, is among them. Goddard, who was General McQuillan's aide, here also. Hughes must be dead, as he was caught at the same time. Some of the boys are screaming for their boxes, and the room is full of the Germans inspecting the equipment of incoming officers. At first the Germans would not let us in the parcel room, but Drake gets this matter cleared up immediately. Dicks, of the 1st Armored Division, is with us in our room.[1] Col. Drake lost a map of the camps, and the Germans are investigating. It now can be announced on the night we left Eichstädt, 66 British officers escaped through a tunnel. This is probably one of the reasons why the Germans started snorting so much about the parcel hut and investigating every piece of equipment of every officer, but even at that many things came through all right. Believe it or not, I still have, at this time, the passport of a German soldier which we had captured at Maknassy, and a G.I. compass.

June 11, 1943 – We issue one BRC parcel per man. Col. Drake very attentive to small details. This tends to irk some men, but I am sure that if we do not all follow one man then the Germans will start having us "sweeping the streets."

June 12, 1943 – We issue 50 cigarettes per man, a gift from the British at Eichstädt. Lt. Thal is brought in, and that accounts for all of those who jumped the train. Some of the Germans are very interesting, and come from all walks of life. One, Knorr, is a lawyer from Berlin and is absolutely sure his side will win. *Hauptman* Menner teaches Italian and geography at the University of Munich.

June 13, 1943 – Palermo has fallen and Sicily is under siege. Another POW brought in today. Some packages issued out.

---

[1] Lt. Col. Maynard W. Files – "Dirty Dicks" ranked Tacey out of our room.

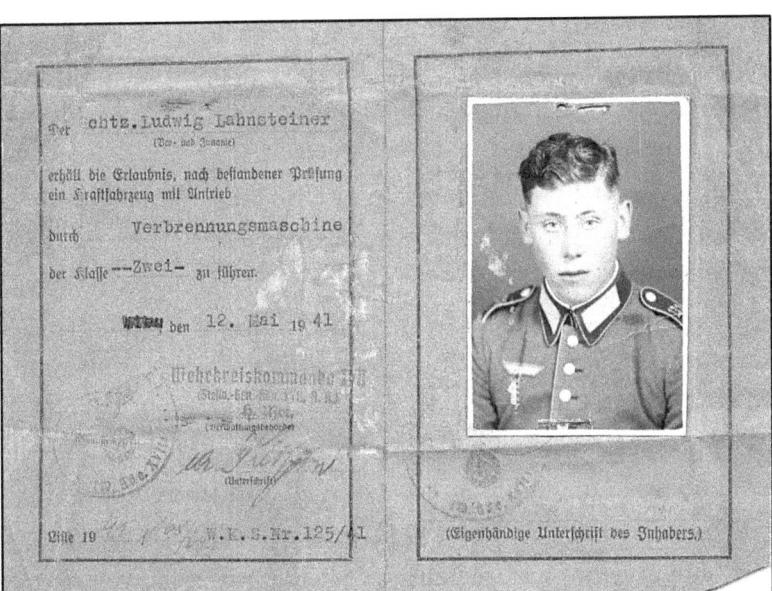

Figure 10-1 ID papers of captured German soldier that Captain Lumpkin managed to keep hidden throughout his captivity

<u>June 14, 1943</u> – Some German holiday, and had quite an argument trying to get the remainder of the packages out. My efforts were to no avail.

<u>June 15, 1943</u> – The Germans are late with their *appell*. Had much paper work in the parcel hut. Some of the tins and tobacco stores are confused. You could not take the parcel to your room, but had to store the tins of food and the extra tobacco in the parcel hut. At first we had an individual box in which each man's private stores were kept. As these were drawn out the Germans would puncture each tin to insure that no food was hoarded for possible escape.

<u>June 16, 1943</u> – There has developed an error in the storeroom of 16 boxes. The only conclusion we can come to is that Bedwell's inventory from Rotenburg was incorrect. Thal is in the hospital.

June 17, 1943 – Issued 176 American Red Cross and 12 Canadian Red Cross parcels. Everyone had a real bash that night. (A bash is when you go all out with the food, and forget about rationing for the next few days.)

June 18, 1943 – Formation today too long. Birds building a nest just above the canteen door. There is a very friendly cat in the compound.[2]

June 19, 1943 – Guards are being changed frequently. We have a new *Unteroffizier* in the parcel hut. Things are running much better in the parcel hut.

June 20, 1943 – The tobacco accounts are finally straightened out, and I had time to read and study Russian.

June 21, 1943 – Have Files in charge of all tobacco stores and I believe that we are getting that organized okay. One day just like the rest.[3]

June 22, 1943 – The *Feldwebel* in the parcel hut is a good soldier. Most Germans are very honest when they understand they are under supervision. Today I gave Schopert an opportunity to take a piece of my candy bar, with no one observing him. He stayed completely away from this temptation.

June 23, 1943 – Lt. Col. Van Vliet and Lt. Chappell from Rotenburg. Lt. Berlinski is the captain of one of the baseball teams. I believe I forgot to mention that Berlinski made the All-American basketball team two years running.

June 24, 1943 – Issued private parcels. Remember sack of candy balls – about 2 oz. and Abraham Lincoln and the futility of it all. (I just cannot recall what was meant by this cryptic entry.) Received 22 lagermarks as pay. Only asked for 30.

---

[2] Gen. John K. Waters – Seems to me that she was always having kittens!
[3] Lt. Col. Maynard W. Files – Do not forget McIntosh, who helped in the parcel store. He was my assistant until his foot gave out.

June 25, 1943 – Col. Drake has conscripted workers for the garden. Probably a good thing, as many men would take no exercise and everyone can eat from the garden.

Lt. Young is back from Posen. Lt. Young is actually an Air officer but was brought into the compound as a ground officer. He had received a very severe wound in the right shoulder from an incendiary bullet. I am afraid he will never have the use of his right arm again.

June 26, 1943 – 26 officers and 18 G.I. orderlies are added to our camp.

June 27, 1943 – Went to church (Catholic) in our small prison church with Dicks and Smith. By the way, this church is inside the compound, separated from the rest of the camp with barbed wire fence, and we have made it off limits for any escape plans.

June 28, 1943 – We worked on the parcels for the next issue, and it is the last of the parcels in sight for the time being.

There are two or three interesting people in the building across the street. (This refers to a building used by the Guard Company as a barracks for the soldiers guarding the camp. I believe that my comment referred to the fact that the housekeeping done in this building was done mostly by some Polish peasants who were brought in to do the housekeeping.)

June 29, 1943 – The parcels are being sweated out and the end is not in sight. (This refers to some private parcels which came into the camp whose return address indicated that they were security parcels. As I recall, we had to hide these until the number of Germans in the parcel hut was diminished, as they were watching us very closely for the first 4 or 5 weeks.)[4]

---

[4] Gen. John K. Waters – Tony, again believe you should not refer to these types of parcels. It might be a breach of security. I have never been allowed to discuss them at any time.

June 30, 1943 – Solved the parcels. Berlinski got balled up on some string.

July 1, 1943 – Issued ARC parcels to each man. Spalding's came in – the real one. (I am sure this refers to another security parcel addressed to Spalding.)[5] Files is sick – has been in the hospital about a week.

July 2, 1943 – The Russian orderlies and the German guards make great store on cigarette butts. (The German guards came in at night, looking for any cigarette butts we may have thrown on the ground. Cigarettes have a great value.)

July 3, 1943 – Dr. Jacobs fixed my teeth. We had a long argument about the effects of Kriegie life on the human being. Jake thinks that we will all probably live much longer, as we are not wearing our stomachs out!

July 4, 1943 – We have a memorial service in chapel, a real meal, and singing at night.

July 5, 1943 – The Swiss commissioner is here, and found that the Germans had not sent our telegrams relative to food. We learn from the Swiss that times are bad in Germany. The quality of their food is poor and there is not much of it. Col. Drake raised holy hell about not sending our telegrams. Shrewdly, Col. Drake had kept a copy of every telegram he had sent to Geneva relative to parcels.

July 6, 1943 – Can converse a little bit with the Russians. Their language is awful. They had many lighters which had been made at Posen – one lighter made from the stem of a safety razor.

July 7, 1943 – Preparing for our last issue of Red Cross parcels. Very skimpy. (As I recall, there was one parcel for either three or four men.)

---

[5] Gen. John K. Waters – Here again – suggest deletion.

July 8, 1943 – The parcel hut is empty. Capt. Spalding is out. Gave me a pencil. (I am not sure, but I believe this refers to a pencil which could be broken up and made into dye for changing the color of cloth.)

July 9, 1943 – It has been rumored that POWs can buy where others cannot, such as eggs, etc. Many rumors flying about "We have taken Crete," "The U.S. is moving to England," "All kinds of secret weapons are being developed," "We are going to receive 500 parcels."

I have enrolled in several courses, including German – which I certainly need, and accounting – which is interesting.

July 10, 1943 – The Germans now admit that Sicily has been taken. The news on the radio is in German. We have an *ersatz* beer party and have the Russians dance for us, which they are very happy to do at the drop of a hat. Their dance is a little more athletic than the buck and wing found among the Negroes' dances at home.

July 11, 1943 – Went to church; talked to "Joe," who is one of the Russian orderlies. I now have some new British trousers.

July 12, 1943 – We issue Canadian Red Cross parcels to everyone. The German soldiers are quite strong in singing. Today they came by, singing "Smiles" in German. Had some difficulty today with Knorr. He attempted to pass a Red Cross crate out the window and I caught him. His argument was that he needed the wood to make a suitcase. My argument was that it was not his to take. I won this argument.

July 13, 1943 – Col. Gershenow is a very interesting man, of the Jewish faith; seems to have plenty of courage, does not mind tackling the Germans verbally on any issue. He seems to be O.K. in every respect. However, he cannot keep his hands to himself.

It is funny how these small things tend to aggravate one when confined as closely as we are.

Files still in the hospital.

Have come to the conclusion that too often in here every man is for himself and the devil take the hindmost... (For the love of me, I cannot recall the incident that prompted this notation.)[6]

July 14, 1943 – Expected news all day but none came. (This refers to the fact that our secret radio was on the blink and we got no news of what was happening on the front.)[7]

July 15, 1943 – Radio is on after being off for two days. The 1st Armored Division had a beer party. 500 British Red Cross parcels received at camp.

July 16, 1943 – The Goons are up in the air about tins going out without being opened. Worked in the garden today.

Tried two by truck. (I am sure this refers to two officers attempting to go out in the vehicle that took out the empty tin cans.)

July 17, 1943 – Escape is the predominant subject. Col. Drake raised hell with Smith in regard to a paper on rationed items. (Cannot recall details.)

July 18, 1943 – News is good about Italy. Allies have given them 72 hours to capitulate before a great mass of bombs will start falling. Went to church.

---

[6] Lt. Col. Maynard W. Files – Your remark about people was due to our friend Dicks hoarding food at Limburg. I bummed food but ate all of mine if you remember. I never saved a damn thing. Also, if you remember, Dicks never took a bath. Drake ordered him to do so. He put his dirty clothes under his pillow.

[7] Lt. Col. Maynard W. Files – We bought the "bird" (radio) from the Supply Sgt. in charge of the tailor shop and the repair shop our first week there, for 700 cigarettes. That is why we had so much trouble with the news. Later, we received the good one.

July 19, 1943 – In the distance you can see several types of fruit trees growing in this area: apple, pear and cherry, and one that looks very much like an apricot.

July 20, 1943 – Read most of the day, and loafed about.

July 21, 1943 – Security getting list out, and new classes being taught in military science.

July 22, 1943 – No lists yet, but names selected by lot. Am not included and am disappointed. So was Smitty; however, Dicks was on the list. Work started amidst much noise and traffic. It is too well advertised! (These last two items refer to our initial tunnel which was started and the security committee selected those who would be the ones to go through the tunnel. However, there was entirely too much noise and loose talk about this matter. I am afraid that it will not come to a full conclusion of getting anyone out.)

July 23, 1943 – Alger on the list, and understand Waters refused. There is quite a bit of work to be done before anything can happen in this respect. (This refers to the tunnel project.)

July 24, 1943 – Prepared parcels for shipment and for issue. Yesterday I received 30 *marks* – a total of 90 that I have received thus far.

July 25, 1943 – Went to church; sermon entitled, "Charity is Queen of Virtues."

July 26, 1943 – Issued BRC. Rumor has it that Mussolini has resigned.

July 27, 1943 – It is rumor time, and this is acknowledged by the Germans. (This refers to a rumor which we started in camp that we were to be moved to the Black Forest. The German sentry found out about the rumor, believed it, and I understand that they have asked Col. Drake if he had heard anything about a movement to the Black Forest)

July 29, 1943 – Mussolini rumored assassinated. There is a ban on fascist meeting in Italy.

Some German generals dropped by and there was a long discussion in the *Kommandanture*. My belief is they are worried over what might happen since Mussolini has gone kaput.

Upon the insistence of Col. Drake I am to go to the station with the German guards to get the Red Cross parcels. Today we did so, and included in the shipment was two barrels of lime. They could almost put it on the wagon, and I could have easily given them assistance in loading it on. However, I refused and this created a considerable amount of argument and yakety yak. They finally blew up in disgust and I was marched back to camp where we picked up some orderlies, went back to the station, and the orderlies loaded the lime on the wagon.

July 30, 1943 – Another German general shows up today. Have been told by one of the guards that he is looking for heroes for the Russian front. Joe, the Russian orderly, came in last night. He reports that the Poles say that Mussolini is dead. Many Russians surround the Germans. The weather is dry and our gardens are drying up. Just back of the camp is a field of grain which has been ripe for more than two weeks but it has not been cut. Could it be that the Germans are short of man power in getting this year's harvest gathered?

July 31, 1943 – Apparently the Germans are up against it. I notice that many small children are working in the fields. Rumor has it that a very important announcement is in the offing.

August 1, 1943 – Went to church. Title of the sermon: "Just as Gold is Tried in the Fire, We Are Being Tried."

Rumor has it that there are 100,000 dead in Hamburg due to an air raid. I am certain that 325 families from Hamburg have been sent to Altburgund (Schubin) for rehabilitation in this area. They are evacuating all large German cities. One German said that in Hamburg the fire was so hot that even the asphalt streets were burning.

Primus left for France today. (I believe this refers to a German who worked in the parcel hut and was a transplanted Frenchman. The Third Reich uses this process quite often in taking a man from one section of Europe as a prisoner and putting him to work for their benefit in another section of Europe.)

<u>August 2, 1943</u> – We issued a half parcel today. Quite a stink rose about the giving of a half of a chocolate bar by each POW to the Hamburg children in this area. Someone had this idea, and it was not too well received by the remainder of the POWs. In the afternoon the Hitler *Jügend* and *Mädchen* marched by. All in all, it was some day. Had a big long talk with the Russian orderlies. The German issue of cheese definitely has worms in it.

<u>August 3, 1943</u> – They finally got some equipment into the field back of the compound and got the entire thing mowed, then all of the women and children helped with its gathering.

Schubin is a very small town about the size of Auxvasse, Missouri.

We can get cold baths, and they will at least enable us to remain clean.

Rumor has it that Goering is dead.

<u>August 4, 1943</u> – Received 800 parcels from Geneva. When picking up the parcels I was able to observe some interesting things about Schubin. All of the buildings have very steep roofs, probably to keep the snow off, and the gutters are concealed in the roof. The Poles are a very sturdy people. They seem to be able to hitch themselves up to the milk carts, potato carts, etc. Tried to pick up a train schedule today at the train station, but was unable to do so.

German kids at the pump.

August 5, 1943 – This time 640 parcels arrived, and everyone seems to be trying to run the parcel hut. Col. Waters went down with me to the railway station. We loaded the wagon so as to be able to ride back. The German driver should be fired. He is the laziest man I have ever seen.

We went on a parole walk and saw the outline of some military trenches. I understand that this area contained some of the very last Polish resistance.

Saw a windmill and the military road. (It could be that this refers to the outline of an old barbed wire compound. The wire was rusty, and it probably was a prisoner compound at one time.)

A complaint has been made to the *Kommandanture*, as we think some of the German postal guards have stolen some of our medical supplies from Geneva.

These parole walks were such that we were allowed to walk in a body, for about two hours, outside of the compound. We were accompanied by the guards, and in order to obtain this privilege we had to give our parole that we would not escape during the time of walk.

August 6, 1943 – The canary went kaput. Used too much current. (This refers to our first radio.) It seems that the condenser will have to be re-wired. Orel has fallen. There are reports of a large number of prisoners taken by the Russians. Refugees from Berlin and Hamburg are being sent to this area.

August 7, 1943 – Learning to play Russian bank. Issued parcels. Sent Files' clothes to him in Vollstein.

August 8, 1943 – Wrote Betty and just sat around playing Russian bank most of the day.

August 9, 1943 – Issued parcels and almost made a mistake. (I am not sure, but I believe this refers to one of the secret parcels getting involved, and we almost did not get it out of the parcel hut.)[8]

August 10, 1943 – About 20 new officers come in. They include Ford, who came in from Eichstädt and from 7-B at Moosbürg. These men were the odds and ends from all over Italy and Germany and some new ones who had been captured in Sicily. Some were paratroopers and some were airborne infantry. Rumor has it that the 1st Armored Division has sent a regiment back to the U.S. All in all, these new men did not know much more than we did. We received 2,000 parcels from Geneva, and we had quite a time unloading them. There was one parcel missing, and we had a real good argument with the Germans at the railroad station. I am quite convinced that the parcel was not in the car, as the seal was unbroken, but at the same time we accused the Germans of stealing our food.

August 11, 1943 – The Germans came by to check on the lost parcel. This included *Hauptman* Zimmerman, the security officer. Zimmerman is a nut! Before the war he operated some type of home furnishing store in Austria. He has delusions of being a hot military man, and you can easily see where Hitler would appeal to this type of mentality. He likes to scream about. Could it be that he is the Nazi undercover man sent here to watch *Oberst* Schneider?

August 12, 1943 – We received some athletic equipment and books from the Swedish YMCA.

August 13, 1943 – 1,995 parcels arrived from Geneva. Five British Red Cross and one tobacco parcel lost The Germans state they will shoot the culprits when found. One of the German guards at the railroad station gave me a bottle of beer.

The local Church has a sign on it forbidding Poles to enter. This sign is also on certain other businesses in the community.

---

[8] Gen. John K. Waters – Suggest deletion.

August 14, 1943 – A British enlisted man, "Basher" Bailey, has been giving us some trouble in the parcel hut. He has seen too much barbed wire and is slightly on the nutty side. Today some private parcels arrived and Bailey started an argument with us rather than the Germans. He got rather violent, and it ended up with us throwing him out of the parcel hut.

August 15, 1943 – Went to church. "Virgin Mary as a Soldier's Patron Saint," was the topic of the sermon. Killer, a German interpreter, is back, wearing a black arm band.

August 16, 1943 – Had another hot argument today with "Basher" and feel rather ashamed about it, as he is probably the victim of having been enclosed in barbed wire too long.

August 17, 1943 – The canary (our radio) sings only when it wants to. Private parcels are starting to come in. The Germans almost caught the canary. (Cannot remember the details.)[9]

August 18, 1943 – Capt. Barker (or Backus) gave a good satire on rumors. In talking to the Germans in the parcel hut, it is evident that the German G.I. is getting fed up with the war.

August 19, 1943 – Some more private parcels arrived. There is nothing that picks up morale in this camp like the arrival of these packages.

August 20, 1943 – A German non-com pulled a very shabby trick on one of the officers relative to an address in Munich. At times they really get your goat (I believe this refers to an incident in which some incoming officer had made contact with a German in Munich. They used a subterfuge, which I cannot recall, to get this officer to identify the address.) This German civilian is probably going to be punished severely.

August 21, 1943 – For recreation, we have started a Quiz Program. It is quite popular between the messes.

---

[9] Gen. John K. Waters – Delete reference to security parcels.

We received 1,800 U.S. parcels and several sacks of private parcels, but no mail.

August 22, 1943 – Gave Joe, the Russian orderly, some cigarettes and he washed one of my shirts. He says the two Ukrainians left the *Oflag* detail to join the German Army.

August 23, 1943 – We issue parcels.

August 24, 1943 – No newspapers. Something is up! There was even an air raid sounded at Schubin.

August 25, 1943 – Berlin reported to have been heavily bombed with one of the largest raids in the war.

August 26, 1943 – For the first time we have the parcel hut storage area almost filled. There were 155 more that came in from Spangenberg.

August 27, 1943 – Have a slight touch of diarrhea. Stayed in bed most of the day. Lots were drawn today for seven parcels addressed to "Any American POW." We received some amusement parcels from the Swedish YMCA. Had quite an argument with Col. Drake regarding the orderlies' share. They did not participate in these parcels, but they were issued wooden suitcases.

August 28, 1943 – Heard a good sermon today: "Baptism may be given by anyone, with the only requirements being the spirit, the ritual, and a flow of water."

I received my first letter from home, from Mark Wallace, dated June 9th.

August 29, 1943 – Received letters from Betty and Glen Hocker.

August 30, 1943 – Letter from Betty, Martha Barksdale, and many of the old MMA boys. I am sweating out a letter to Geneva. (Believe this refers to the fact that we are attempting to get Schubin to be designated a warehouse point for Red Cross parcels.)

September 1, 1943 – Files back and had many tales of the treatment of prisoners.

Apparently there is a different classification according to nationalities, Norwegian, British, Dutch and Jews the low men on the totem pole.

September 2, 1943 – Letters and photos from home. Col. Drake called to Posen to talk to the British high command.

Capt. Bernie "Chief" Bolton knocked apples off the ground. (Do not recall what this meant)

September 3, 1943 – Col. Drake told of trip to Posen. We are complimented on our conduct. There was an air raid siren at 1600 hours.

September 4, 1943 – Swapped around and obtained a pipe, from which I scrapped all varnish. Dicks, Jones, Files and I are playing a lot of Parcheesi. We are in contact with many friends. (This refers to the fact that we are able to write back, through certain other officers and me, letters that can carry a message to the headquarters in London.)[10]

September 5, 1943 – To Church. A good sermon on prayer.

September 6, 1943 – Issued parcels, and studied Russian with Joe.

September 7, 1943 – Got in about 5-mile walk (a parole walk.) Soil in this area seems to be poor, sandy, and rather porous. Woods are neat and pretty; the village is dirty. In horsing around, one officer hit a guard over the head with a rock. Fortunately, he had a sense of humor and understood that no harm had been intended.

September 8, 1943 – Files and Dicks are cheesy Parcheesi players. Tramped the spinach down.

---

[10] Gen. John K. Waters – A security item that should not be revealed.

September 9, 1943 – Believe Italy is *kaput*. Studied most of the day. Smith moved out (Believe this refers to Captain Smith moving out of our room.)[11]

September 10, 1943 – Five new officers and the 19(17?) returned after a bitter experience in an Oflag near Berlin. The Germans tried to get information from them. Lt. N. C. Tacey, of Springfield (Holyoke?), Mass., just came in and is now our new roommate. I was able to draw a good U.S. razor and a toothbrush.

September 11, 1943 – Had another walk, and played bridge for the first time tonight.

September 12, 1943 – Attended Church, and read most of the day.

September 13, 1943 – Received some parcels and noted some air flasks in the station. Reported this to security. The German guards were rather tired today and our detail walked faster than they could keep up with us. Knorr kept yapping "Slowly, slowly." Knorr is a true nut.

September 14, 1943 – Had an air alert today.

September 15, 1943 – Find out from the Germans that the air alert was caused by five Russian planes which were at about 20,000 feet. Some parcels arrived today.

September 16, 1943 – Got into quite an argument with one of the guards about the war. He finally admitted that the war would not last forever, and that they were losing in Italy.

Had a chance to be in Willie Krick's home. It was very nice. When he is not soldiering, he is the local printer. Certain houses in this village are designated as being suitable only for Poles.

---

[11] Lt. Col. Maynard W. Files – Smitty left our room because of Dicks, and we got Jones. Thank God!

September 17, 1943 – Received two carloads of parcels and we worked all day unloading the lot. Had a strong argument with Knorr about some letters. (Do not recall the details.)

September 18, 1943 – The Germans show us a motion picture in the camp, including a newsreel. There is no doubt that the news is heavily censored in Germany, and to listen to them discuss the merits of our equipment compared to theirs made the whole thing rather ludicrous.

September 19, 1943 – Worked on the parcel hut books most of the day and failed to go to Church. The Hitler *Jugend*, who are in camp somewhere near here, marched by today with their drums, banners and short trousers.

September 20, 1943 – I saved Bingham.[12] (Do not recall.) There are five Italian officers here in Schubin. The Germans say they are to be turned in to this lager. One is reported to be a general. The Swiss legation was here. Received a box from home, with the candy removed. (Do not recall too many of the details of the above cryptic notes.)

September 21, 1943 – Drew the lucky number today and got a box addressed to "Any American POW" from Mr. Seymour Knox, of 269 Delaware Avenue, Buffalo, New York. Was kidded quite a bit about drawing his parcel.

September 22, 1943 – We have rearranged the racks, and issued tasks at the hut. Played bridge most of the afternoon.

September 23, 1943 – Received a letter from Betty, took a parole walk, and played a new game – Lexicon.

September 24, 1943 – Had my picture taken yesterday by Popakofki, an interpreter from the *Kommandanture*.

---

[12] Lt. Billy Bingham – I remember. The Germans caught a book containing G2 information addressed to me and you disposed of the book which was given to Lt. Col. Alger.

September 25, 1943 – The guards about the lager have been redistributed, and apparently some of them are on the way to the Russian front.

September 26, 1943 – Heard Father Cain speak on "Christ, the Perfect Man." Lt. Tacey has started writing his novel. I witnessed the preface. The weather is starting to be bad, with some rain and much colder. The Hitler *Jügend* marched all morning.

September 27, 1943 – At the parcel hut today got into quite a discussion of the Schützenfest with one of the guards. The Charleston, South Carolina, Rifle Club used to have one of these each year, at which everyone drank beer and fired at targets.

September 28, 1943 – Was able to take another walk today. Sanitary conditions in Poland are poor, farm houses dirty, open wells. Most of the Polish homes are thatched. There is some moss growing in the thatch.

September 29, 1943 – Took a bath – No singing. (I believe this refers to the radio not operating.)

September 30, 1943 – Walked around the compound; talked to one of the guards in the parcel hut about the Hitler Youth Movement in Germany. The kids are divided into two groups: 8 to 14 and 14 to 17. For six months they are in attendance at a camp where there is much exercise and some study. They then return home and attend school for six months. There is no cost to be borne by the parents. He seemed to be thoroughly sold on this movement.

Was surprised to hear one of the Polish workers speak English today. (I cannot recall his conversation.) These men are brought into the camp for specialized work such as repairing the ovens, electrical fixtures, etc. The German guards in the parcel hut say that times are bad in Germany. They know that they are retreating on both fronts.

October 1, 1943 – Played bridge most of the day.

October 2, 1943 – Lt. Col. Yardley, a paratrooper, came in. He had been captured in Italy September 15th. Rumors at the present time are thick, furious and good. (Cannot recall the details.)

October 3, 1943 – Music at the Church today excellent. Played bridge in the afternoon.

October 4, 1943 – On parole walk today, noticed there was a body lying in state in the German chapel. The Polish section of this town is absolutely filthy.

October 5, 1943 – There was a hurried-up try today by four officers to escape and it failed.

October 6, 1943 – Van Vliet, Chappel, Aten and Higgins attempt to cut through the wire and are caught red-handed, with maps, tools, food, etc. The Germans immediately had an *appell*. They had a very difficult time attempting to count everyone, after they arrived at the figure we later found that Schultz was asleep upstairs and had not been counted. Could it be that the Germans themselves do not know how many prisoners are in the camp?

October 7, 1943 – Rumors – and more rumors – one of which is that the camp had better be ready for a big shakedown search by the *Gestapo*. Obtained this small item during the walk today, in talking with one of the German guards. (The Germans were very anxious that the *Gestapo* not find anything in the camp that would indicate we were not good little boys.)

October 8, 1943 – *Feldwebel* Schopert on three weeks leave, but swears he will be back at the same job. I certainly hope so, as I believe he is a good man and I know that he is extremely honest. Many more rumors about the *Gestapo* search, and everyone is running around hiding things in preparation. Seven new officers are brought in today. They were captured in Salerno on September 9th. Morale of camp is good. I read most of the afternoon.

October 9, 1943 – Received three letters; one from Nelson Rowe, who is handling our advertising at MMA. We play quite a bit of bridge.

October 10, 1943 – The *Gestapo* arrived as scheduled and searched the rooms of all the four who had escaped. There was quite a bit of excitement, and a mad rush to get everything hidden. *Oberst* Schneider came out and gave us a talk (sounding like a bull) which was translated by Minner (sounding like a mouse). The gist of it was, "Do not try to escape or you will be shot."

October 11, 1943 – Played bridge most of the afternoon.

October 12, 1943 – Talked to Young. He knew Farrell, who had formerly been on the faculty of MMA.

October 13, 1943 – Received much personal mail today. Heard from Aunt Mary, Oliver Marshall, several MMA alumni, and Major Nunn of the MMA faculty.

October 14, 1943 – Played bridge most of the afternoon with Englehaardt as my partner.

October 15, 1943 – Received a tobacco parcel from Betty.

October 16, 1943 – Col. Drake and Bergeson go to Posen today in regard to the repatriation of Bailey, Young and Morgan. Thirty new officers are due in today. (Young, as I may have written, was the Air Corps lieutenant who had been wounded in the shoulder with an incendiary bullet and would probably lose the use of his arm for the remainder of his life.)

October 17, 1943 – To Church. Heard a good sermon on Fosdick's idea of the present conception of religion. I am reading an excellent book on the psychology of human behavior.

October 18, 1943 – We are starting some studies in camp, and I am enrolling in one of the courses on common law.

October 19, 1943 – Thirty new officers came in. It seems they were in a POW camp in Italy when the Italian government fell. They report that the senior officer held all of the camp under orders to remain in the camp and to make no attempt to escape. Received a private parcel from home.

October 20, 1943 – Took a bath. Thirty more officers in from the 36th Division. We now have 322 (284 officers and 38 orderlies) in the compound. I received a very nice letter from General Ward and Capt. Hatfield. Ward reminded me to keep my eyes open, which I have been trying to do.

October 21, 1943 – Wrote the International Red Cross at Geneva. Took a walk around the compound.

October 22, 1943 – The camp received about 25,000 British Red Cross cigarettes which had been sent to the Serbian POWs at this compound.

I am quite certain that our lager had been used for other nationalities before we were sent here. As I understand it, it was originally built to hold French and Polish POWs. These were later moved out and the lager was filled with British POWs. I do know that one of the men I have since met, in the Dairy Queen business, Joe Phillips of Laurel, Mississippi, had been a POW in the same compound, and he was one of the Americans who flew with the Royal Air Force before America entered the war.

Rumor has it that we are going to get all the Montroys (sic?, Fading ink makes it hard to read) equipment if they are to be repatriated.

October 23, 1943 – Received mail from Nelson Rowe and Gen. Ward. Wrote Betty and Gen. Ward.

October 24, 1943 – Father Brock delivered the sermon today. Could not quite follow his thinking to well.

October 25, 1943 – Issued boxes, rearranged the orderlies and their requests.

October 26, 1943 – Talked to Joe. He has two sisters. One works in Moscow. He is a 7 month veteran in the Finnish war. Said it was extremely cold in Finland.

October 27, 1943 – Many rumors and much talk of the East Front. (Cannot recall.)

October 28, 1943 – Packed up Bonami and two doctors to go to a *Stalag*. (Do not recall the details of why Bonami was included.)

October 29, 1943 – The camp put on a play and it was very good. The orchestra was particularly good. We have been able to get some instruments through the Swedish YMCA.

October 30, 1943 – Louflier took Smith's cigarette lighter and we all raised a stink. (Louflier was kind of a thickheaded German who worked in the parcel hut and later was assigned to German security detail. I do not recall the exact reason why he seized this lighter but do recall that we got it back after much argument.)

October 31, 1943 – Sgt. David Edward Scrace, of 30 Manor Road, Tumbridge Wells, England, came in and he is going to Wallstein – a rather plucky, self-reliant Britisher.

November 1, 1943 – We wrote the Swiss Legation and the International Red Cross. 14 new officers came in.

Knorr was infuriated today by finding a dog biscuit in a cigarette box. (Cannot recall the details of this.)

Got into quite a fuss with the German security regarding the storage of Red Cross parcels. Col. Drake certainly has the Germans under his thumb. (I am quite certain this refers to an incident in which the Germans wished to move some of the parcels across the street to their barracks for what they call "safe keeping". Col. Drake insisted that everything addressed to us be brought to the compound, opened in our presence, and remain in the compound. He won his point.)

November 2, 1943 – The argument still continues with the Germans. We finally move some of the parcels to another building in order to relieve the weight on the floor. There was a great deal of face-saving in this maneuver.

November 3, 1943 – Have started studying Italian under Lt. Cipariani and have dropped the class in German as it is apparent that I should not learn to speak German too well. In talking with the Germans it is best to give them the impression you wish, rather than the exact details.

November 4, 1943 – 12 new officers came in. Moved some more parcels to the new building. One German is a farmer and lives nearby. (Could this refer to Willie Kricks, who is a German soldier who has several hours off each week to continue his job as the local printer for the town of Schubin?) One of the Russian orderlies is a pretty savvy character. He was a petroleum engineer. We had quite a discussion on trigonometric functions.

November 5, 1943 – Opened parcels and tried to straighten out the invoices and bills of lading. These were called *Frachtbriefs*.

November 6, 1943 – Played a trick on Knorr. Amon Carter and Buschman played one on me. (Cannot recall.)

November 7, 1943 – Getting very cold. Spent most of the afternoon reading and helping Files with analytic geometry. Files, by the way, is studying college math with the idea of finishing his degree. He lacks only a few hours of having a bachelor's degree from the University of Maine. (As I recall, the university gave him this privilege, and he did complete his college education while a POW.)[13]

November 8, 1943 – Issued parcels and finally got the invoices straight. The YMCA commissioner, an old man from

---

[13] Lt. Col. Maynard W. Files – yes, my wife received it with hers in Dec. 1943.

Denmark, was here. He was most interesting.[14] The Germans are watching every move he makes, but even so he was able to tell us some of the hard times the Germans are now having with their manufacture and railroad complex.

Got into a squabble over a shoe repair kit from the Red Cross. (I recall this incident very well.) We received a keg containing half soles, shoe tacks and a small knife, from the Red Cross. The keg, about the size of a nail keg, had been opened and in checking the contents with the invoice there were two half-soles missing. While it was very minor, at the same time I screamed that somebody in the Third and Last Reich had stolen leather that had been issued to us as internees. We had quite a hot argument with *Hauptman* Merck, who finally took the details to talk it over with the *Kommandanture*. He came back with a long face and told me that the *Kommandanture* was going to hold him personally responsible. Merck never had anything to do with it in any way, shape or form, and had not even seen the keg until it arrived in the parcel hut. Merck was somewhat "shook up" over the matter. I suggested to him that we frame Knorr and state that Knorr had had his hands in the keg. He seemed to be well taken by this idea and assured me that it would be one way in which we could get rid of Knorr, who is a pain in the neck to the POWs as well as the better element of the members of the German Army. Frankly, I think Knorr is an under-cover Nazi and is probably in one of Himmler's outfits.

<u>November 9, 1943</u> – On the parole walk today had an opportunity to talk to a Polish woman when the guard was not looking. The morale of the local Polish peasants is very good.

Churchill's speech lowered the spirits of the POWs a great deal. (Cannot recall what phrase he used, unless it was some threat to turn Germany into a goat pasture.)

---

[14] Gen. John K. Waters – His name was Mr. Cedergrin I believe.

November 10, 1943 – Unable to take baths. It is very cold and the German railway system is not able to deliver coal. Anyone can take a cold bath. I finally took one, even though it took a long while. Extremely cold!!

November 11, 1943 – Not much doing except many protests to the Germans. Jones ill. (Do not recall what the protests were about. – Probably about nothing, but were a good way to keep our morale up and keep the Germans on the defensive.)

November 12, 1943 – *Oberst* Schneider says that the 1939 Geneva Convention is out, and that we will have to do as he says. This leaves us nothing to do but to kick on this matter to the Swiss.

Some new orderlies came in from Montroys and brought a chest of tools and some theater props.

November 13, 1943 – Saw a German picture. Their films are all very suggestive. The title of the film, "A Well Cut Woman." The news is good from the canary and also in letters from home.

(In case I did not mention it, all outgoing and incoming mail was very severely censored. Sometimes they would merely cut out the pages they did not wish to fall into our hands, and sometimes they simply withheld the entire letter. I am quite certain that many of our letters were never mailed, for the same reason.) The attitude towards Col. Drake has changed considerably. He is looked upon more favorably than he was at first. This group certainly needs a strong hand if we are not going to be thrown out into the streets to sweep them along with the Poles.

November 14, 1943 – I am reading a lot of Damon Runyon.

November 15, 1943 – Issued parcels and rechecked the invoices.

November 16, 1943 – On a parole walk today spoke some Italian to a Pole who thoroughly understood me. The morale of the Poles is very good.

November 17, 1943 – Took another cold bath, and saw the doctor today relative to my finger which seems to be getting arthritic. Captain Jones is a good man and a lot of help in the parcel hut. Certainly has no use for Germans.

Buschman is being tried for stealing the half soles mentioned several days back. I was called out to testify and I did so on his behalf as he had nothing whatsoever to do with it. Buschman is a very nice looking young German, until he takes his hat off and then you can see that he has not a hair on his head. *Hauptman* Zimmerman was trying to pin this stealing on Buschman rather than have it fall on Knorr, who is his protégé. Buschman is certainly not connected with this deal.

November 18, 1943 – Even though we keep Maw, a cat, in our parcel hut, and she has kittens about every eight weeks, there are some mice getting into some of the boxes and eating the dried fruit (prunes).[15]

November 19, 1943 – More new officers in. Lt. Col. Goller was one of them. He had been captured at Bengazi. He was a military observer with the British Army. He had tried to escape, got between the lines, and was recaptured by the Germans. He told of being befriended by the Italians, and two Italian children in one family were shot for the family's action in befriending him. I recall Goller, as he had short papers, later printed into a manual, on some of the Libyan maneuvers.

November 20, 1943 – Bougainville is reported by the German papers as being a great Jap victory.

November 21, 1943 – I am reading "The Horse and Buggy Doctor."

---

[15] Lt. Col. Maynard W. Files – Maw had 4 doctors assisting in delivery, Salerno, (the Blonde from S.C.), Borgen from Iowa, and Jacobs.

November 22, 1943 – On parole walk today we go into a new area south of Schubin. All of this country very much the same – flat, with a little roll to it, and sandy.

November 23, 1943 – Received a food parcel from home, and it came in good time. As I recall, it was something like 14 weeks in delivery.

November 24, 1943 – Bath today, and a big day! Tried to get a list of S.A.O. parcels. (Cannot recall the details.)

November 25, 1943 – Big day, with good meals: millet porridge, Red Cross stew, and for the second meal: Prem, vegetable, potatoes and pudding. It was really good!

November 26, 1943 – Our theater group is producing "Brother Orchid."

Willie Kricks, in the parcel hut, has an unusual education. In some 7 years of schooling, he has a pretty good understanding of English history, American history, and basic mathematics. At the same time he speaks good Polish, good German, and a smattering of English. Willie has a medal to prove that he participated (probably as a ticket taker) in the Olympics in Berlin. He is quite a gambler and a poor chess player. He bets Jones a bottle of Schnapps for each game and at the present time owes Jones 25 or 30 bottles, which of course will never be paid.

November 27, 1943 – We received a large number of pillows from the British Red Cross. These were turned over to the hospital. Much rather something else had been received, but beggars cannot be choosers.

November 28, 1943 – Read "The Country Doctor" and slept most of the day.

November 29, 1943 – Went on a parole walk and had an opportunity to talk to Hans, one of the armed guards, on this parole. (We protested to the Germans that since it was a parole walk there should not be an armed guard. The guard is along to protect us from the Poles – according to the Germans!!) I am surprised that the battle of Africa is still being fought so much. Everybody rehashes his little part.

Received a distressing letter from Hocker relative to the administration at MMA. He fears that he is being marked by Stribling and is going to have a hard year. I sincerely hope that this is not so.

November 30, 1943 – Joe brought up two new Russians: Koslow and Mikell. The four of us trying to talk Russian creates bedlam in the room.

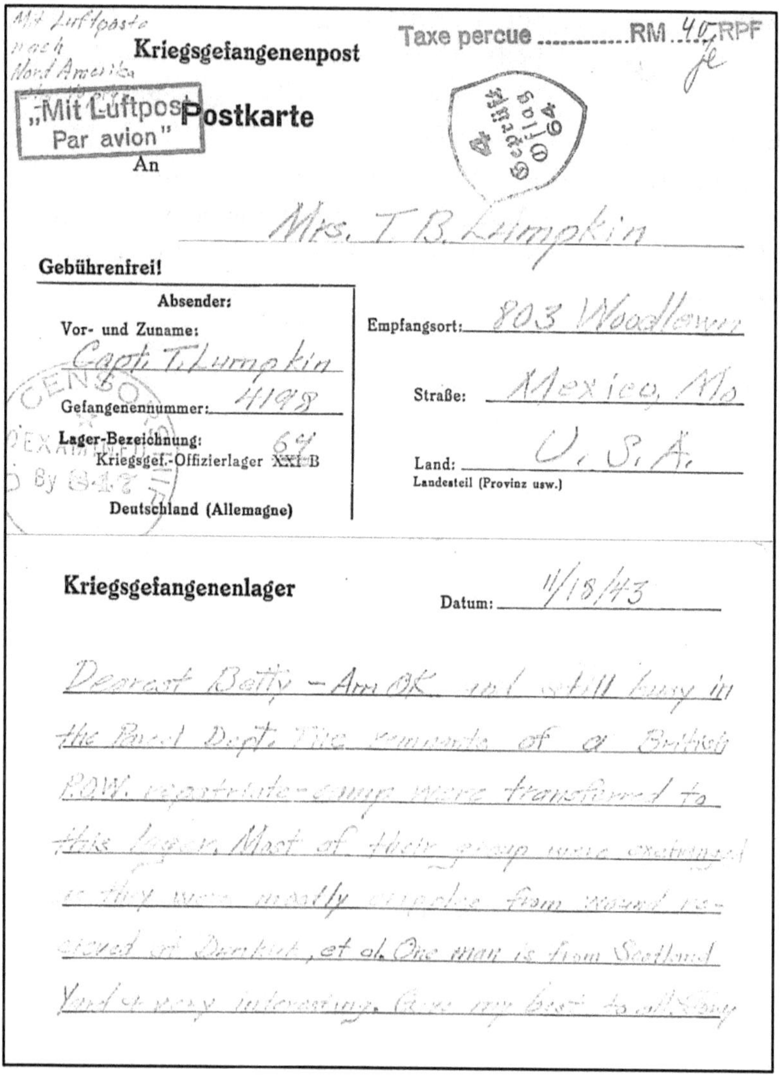

Mit Luftpost nach Nord Amerika

Kriegsgefangenenpost

„Mit Luftpost Par avion"

Postkarte

An

Taxe percue ....RM 40 RPF

Geprüft 4 Oflag 64

Mrs. T. B. Lumpkin

Gebührenfrei!

Absender:

Vor- und Zuname: Capt. T. Lumpkin

Gefangenennummer: 4198

Lager-Bezeichnung: Kriegsgef.-Offizierlager ~~XXI~~ B 64

Deutschland (Allemagne)

CENSOR EXAMINED By 842

Empfangsort: 803 Woodlawn

Straße: Mexico, Mo

Land: U. S. A.

Landesteil (Provinz usw.)

Kriegsgefangenenlager

Datum: 11/18/43

Dearest Betty – Am OK and still busy in the Parcel Dept. The remnants of a British POW repatriate-group were transferred to this lager. Most of their group were exchanged as they were mostly cripples from wounds received at Dunkirk, et al. One man is from Scotland Yard & very interesting. Give my best to all. Tony

Figure 10-2 One of many letters Capt. Lumpkin wrote to his wife, Betty. Each passed through German and U.S. censors before being delivered.

Chapter 11

German Plans go *Kaput*

December 1, 1943 – The security group from the German *Kommandanture* have ordered all parcels opened in their presence. After working out a plan according to their thinking, they got it all balled up and washed their hands of the matter, letting us do it in our old way. (As I recall this instance, they had some system in which they wished to have every can opened. We protested that it would cause some of the food to spoil. They agreed that such might be the case and finally decided that a can would be completely opened at both ends and everything dumped on a plate. Of course this was an inconvenience to all of the POWs, so the parcel hut group instituted a slow-down and at the rate we were going it would take almost three days to issue parcels. This of course tied up the Germans, who were most anxious to get out of the hut and away from this sticky problem. They finally went back to the old system of puncturing a nail hole in each can as it was issued. This anecdote points up the fact that often the Germans, who were such great planners, would over plan a project and tangle themselves up in a mass of details, which made the original plan go *kaput*.)

December 2, 1943 – Lt. Bonomi's equipment came in and some articles were stolen. I squawked and the Germans all got excited, but I could not pin this on Knorr, as he was on leave.

December 3, 1943 – Berlin really got a pasting. The papers say that Japan reports that the Germans have peace feelers out.

December 4, 1943 – The German papers are bragging that they have a new secret weapon and that it goes into effect tomorrow. As to what this weapon is seems to worry some of the boys. Could it be reprisals? Koslow came in today to help me with my Russian.

December 5, 1943 – Cold; snow; weather very bad.

December 6, 1943 – Saw a Sherlock Holmes picture. It was very poor.

December 7, 1943 – Had trouble with some books. (Am not sure, but believe this refers to the Germans having brought in some 12 or 14 copies of *Mien Kampf*. We refused to issue them until we had censored the book, just as they censor our books sent to us from the Swedish YMCA.)[1]

December 8, 1943 – The German newspapers call Roosevelt, Churchill, etc., a bunch of gangsters. The allies are calling upon Germany to quit.

December 9, 1943 – On the parole walk today, lost a package of cigarettes. (Cannot recall details, but believe this refers to giving some cigarettes to one of the Polish farmers.) The German papers have goofed up in showing some of their tanks in the Vatican City. The papers say that hate is the answer to the bombing of Berlin.

December 10, 1943 – The German government is now asking girls 14 years of age to volunteer for work service. There is quite an article in the German papers about Patton striking a

---

[1] Gen. John K. Waters – This is true.

wounded soldier. These papers of course grab anything for propaganda use.

From the canary I understand that the stock market is rising sharply on the war news.

One of the POWs has made a Christmas tree and decorated it with tin cans.

In a discussion with the Germans in the parcel hut, it seems that they take their Communist and their Jewish question very seriously. They say the Poles cannot organize themselves, and the country around here seems to bear this out. Many of the prisoners are now talking of what they will do after the war is over. One group is talking of starting a leisure camp for the working girls. Knorr seen with two very beautiful girls yesterday. He told me they were from Germany when I accused him of fraternizing with the Poles, who he says are lower than pigs. He tells me there is an order making it strictly forbidden for a German soldier to date a Pole.

December 11, 1943 – *Hauptman* Menner has not returned from Berlin. Rumor has it that he was caught in an air raid and was killed.

December 12, 1943 – Christmas parcels and some clothing parcels came in today. On the trip from Bonhof, one of the small kids (Polish) gave me the real house. (I am not sure but I think this merely refers to a kid giving me the V for Victory sign.)

December 13, 1943 – I am reading Van Loon's "Story of Mankind." Stooged for the first time while the canary was singing. (Stooging was a rather complicated device that was used to insure that we knew where every German in the compound was during that time. Particularly was it important to know the moment any new ones entered the gate. That was my job for that night.)

December 14, 1943 – The YMCA has issued us some blank books of regular size, which may be used as diaries. (As it later turned out, this was a rather dangerous issue, as many of the men were writing down facts which should not have been reproduced for German eyes. There is probably much of this later on, but I do recall that several officers very foolishly wrote down their opinions and the facts of camp life which later were rather embarrassing to the group as a whole.)

December 15, 1943 – Studied with another Russian orderly. His family had been taken from Krokov and sent to Austria. He was a sergeant of artillery in the army, and prior to that he had been a railroad engineer. He was quite a braggart about the fact that the Trans-Siberian railroad operated on a 7-day schedule between Leningrad and the Pacific Coast. Later on, after much questioning, I find that the train can actually make it in about 4 ½ days, so they go like the devil for 2 or 3 days, just in case they have a break-down before they get to the other end. If they find they are going to arrive too soon they merely pull into a siding and wait for a day or so.

December 16, 1943 – *Hauptman* Menner has been found in a hospital in Saxony. (Do not recall the rest of the details.)

December 17, 1943 – Am just about ready to learn Russian. Russian is a most difficult language. I have had to learn a brand new alphabet. After learning the alphabet one can then add words, and after a sufficient number of words you can then add grammar, etc.

December 18, 1943 – I drew a towel today as part of our regular Red Cross issue. A towel is certainly a wonderful thing to have. I have asked the Swedish YMCA for a Russian-English and an English-Russian dictionary.

December 19, 1943 – Two doctors, Barkus and Jacobs, left for a Stalag. We had much trouble getting their equipment past the Germans.

December 20, 1943 – Continued study of Russian. Was slightly ill tonight from leaky coal gas fumes.

December 21, 1943 – Wrote Geneva in an attempt to get my invoices correct. Weather very cold and icy.

December 22, 1943 – Took a parole walk. Very slippery. Capt. Jones received his first letter since he was captured the 17th of last February.

December 23, 1943 – Our stove is kaput. Our stoves are handmade from tiles/ and once you get a bed of hot coals the secret is to cut off all air. The stove is about 6 feet long, 5 ½ feet wide and 4 feet across – the most efficient stove for using a small amount of fuel.

Tonight the Polish chimney sweep came in and gave this stove the works. We also had a box of cardboard brought up from the parcel hut, and for the first time in a long while we really got the room warm.

December 24, 1943 – We issued parcels. I am going great guns with my study of Russian.

December 25, 1943 – Jake gave me a drink that they had distilled. Had many Christmas greetings. Thought of home and the kids.

December 26, 1943 – Jones seems to be getting his mail O.K. now, as he received much today.

December 27, 1943 – This is a slow week. Too many thoughts of Christmas. Received a parcel from The War Prisoners Benefit Association, 156 Fifth Ave., New York, #2966. This parcel really set me up, with a towel, sugar and a deck of cards.

December 28, 1943 – Kozilowski, a German interpreter, gave me a picture of the camp building. It is very cold and snowing.

December 29, 1943 – Reading several books.

December 30, 1943 – The Boys are still re-fighting the battles of Oran, Algiers, and Africa.

December 31, 1943 – There is a big party tonight, with much gambling, games of chance, using lagermarks. It is amazing what people can do with improvisations. Received a tobacco parcel from Betty.

January 1, 1944 – A new year, and much study of Russian. This place should be named for the study of the Battle of Africa, or an Old Soldiers' Home.

January 2, 1944 – Wrote the Swiss regarding parcels. One of my Russian instructors was an officer in the Red Army.[2] He is keeping it very quiet. The Germans tell me it is *verboten* for SS troops to gamble. I doubt this very much.

The news on the canary is good. The Germans are cracking up; very much so in the last few days.

January 3, 1944 – A letter from Glen Hocker. He is really low about the MMA situation.

The Red Army is coming like hell. Attitude of the Germans has definitely changed.

We are getting many special parcels. (I am sure this refers to our secret parcels.)[3]

January 4, 1944 – Studying Russian very hard, and trying to write its script. My teacher is a real gem and has given me his past history in the Red Army. He is an officer but is passing himself off as an enlisted man.

January 5, 1944 – Got a warm bath today and really needed it.

January 6, 1944 – Wrote to Mr. Mumford, Johnny's father in England, and thanked him for writing Betty and me. Johnny

---

[2] Gen. John K. Waters – As I recall, Russian officers of the rank of major or below were put in camps with Russian enlisted men. The Germans refused to differentiate below Lt. Col.

[3] Gen. John K. Waters – Recommend omission.

had apparently written his father who wrote Betty that I had been with Johnny in Eichstädt.

January 7, 1944 – Much study.

January 8, 1944 – Studying and reading.

January 9, 1944 – Lights in the compound on the blink. We live and eat by light made from a can of British oleo. Not very much light!

January 10, 1944 – Capt. Richard H. Torrence, of Waco, Texas, collapsed this morning and died about 9:30.[4]

January 11, 1944 – A real hot argument with Knorr relative to tins being punctured. He found one can in which the nail had only dented the metal.

January 12, 1944 – The Germans finally get the lights on, and this also gives us water as the water system is based on pumping from an underground well.

January 13, 1944 – Dr. Jacobs (Paul G.) filled a tooth for me and did a very good job. His drill was made from a small nail which he had fashioned into a bit and had hardened. With one of the cameras which had been sneaked into camp, was able to get pictures of the Missouri group and the occupants of #21.[5]

January 14, 1944 – Rumor has it that the Russian orderlies are to be sent away. Hope that I can get my homemade dictionary completed in time.

Capt. Torrence was buried today in the Schubin cemetery. The *Wehrmacht* sent a wreath and honored him with volleys over the grave.

January 15, 1944 – A Russian orderly tried to steal a can of meat and was caught. (Do not recall the details.)

---

[4] Gen. John K. Waters – Note: As I recall this happened during *"appel"* – I think he had some sort of a throat obstruction – (instantaneous).
Lt. Col. Maynard W. Files – No to above. He died of apoplexy.

[5] Gen. John K. Waters – Leave out fact that it was sneaked into camp.

January 16, 1944 – I am reading a book on Cortez. Study Russian in the afternoon and play bridge at night.

January 17, 1944 – The tin store operation is changed by order of the S.A.O. No food to leave the tin store in the original cans. This creates quite a rat race, and the Germans do not like it. I am not sure, but believe this was done in order to force the Germans to quit putting in too many rules about the tin store operation.

Knorr and Louflier (Weasel and Ferret) came into room 21. Louflier is Knorr's stooge. Before the war he was a clean-up janitor in a bathhouse, the two of them together look very much like a pair of old rats.

Jake and I are having fun with rumors; even have the Germans believing them; one of them being that a Russian paratrooper has been flown into camp and the Germans cannot recognize him.

January 19, 1944 – Still studying Russian.

January 20, 1944 – Some of the Russian orderlies being sent to Posen.

January 21, 1944 – Reconciled the inventory and the parcels we have on hand.

January 22, 1944 – The remainder of the Russian orderlies are leaving. I hate to see them go. They have been a rather cheerful lot, and certainly have been a great deal of help in my study of Russian.

Jones says that a new dam is going in and it will cover his farm. He is greatly worried over this. (It later came out that this farm is part of the Oak Ridge development.)

January 23, 1944 – The news is good for the last few days. (Cannot recall.) There are rumors that there will be a big exchange of prisoners.

Went to Church. Father Brock very difficult to understand.

January 24, 1944 – Go on a parole walk. Received mail from Betty and Glen.

January 25, 1944 – News not so good on the East Front, but the South Front is picking up. Received two tobacco parcels from Betty.

January 26, 1944 – Larry Allen, a war correspondent, is a POW in camp. As a news analyst we have used him to rewrite the German news extracted from the German papers. Today he had a tooth pulled, and our news service is severely crippled.

A German general is inspecting the camp today or tomorrow.

Dates on tobacco parcels indicate that they were mailed 9-11, 11-10, 11-11 and 1-10.

January 27, 1944 – Another tobacco parcel dated 11-11 received from Betty.

January 28, 1944 – Schopert and Knorr are to be sent to the East Front. Hate to see Schopert leave, as he is a good man.

Received pictures from Betty.

January 29, 1944 – Tried to get my Russian together for the final break-up.

January 30, 1944 – The Swiss have sent me a French dictionary.

January 31, 1944 – Betty is a real marvel at sending me the proper things. Received a parcel today and there was not one ounce of superfluous articles. Some of the packages received by the POWs have had such nonsensical items as saltine crackers, or a glass jar of candy, of which the glass weighed more than the candy. One officer actually received a letter in place of a parcel. These parcel labels are sent out by our War Department and his family had taken the label and pasted it on a letter. In his case we were able to give him a parcel which had been sent to Capt. Torrance. I am sure no one minded.

February 1, 1944 – A bombed-out refugee from Berlin is now attached to the parcel hut for work. He is a dried-up, funny-looking little fellow, and seems to be scared to death of all Americans.

February 2, 1944 – Louflier is really getting worried about our pail of sand. (I am quite certain that this refers to a made up story of a great "tunnelmachine" – machine which Jake and I told Louflier we had built – that it ran on gas and that we needed about 1½ gallons of gasoline, for which we were willing to pay 100 American cigarettes. Louflier, as a member of the German security, is afraid that we actually have a machine, but he doesn't know it until he can actually find it. He wants to see the machine before he will get us the gasoline, and of course this creates more confusion. It just shows how silly the German organized mind can be at times.

February 3, 1944 – Received another long letter from Nelson Rowe in Kansas City. Nice of him to write!

February 4, 1944 – Larry Allen is a Pulitzer Prize winner, and seems to be a very good egg. He covered the Spanish Civil War and has many friends in that area.

February 5, 1944 – No water in the compound. We hear many glowing reports on the treatment of POWs in America. Understand that many of the higher-ranking officers are stationed at White Sulphur Springs, VA. Our rations are not good.

February 6, 1944 – Read "Action at Aquila" and took a parole walk.

February 7, 1944 – Received some packages from YMCA. These were books and some hospital supplies.

February 8, 1944 – The British orderlies left, and all were sorry to see them go. Schultz not sorry to see go. (This refers to Lt. Schultz, whom we passed off as a British enlisted man and he left with the British orderlies for their *Stalag*. The plan was, Schultz could make an escape better from a *Stalag* then he could from this *Oflag*.)

February 9, 1944 – Ernie Pyle's book, (*Here is Your War*), arrived, and the Germans saw it before I got to it. However, I sneaked it out and had a preview. It is a very popular book at the camp. At one time there were 18 people reading it at the same time, and many others wanted it be put on the reserve list.

February 10, 1944 – After much fussing, the Germans took my book and gave me a receipt for same. I almost got put in the "bunker" for it.

February 11, 1944 – The book is returned with a request that I do not pass it about. *Hauptman* Minner made the request, and he apologized to Col. Drake.

February 12, 1944 – Another story of a house taken at Casino. (This refers to our radio news which was filled day after day after day with another house or another square foot of ground being taken at Casino. It must have been a really tough battle.)

February 13, 1944 – Have started razzing the rough, tough, two-gun slinging man-eaters of Africa. (Believe this came about from hearing so much about what happened in North Africa, that finally one day I squared off and said that I did not see how it was possible that mere barbed wire and a few rifles could keep these toughies in a compound.)

February 14, 1944 – The winters are sure cold, and this staying in is working on all of us.

February 15, 1944 – We had an inspection yesterday and it was probably a good thing to get some of us up and moving about and cleaning our quarters.

February 16, 1944 – 28 new officers arrived. Some had some real tales to tell. A British officer had his ribs stove in trying to keep a German soldier from horsewhipping a Polish pregnant woman.

February 17, 1944 – Since my German is so bad, I have started studying it again with Dr. Jacobs in the hospital.

February 18, 1944 – Jake and I having a race with the rumors. Started one today that the SS is coming in to take over, and within an hour and a half Louflier asked me if I knew anything about it. I told him, "Yes – we had it straight from the Polish underground."

February 19, 1944 – Willie Kricks is a simple soul. He is proud as Punch today that we voted him "The Chief Interpreter in the Parcel Hut – Just in Case of Fire Only".

The Germans are easing up. The *Oberst* has turned over the entire compound and is letting us have some later lights.

February 21, 1944 – The German newspapers announce the forward-pressing victorious German Army is advancing towards the west – and this is a description of the East Front condition. Somebody really goofed on this one. Buschman has gone to Leipsig, his hometown, as his home had been bombed.

February 22, 1944 – Lt. Fisher returned blanket by the Germans; had a time.

February 23, 1944 – A letter from Glen Hocker says that our tank named "Missouri Military Academy" had made the Associated Press Wire.

February 24, 1944 – Lt. Curtis Jones injured by a loaf of bread falling from his locker on his foot. We are all certain that this bread is made from wood. Had another gambling night tonight. The parole walk called off.

February 25, 1944 – An air raid yesterday was given as the reason for calling off the walk. Jake to Gniesman, where he saw our planes yesterday.

Maw about to have more kittens.

Some book parcels arrive, as well as some private parcels, some of which were packed with ridiculous items. One man received two glass jars of olives.

February 26, 1944 – Jake leaving for Vienna. Jones received another parcel. (Believe this was a secret parcel.)[6]

Major Meacham's cigarette case from Sidi Bou Sid arrived. (Don't recall.) There is a rumor that we have a traitor in the camp.[7]

February 27, 1944 – Read and then took a walk around the compound in the fresh air. Noticed that most of the Germans off today were drunk as coots this afternoon but do not know why.

February 28, 1944 – Drew 60 lagermarks for the month of January. Issued parcels and had quite a problem in giving the orderlies their choice.

The German papers certainly lay on the propaganda. Many caricatures on the action of our soldiers in Naples, of President Roosevelt, Vice-President Wallace, and Winston Churchill.

March 1, 1944 – Goebbels predicts in the papers that the very worst will happen if the invasion succeeds.

There is a rumor of 50,000 POWs being repatriated.

Rumor has it that Finland wants to quit the war.

Matches from British Red Cross came in and are given to POWs. O.K. to take from parcel room, but Germans raised hell about the issue.

Harnisher is over the barrel. (Cannot recall the details of this too well.) Harnisher was a worker in the parcel hut who was a Protestant minister and about as thick-headed a German as you will ever find. He never quite understood anything unless it was given as an order; then he would treat an order

---

[6] Gen. John K. Waters – Omit reference to "secret parcels."

[7] Lt. Col. Maynard W. Files – It was allegedly a Dutch soldier in U.S. uniform that we did not accept and he was refused by the Germans.

from a superior officer with the same sincerity regardless of whether the officer was a German or an American. One of his tender spots was to needle him about the fact that Hitler had Pastor Niemöller[8] in the concentration camp, when actually he was one of the submarine heroes of the Old German Navy.

March 2, 1944 – Took a bath.

Harnisher caused trouble about the rations. However, after much argument he finally let them go through.

March 3, 1944 – There is a rumor that the *Gestapo* will be sent here to make a search. It seems that the Italians in another POW camp have been found with some guns.

March 4, 1944 – We get everything prepared for a possible search. This includes any canned goods we have for escape, the radio, and all contraband items.

The orderlies are having a hard time trying to choose which parcel.

March 5, 1944 – All of us, including the Germans, are expecting the *Gestapo*. There was a carload of clothes at the station. (I believe this refers to some gas cylinders which I noticed at the station during one of my trips to the station.)

The people are very friendly, and our G.I. orderlies were giving some of the girls the usual G.I. signs. The guard ignored everything.

March 6, 1944 – I took a walk of several miles in the compound. This is done by walking around our allowed perimeter.

Larry Allen gave a talk on Franco and Spain. He was a correspondent during the Spanish Civil War.

---

[8] Pastor Martin Niemöller was a former U-boat captain and Iron Cross recipient who became an anti-Nazi theologian. He was imprisoned in concentration camps from 1937 – 1945.

March 7, 1944 – "Bull" (This was a German interpreter) was with the Colonel and the Swiss at noon, and the Colonel excused him from the conference. However, Zimmerman heard of this and ordered "Bull" back to the conference.

Had an argument with *Gefreiter* Brandis, who was censoring some sheet music we received. I found that Brandis was an orchestra leader in Hamburg and was attempting to copy this music for his own orchestra after the war.

March 8, 1944 – E.S.U. (German Red Cross) and the Swiss are here. The Germans want to take some pictures showing the tables with table cloths on and what looks like big steaming meals. Col. Drake refused to cooperate. He sure knows how to handle these Germans. He stated no pictures were to be taken unless they show the actual conditions.

Sgt. Carn Godsey's music.

March 9, 1944 – Argument resumed today about the Red Cross pictures which the Germans want taken. Col. Drake tells them that it will be done only on a War Department order.

We live very close in this compound, and I am certain that at times we get on each other's nerves.

March 10, 1944 – Lt. Harry Abrahams, a Jew, was sent to 3B so as to keep from being repatriated.

Play with shadow.

One German seems to be O.K. and has tipped us off as to the search. Could it be that the old German colonel is most anxious that the *Gestapo* find nothing?

March 11, 1944 – Willie Kricks has this day been appointed the "Head *Führer* of the Fire Fighting Group of the Parcel Hut" and seems to be much elated with this new rank.

March 12, 1944 – Was interviewed by Larry Allen for our camp paper.

Playing lots of bridge with Bingham. (He had never played bridge before but had a very sharp mind, particularly in connection with mathematics.) One morning we outlined the probabilities of the strength in a bridge hand, and in the early afternoon we arranged some of our own personal signals. That night we played bridge with some of the camp experts, announcing we would bet them 5,000 points. We ran up 5,000 points in a very few hands, and let it seesaw back and forth until the other team had had enough.

(One hand in particular stands out. I had an ace-high tenace of hearts and Bingham had four small hearts. We wound up with Bingham bidding 4 hearts and playing my hand as dummy. The opposing side had five hearts in a king-high tenace to the right of dummy. With the proper signals, we caught every one of their hearts. After the hand, Col. Cooler told Bingham, "Young man, I have played lots of bridge but that is the finest played hand I have ever seen.")[9]

March 13, 1944 – Received some occupational therapy parcels. These therapy parcels contained bits of string, leather, spools, etc., which the POWs can use in making things.

March 14, 1944 – Bought 21 lithographical prints of German war scenes. Two or three of them are very good.

March 15, 1944 – The Inspector General – or the General of all POW camps – visited the camp today. The German discipline, as evidenced by the local troops, was excellent.

March 16, 1944 – Got a bath, and received much mail today; some of it was hooked out without going through Kozlowski, the German interpreter. This was done by Amon Carter. It is possible we might be able to investigate this avenue of direct mail a little more closely.

March 17, 1944 – We were marched to a picture show under guard in the afternoon to see a short on the care of babies,

---

[9] Lt. Col. Maynard W. Files – You also used to stack hands with Jones and I against Bingham and you.

a newsreel, and a color film, "Women are Better Diplomats." All speech was in German; however, everyone enjoyed getting out.

Our own theatrical group put on a play – *"The Man Who Came to Dinner"* at night. It was very good, and even attended by several Germans – armed with rifles, of course.

<u>March 18, 1944</u> – Box received from Betty with candy, sugar and Nescafe. Left the States the first part of January. Betty has certainly been excellent in preparing and getting the right things to me. The war news as published by the German newspapers is, of course, very much behind that which we receive over our "canary." The Germans are finally admitting that their lines are pulling in towards Berlin.

<u>March 19, 1944</u> – The Russians are driving very strongly, and it looks as if they will get us out of this before long.

<u>March 20, 1944</u> – The Germans have ordered us to open all cans completely. We have squawked about this, and in order to keep it somewhat under control have insisted that they do all of the work. This, of course, involves more soldiers and has been a great hindrance to them.

<u>March 21, 1944</u> – Played bridge this afternoon with Bingham.

<u>March 22, 1944</u> – The Swiss are here and say that they expect the war to be over in six months.

<u>March 23, 1944</u> – The parcel store is being done over and had a talk with the German guard and the Polish worker. (Cannot recall the conversation.)

<u>March 24, 1944</u> – The Germans are giving us another type of parole to sign for the picture shows. We are not signing it.

(Do not have the details as to this type of parole, and should check with Col. Drake or Col. Waters.)[10]

March 25, 1944 – The goons are up to it again – the lights out earlier than they had promised. I have a very strong suspicion that the German nation as a whole is short of fuel for power as well as warmth. No doubt the curtailment of lights and the severe rationing of coal is one of the by-products of their war economy.

March 26, 1944 – Read most of the day.

March 27, 1944 – The Germans are changing the number and the times of the *appells*. At the present time, we are to have three, and they will be at any hour of the day. The Germans showed us a newsreel of the west wall. Looks like it might be hard to break.

Harnisher, the dumb clout, says he does not understand me. (I believe this refers to me calling him an eight ball, and he spent a great deal of time attempting to determine just what an *acht ball* really was.)

March 28, 1944 – I am giving parcels to Lt. Wilcher (Bill) Stotts – those I cannot forward. (I believe this refers to Lt. Stotts having trouble getting parcels from his home. He just seemed not to receive any. Also, the German mail was not the most efficient, as, often, parcels were shipped to us for French POWs who had been out of the Schubin compound for over two years. We had no way of knowing where these POWs were, and when the address was blurred it was almost impossible to forward same.)

March 28, 1944 – Very strong rumors of a *Gestapo* search.

---

[10] Gen. John K. Waters – I remember this – but not too well. It compromised our position & indicated a form of an allegiance to the Germans that was not honorable.

March 29, 1944 – For the first time, we are having a problem with the packing of Red Cross parcels. Some are showing up with coffee and some without. There is quite a heated argument going on here in the camp, as it is claimed that we have ways of knowing how the packages are packed. The markings on the outside of the containers are identical. I guess this criticism is just something that must be accepted.

Saw a German picture, "The Second Shot." The plot was very complicated. (Cannot recall the details.)

A carload of the Swiss arrived from Geneva today.

April 1, 1944 – This is my anniversary of one year of captivity.

I am surprised at the loud talking of the "personality boys." They seem to talk all of the time, and as loud as they can shout, and about nothing. A psychologist might interpret this as one of nature's defense mechanisms creeping into our unusual type of living.

April 2, 1944 – The German guards come in and search, but they are very poor at it. Their heart is simply not in it. One German took some cigars, for which we set up a terrific squawk. Some others took some security items which I had cached, and some "looks like club cards."

April 3, 1944 – Issue parcels today and find out that I am not on the next escape plan. I am truly sorry of this, as I believe I could survive outside as well as any of them.

April 4, 1944 – Schopert is back and happy as a lark. The POW theater has been putting on a variety show which is very good.

April 5, 1944 – We received some parcels from the Swedish YMCA. Willie Kricks, the German who works in the parcel hut, is learning all of our curse words and uses them in the craziest manner. (This refers to Willie learning some of the ribald G.I. songs in English.)

Dills are really good. My conscience in this matter is neither happy nor unhappy. (This refers to an item of interest. I found a way of picking the lock to the German storeroom in the basement of the main building. One Sunday afternoon I made my way into the storeroom and found among the food items a broken sack of sugar and a broken barrel of dill pickles. I loaded up three Red Cross parcel boxes with the German sugar, and two with dill pickles. I was afraid to take too much for fear that this would be found out. I then slipped back through my entrance and re-picked the lock so that it appeared to be secure, and no evidence of an entrance having been made. I was able to repeat this 6 or 8 times, taking care each time never to open anything that had not already been opened. On one trip there was some delicious apple jam. While I kept one box for myself and my roommates, I gave the others out to Col. Drake and the hospital. We all agreed that it would be best not to tell anyone of the escapade.

April 6, 1944 – One POW, Captain (I don't have his name), very foolishly remarked in his log book that the West Pointers and the National Guard and the organized reserves are not always like ticks in the same bed, so now all private papers are to be censored. I have kept mine in such a cryptic manner, without reference to any particular personality, that it passed O.K.

April 7, 1944 – The Little Theater had a show this morning. We had much religious singing at night.

April 8, 1944 – The sun is out, and bright, and we issue parcels with jam. It was really good.

April 9, 1944 (**Easter**) – A good service held in the theater by Lt. Carpes. Lt. Russ Ford has done wonders with his glee club group.

April 10, 1944 – Lt. Francis Tripp Jr. is writing letters to his family in his log book. I believe he has one child whom he has never seen.

As another hobby, I have undertaken the grafting of a few buds in some fir trees.

Got in a hot argument (using my poor German) with two brown shirters outside the fence. They had just gotten down from a wagon to beat up a Pole for not returning the Nazi salute. They are the worst bullies I have ever seen.[11]

April 11, 1944 – Had a hot argument with *Hauptman* Merck in the parcel hut about the brown shirts. Knorr came in about that time and that made it even worse. They threatened to take me over to the "bunker" but backed down when I told them that I would close the parcel hut if I went, and this in turn would cause a greater argument with the Swiss.

April 12, 1944 – Maw and her two kittens are being transferred to the parcel hut as we saw a mouse.

April 13, 1944 – The German doctor refused to work on a patient (an enlisted man) who failed to salute him. He later came down to the parcel hut and tried to steal some medicine parcels for his department. Every German has clammed up when I tried to get his name. Somebody should get that guy.

April 14, 1944 – Worked in the garden and am very tired. Files, who has been in the hospital for the past days is now back in the room.

April 15, 1944 – Many book parcels received from the YMCA.

I submit two plans to the security group for approval. They want to think it over.

---

[11] Gen. John K. Waters – This made the whole camp mad. The Pole was dressed in his best clothing and with his girl.

April 16, 1944 – Plans O.K'd after security sees it. (Cannot recall the exact details but believe this referred to the possibility of using a balloon to go over the wire. Crazy as it may sound, it would be possible for us to have some balloons sent in.)

April 17, 1944 – Another red hot argument with Knorr. He is one smart German – had been a lawyer in Berlin. He is the enlisted man who patrols the camp for internal security. He is sure that we are digging a tunnel from the parcel hut, and is nosing around all of the time. Today I ordered him out of the parcel hut and told him he was not to return unless accompanied by a German officer of my rank or higher rank; that I did not recognize him as a military equal. Frankly, I hated to say all of this, as I have very high respect for his ability, but certainly despise his personality.

April 18, 1944 – Received 300 Export (brand name) cigarettes from Mrs. Charles Gurney, 269 Delaware Avenue, Buffalo, New York, #6634.

April 19, 1944 – We are having some argument with the Germans relative to the issuance of medical parcels. (I am not sure of the details, but believe we have in these parcels certain medicines which the German Army itself is unable to obtain. In the course of the argument it has come up that the Germans are in short supply of sulfa drugs.)[12]

April 20, 1944 – 103 new POWs arrived from Italy. They say the fighting is very bad. Many losses, many missing and much dead in the Canal.

April 21, 1944 – Issued parcels to the new POWs. One Major in the group. He had looked as if he just graduated from West Point about three or four weeks ago. His first request was for a private room. This character is so young and

---

[12] Lt. Col. Maynard W. Files – It was sulpha drugs that I received.

inexperienced in handling the Germans, I am sure we are going to have trouble with him.[13]

April 22, 1944 – Wrote to the Red Cross. *Oberst* Schneider is replacing the lockers with better ones. (Do not recall details.) We have not received mail for the past several weeks. It seems as if the invasion is going to be late.

April 23, 1944 – No mail. The boys are getting along O.K. but their signs are faint at times. (I believe this refers to the tunnel. There were several times we were almost caught. One time the ceiling of one of the rooms fell in from the weight of the dirt we had stored above. Believe it or not, we actually sewed the plaster back to the ceiling. Another incident this tunnel started out through an old stove, and we barely got the stove back in place before the Germans arrived for an unexpected search of the building.)

(We kept the Germans busy looking in the obvious places for tunnels, two of which are worthy of reporting on these pages. It was the time of year to dig up for our garden, so I told Knorr that I was going to let him in on something – that I had been kept out of the escape group and the others were building a tunnel but would not let me participate. When he asked where the tunnel was I insinuated that it was in the garden area. The next day a group of 150 Germans came in with spades and dug up the entire area and broke the ground up nicely for us to do our planting!)

(Another one was a trick employed by Dr. Jacobs and myself. Capt. Jacobs and I let it be known that we were feuding and on the verge of a fight for two or three days. One day, as Knorr was walking past one of the buildings, I rushed out with a box of sand to throw at Jacobs. Jake saw it coming, dodged and the box fell at Knorr's feet. The box contained this very

---

[13] Gen. John K. Waters – ? Must have been a 2nd lieutenant if just out of West Point.

yellow sand which is about 25' below the surface in the Schubin area. The following day the Germans came in and dug up the basement.)

April 24, 1944 – Lt. Bob Young, the officer who had arrived at the camp a few days after we got it organized, is back at the Marine Reserve Hospital. His home is in Worcester, Ohio. Bob was shot in the shoulder with an incendiary bullet, and it is doubtful whether he will ever have the use of that arm again. He had been repatriated.

April 25, 1944 – My plans for escape were turned down. Col. Drake argued that I should not claim to be insane, as it is sometimes most difficult to prove that you are sane, once the stigma is attached to you. The Germans would repatriate any person who was mentally disturbed.

April 26, 1944 – Jones still in the hospital with a broken ankle. (For some reason, I do not recall the details of this.)

April 27, 1944 – We received the new lockers, which do seem to give us more space. We are transferring some of the officers to the other buildings. (This came about through a very hot argument by Col. Drake, stating that we were too crowded. The Germans made a big show of measuring all of the available floor space. Col. Drake finally told them that we were entirely too crowded.)

April 28, 1944 – In the last batch of POWs, there were two young majors not over 23 years of age. – Haggard and Crandall. They have insisted on having a room to themselves, and have, in general, started off on the wrong foot. We have a system in the camp in which only some 20 of us are permitted to talk to Germans. These two inexperienced officers are apparently paying no attention to that rule, and are attempting to bribe Germans for favors. This greatly interferes with the law of supply and demand of cigarettes with the Germans. If we are to get any information from the Germans, or any item, one of the

20 of us will do the negotiating, and thus far we have kept the price of cigarettes up to a very high standard. These two men are threatening to break our market.

April 29, 1944 – We are expecting the invasion tonight. Six security parcels came in today, which created quite a hassle in getting them all by the Germans. We were successful and all of them turned over to the security committee.[14]

April 30, 1944 – Went to Church to hear the new preacher. He is not ordained but is very good.[15]

May 1, 1944 – This is a German holiday and we are expecting the invasion. Col. Drake to Posen to appear before the Repatriation Board.

Had a fight with the Germans relative to food items issued from the parcel hut. (Do not recall the details.)

May 2, 1944 – Col. Drake passed the Repatriation Board.

Three more security parcels in. I have often wondered what will happen when one of these parcels has its label torn off and is inadvertently opened by the wrong person.[16]

Talked to Larry Allen about getting news home. (Do not recall the details.)

May 3, 1944 – The repatriated boys are all getting excited about going home.

May 4, 1944 – On the trip into the warehouse today was able to bring back some onions. They were delicious.

May 6, 1944 – I am reading a number of detective novels.

Larry Allen received some wine from Spain. After much fussing with the Germans we said it was for religious purposes and were able to get through a bottle at a time.

---

[14] Gen. John K. Waters – To be rewritten because of reference to security.
[15] Lt. Col. Maynard W. Files – Paul Karns from the 9th Div.
[16] Gen. John K. Waters – Kill.

We have held all bottles until the total package could be passed through. Tonight we had a good drunk.

May 7, 1944 – The repatriated prisoners are not leaving until a later date. The Germans have issued us sheets. What next?!! They are sure they are going to lose the war now.

May 8, 1944 – Larry Allen left for a Llag to be repatriated and sent home. He promised to write Betty and the gang.

May 9, 1944 – Onions, pickles, and black pepper are sorely needed in the camp. (Don't recall the details of this entry.)

May 10, 1944 – Took a long hike around the compound and it made me feel rather weak. We just don't get enough food.

May 11, 1944 – The War Department commands us not to write home about the conditions in the POW camp. (I am not sure, but I believe this refers to the fact that we were told by the German *Oberst* that these letters would simply not be forwarded.)

May 12, 1944 – A German motion picture was shown in camp. (I believe this refers to a series of newsreels which were shown for German consumption of the different type of armament and armor used by the American troops. I recall that one of the scenes was an American tank being unable to pull up the side of a hill, and a German tank climbed it very readily. It also showed several planes which had been captured intact. Quite a bit of propaganda made of this. Anyone understanding equipment would know that our machines operated on a high octane gas, whereas the German machines would operate on potato gasoline or a very low grade gas.)

May 13, 1944 – Lt. Solomon (Sol) Levy warmed the boys with his violin playing. (I am not sure that I had this officer's name correctly, but do remember that we had a terrific violin player in the compound.)[17]

---

[17] Gen. John K. Waters – Lt. Joe Friedman was another one.

May 14, 1944 – Read and walked most of the day.

May 15, 1944 – Issued some parcels to the boys in jail. (As I recall, we had several boys in the "bunker."[18] Due to the efforts of Col. Drake, we insisted that they be allowed to have their regular Red Cross parcels. In this particular instance, we had some boys who had created a scene in the compound by feigning drunkenness. This caused their arrest by the German guards and they were given a small sentence in the "bunker." The reason for this was that it was thought that it would be easier to escape from the "bunker" than it was from the compound.)

May 16, 1944 – The drunkards got out last night for a short time. Three were caught and two are still out. Van Vliet was unable to get out of the "bunker" as he could not work the lock. Two were caught about twilight.

Had an argument with Knorr about a razor and an indelible pencil. (Do not recall the details.)

May 17, 1944 – We are expecting a *Gestapo* search. Just to play it safe I have hidden this diary.

May 18, 1944 – Higgins and Aten are caught and returned by the Germans but they would not let Col. Drake talk to them. He immediately fired off a blistering letter to the Swiss. That guy certainly has the measure of the Germans.

May 19, 1944 – A long discussion with *SS* regarding Files and the parcel situation. (Do not recall the details.)

May 20, 1944 – Col. Drake has canceled all escape plans until definite news of the two escapees is in his hands.

May 21, 1944 – Have just about completed a course on Earl Stanley Gardner.

---

[18] Lt. Col. Maynard W. Files – Lt. Aten, Lt. Chappel, Lt. Thal, Lt. Higgins & Lt. Col. Van Vliet.

May 22, 1944 – Issued British parcels and collected lots of cigarettes and soap for US, British and Russians in Wallstein POW camp. (This refers to the fact that we had excess soap and actually excess cigarettes, as we received cigarette parcels direct from home and also all American parcels had a cake of soap in them. Rather than have this soap be around where it could be picked up, the soap was taken from each parcel and then when anyone needed soap for any reason whatsoever they could always get it at the parcel hut.)

May 23, 1944 – Found a couple of books in the library on astronomy and have taken it up as an additional subject.

May 24, 1944 – The two escapees are back in the compound O.K. No bad luck yet.

May 25, 1944 – Two wagon loads of Polish peasants drove by today and returned our greetings by waving to us. They were immediately picked up by the Germans and sent to a concentration camp.

May 26, 1944 – The Germans have another holiday, as Sunday is Pentecost.

May 27, 1944 – Issued Red Cross parcels and some private parcels.

May 28, 1944 – I am re-reading Don Quixote.

May 29, 1944 – *Feldwebel* Schopert opened up. (Do not recall the details.)

They drew yesterday for nuts and fish. (Do not recall the details.)[19]

May 30, 1944 – Issued to the lucky numbers and some did not come down.

May 31, 1944 – Some of the boys are playing much basketball, volleyball, handball, and baseball.

---

[19] Lt. Col. Maynard W. Files – British & Norwegian gifts – had a raffle.

June 1, 1944 – Everyone is getting ready for the anniversary which is to be held on the 6th. (Believe it or not, this date was selected by us as an anniversary day, and had no connection whatsoever with the Normandy invasion date.)

June 2, 1944 – Schopert requested that we issue tomorrow, as they have a holiday on Sunday. It is Pentecost and it shows the effect of the union of Church and State.

June 3, 1944 – The Fifth Army in Italy is going great guns, according to the canary.

June 4, 1944 – The morale is down.

All are prepared to spend some time in this camp.

June 5, 1944 – A new German – small, lame, and a veteran of the East Front, has been assigned to the parcel hut.[20]

The can openers furnished by the Germans and operated by them are broken and it really slows up the Germans.

The new German lost all of his toes at Stalingrad. He says he is lucky to be alive.

---

[20] Lt. Col. Maynard W. Files – "Shorty." Two frozen feet. All toes amputated on both feet.

Chapter 12

D-Day and a Celebration

June 6, 1944 – At last the invasion! Rome falls and more parcels arrive. Our anniversary program is a huge success. Mr. Söderberg, of the Swedish YMCA, gave us a very heartening talk.

The fact that we had the celebration on the date of the invasion absolutely confused the German sentries. They were sure that we had news of it. I remember *Hauptman* Merck questioning me very closely as to why we picked that date, and I assured him that it was just another day. I knew the invasion had occurred, from the announcement over the canary. The Germans made no mention of it, but they doubled to guard around the compound and there were some anxious discussions among the groups of Germans one could see on the other side of the wire.[1]

June 7, 1944 – Morale is tops and everyone is giving the Germans hell. We have promised Louflier and Knorr that when the war is over they will be sent to the salt mines. *Zu die salz minne!* Louflier was such a clown and such a dummy that he actually believed it. Knorr was much sharper and crafty of wit

---

[1] Lt. Col. Maynard W. Files – Merck was very nice. A good soldier but a Nazi. He observed our acts of rank over his.

and had enough self-confidence to face this possibility as a real soldier. While I had my arguments with Knorr, I still have to admit he was a pretty good soldier.

June 8, 1944 – Still much ribbing with the Germans. They say that our First Armored Division had been wiped out. I told them to go back and pack for the salt mines. We are getting the canary twice a day. I believe that some Germans are actually glad that the invasion has started. The officiousness of the Germans is picking up. Dr. Marti, the International Red Cross representative, was here to take pictures and Col. Drake flatly said "No." Marti left in a huff and said he would never do anything more for the POW. He said the U.S. had too much money.

June 9, 1944 – Lord Haw Haw is sure bleeding. Our POW camp was rigged for loud speakers. Often the Germans would play Wagner and many of the classics. Any propaganda for their side was immediately beamed to the POWs. *Lord Haw Haw* was our special diet. To really understand the entry for this day one should look at the cartoons contained in my scrapbook which depict how the Germans pictured us as a bunch of barbaric gangsters.

June 10, 1944 – The German *Wehrmacht* announces that they will push the invasion force into the sea.

June 11, 1944 – We received 500 parcels from Spangenberg. I go down to the station with Schopert. Got in a hot argument with the *Bahnhofmeister*. Schopert took my side and ordered him back into the railroad station. Schopert is a good man.

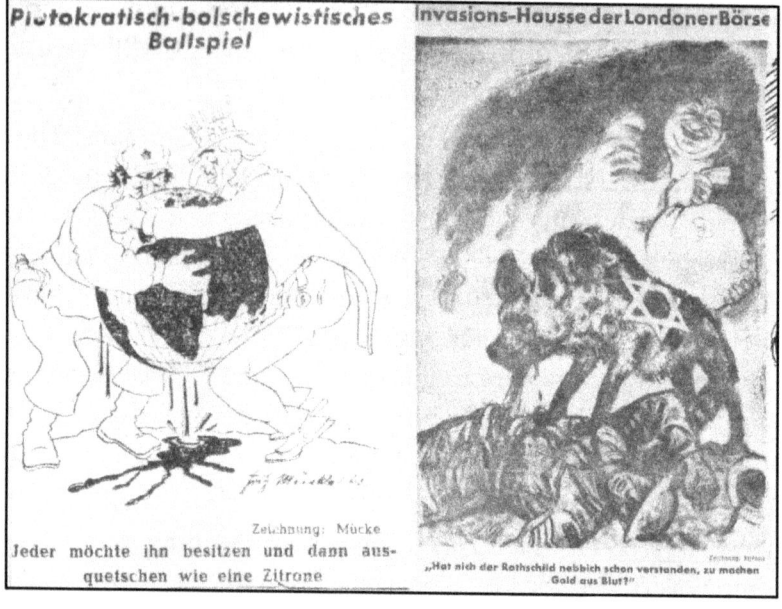

Figure 12-1 *German newspaper wartime propaganda cartoons depicting allies as barbaric gangsters. The first one roughly translates to "Everyone wants to possess it and then like a lemon." The second translates to "Not the Rothschild has already understood" referring to the Jewish Rothschild banking family.*

June 12, 1944 – The German can openers have completely broken down and the German system of opening each can is really in a fouled-up condition. They have to issue parcels over two days, and Col. Drake insists that it all be done in one day. A good hot argument has started on this. Drake's position is that if they would go back to the old system of merely putting a nail hole in each can we would receive our parcels as per schedule. Their new order of fully opening each can is an act of harassment upon helpless POWs. This is a very delicate situation for the Germans, for if they press too hard they realize that Drake can make quite a mountain out of this molehill. If they do not press hard enough they will have to issue the cans as they did in the past, which gives us some opportunity to store food for possible escapes.

Schopert has been transferred out again. Believe it or not, we immediately requested that he be transferred back. *Oberst* Schneider has said that he will do what he can to have Schopert returned.

<u>June 13, 1944</u> – The Swedish YMCA has sent us a curtain. (I faintly recall that we had quite an argument with the Germans, but insisted that this curtain be passed through for the use of our little theater.)

<u>June 14, 1944</u> – Had a red-hot argument with Knorr today relative to a knife taken from Amon Carter. I am finally getting Knorr down to where he will not start an argument with me. I believe that I have been able to get the best of him even though we may lose an argument now and then. (As I recall, we got the knife back but lost the curtain.) I will have to let Drake get the curtain back for us.

<u>June 15, 1944</u> – Our canary needs a transformer. This was purchased for cigarettes from the Germans. If you can soften one of these goons you can buy almost anything. Of course, the German takes his life in his hands when he deals with us.

<u>June 16, 1944</u> – We have a central cooking unit which cooks the German issue of potatoes, millet, cabbage and turnips. Today we worked out a deal to have gravy, by having each mess contribute 1 teaspoonful of dried milk.

<u>June 17, 1944</u> – The garden space has been broken up and assigned by messes. My mess is to take care of the beets. By dropping a hint that there is a tunnel in that area we got a platoon in here digging it up! They seem to bite on that every time.[2]

---

[2] This was one of Captain Lumpkin's favorite stories. When the camp started work on a garden, they found the ground extremely hard to work with the

Figure 12-2 From left to right: 1st Lt. LeRoy Ihrie, Captain Tony Lumpkin, 1st Lt. Henry Haynes, and 1st Lt. Amon Carter Jr. in the "Parcel Hut" at Oflag 64

Harnisher, the student of theology – and a dim wit if there ever was one, – has left for officers' school. I do not believe he will ever make it.

<u>June 18, 1944</u> – Most of the day spent reading and playing baseball.

<u>June 19, 1944</u> – Go to the station today for parcels. Some Polish kids quickly consumed a piece of a "D" bar which was offered to them. Willie Kricks was one of my guards. We

---

garden tools they had. They simply started a rumor that there was a tunnel in the area, and the Germans brought in a platoon to dig up the soil looking for a tunnel and, therefore, loosen the dirt for their garden.

worked through the meal issue time and he took me by his home and gave me some bread and butter – the first fresh bread I had eaten in some time.

June 20, 1944 – Unable to unload the car yesterday and returned today to finish the job. While at the station an air raid siren sounded, but saw no planes.

June 21, 1944 – The transformer came and was out and in again – it has been found that a part was missing from it.

June 22, 1944 – The Hitler *Jügend* have gathered for some kind of a conclave near here. There is much singing, marching, drum beating, etc.

Lt. Howard "Boomer" Holder and I got to the gate. I believe this refers to an escape plan which someone worked up, the success of which depended upon whether or not the front gate could be unlocked. In the camp we had a professional housebreaker who could make keys to open any lock provided he got close enough to it. We worked out a plan of walking down to the gate and demanding to see the *Kommandant*. This caused a great deal of consternation and argument with the German soldiers, who of course would never send for the German Colonel. This took about 15 or 20 minutes and we were permitted to stand at the gate. Fortunately, our shoes were untied and this gave us an opportunity to stoop down and everyone got a good look at the lock. The officer (housebreaker) came back and made a key for this gate lock.

June 23, 1944 – The news is good, both the straight and the indirect. (Believe this refers to good news from our canary as well as from the German papers. The German newspapers of course slanted everything to sound like either a very costly gain by the allies or a smashing victory for the Germans.)

Maw had another litter of kittens. I believe the father is the largest tomcat I have ever seen. The distance between his eyes is wider than the palm of my hand. I can put my hands in front of his eyes and still see both of them. I always got a bang out of this tomcat. I had a pair of mittens, made from a German blanket. These went over some gloves; hence my hands were rather well padded. This tomcat had a vicious temper and on the slightest provocation would whirl around and peel the skin off of anyone who might advance a hand to give him a pat. I think we got along because my gloves were too thick for him to do any damage. Maw was a very immoral animal and had kittens not only by this tomcat but also by some of her own children.

June 24, 1944 – Three new officers in. One had lived for 9 months in Italy, on the loose. The only reason he was picked up was that some of the British who were traveling with him got drunk.

June 25, 1944 – Studied German and unloaded a wagon.

June 26, 1944 – A Polish girl brought us some water at the freight yard. I gave her a piece of a "D" bar.

June 27, 1944 – Lt. Geist has made the key to open the gate.

June 28, 1944 – A kit of theater equipment came in. Knorr missed a book that had been removed before it had been *gepruft*. We had quite a hassle in distracting that cunning goon's attention until we could get the book back in place.

June 29, 1944 – Mr. Söderberg of the Swedish YMCA, here, and we made records to be sent home. Wrote Bingham for him. (Do not recall the details.)

June 30, 1944 – The Germans are getting nervous and are sure that we are digging tunnels out of the camp in all directions. They are blasting the bottom of their protective trench in order to see if they can't cave in any possible tunnels.

July 1, 1944 – Another argument with the German security. We received some boxing gloves. After they had been inspected for any maps, etc., the Germans still withheld passing them on, for no reason.

July 2, 1944 – Big pup for Fourth of July. (Do not recall.)

Knorr, *Hauptman* Merck and I have an agreement (I do not recall the agreement or why it was written this way, as Merck absolutely detested Knorr.)

July 3, 1944 – Much athletic equipment received from the YMCA.

July 4, 1944 – The *SS* band played. We even had the Star Spangled Banner, but they didn't furnish us a flag. There were many carnival activities, horse races, athletic events, etc.

July 5, 1944 – Another Larry Allen parcel came in and is gratefully received. (Believe that this refers to some wine that some of Allen's friends in Madrid sent to him. Since we had had such an argument about the wine the last time, we just slipped it through as a security parcel.)

July 6, 1944 – There is a rumor of a *Gestapo* search in the very near future.

July 7, 1944 – There is no search today, but two cars of German officers stopped outside and I sent a man out. (I do not understand what is meant by this.)

July 8, 1944 – Strong rumors that we will receive many more POWs at Schubin.

July 9, 1944 – I may be able to get in on the next planned escape.

July 10, 1944 – I am on the plan and in "D's" group. (Do not recall "D".)

July 11, 1944 – Received a copy of "The Robe" from Aunt Besse and Aunt Calla.

July 12, 1944 – A tobacco parcel and a food parcel came from Betty. The candy was excellent, but the powdered coffee had solidified.

July 13, 1944 – Files and Hansen parcels are in. I am sure this refers to security parcels. We were told that one would come in for Capt. Files and one for Lt. Hansen. Since these men worked in the parcel hut and were well known to the guards it made it a rather ticklish item. We requested that no future security parcels be sent to anyone working in the hut, as it made a very difficult problem of hiding the parcel before the Germans could see the label. Needless to say, we were glad to get both of these parcels out of the hut as promptly as possible.[3]

July 14, 1944 – Burgman came in and we talked of dogs while he sniped at butts. (Believe this refers to a German recently assigned to the parcel hut, who picked up every cigarette butt we ever dropped.)

July 15, 1944 – Played some volleyball.

---

[3] General John K. Waters – Revise to kill reference to nature of parcels.

Chapter 13

Camp Population Swells

July 16, 1944 – The POWs from the West Front are coming in. It must have been quite an affair.

July 17, 1944 – Col. Millet, one of the new prisoners, outranks Col. Drake. I look on this with a great deal of misgiving, as I understand that Millet has already been buffaloed by the Germans. They actually had him out doing work as a POW. When this story gets to the local Germans, it will make Drake's position that much harder to maintain.[1]

July 18, 1944 – Another Larry Allen parcel arrived, bringing great happiness to all and some worry as well as happiness to me. (I believe we all got drunk off this batch of wine.)

Many explosions. (Not sure what this refers to but believe that we could hear, from time to time, heavy detonation in the distance.)[2]

---

[1] General John K. Waters – However, Col. Drake did not relinquish command, I am glad to say.
[2] General John K. Waters – Probably air attack at Posen – where airplane engines were being assembled.
Lt. Col. Maynard W. Files – I think it was an attack on a V1 site.

July 19, 1944 – A carload of parcels came in today, both private and Red Cross. I received four cartons of Luckies.

July 20, 1944 – Hitler is reported hurt by a bomb, and the army is in semi-revolt.[3]

July 21, 1944 – Private Heathcoate found out, and Knorr is in a jam with Col. Drake for pulling a pistol on an officer. (The Heathcoate affair referred to a British enlisted man who changed places with an American officer when the British enlisted men were transferred out of *Oflag 64*. We carried Heathcoate on our rolls as the missing officer, and the missing officer assumed Heathcoate's identity. Later, our officer escaped from a British enlisted man's camp and almost got back to allied lines.)

The Knorr incident above referred to Knorr getting in an argument with a Jewish lieutenant in camp. Knorr, a militant Nazi, got almost in a white heat when arguing with this Jew. While I did not see the argument, I was told that he got completely white with rage and drew his pistol. This type of incident was just made for Col. Drake. He immediately insisted that Knorr be banned from the camp, or would never be permitted in the camp armed with small arms.

July 22, 1944 – We go down to the station again today and pick up private parcels. The Germans had an order stating that POWs will not walk on the sidewalk. In the past I have simply disregarded it, but today for some reason the argument was carried back to the *Kommandanture*. *Hauptman* Minner apologized very profusely but insisted that he had his orders. After this argument had seesawed back and forth for two or three hours, it was worked out that I will ride on the wagon instead of walking. I am not sure whether I won this argument

---

[3] General John K. Waters – This is the attempted assassination of 20 July – of which much has been written.

or not, but we did have a lot of fun, and caused the Germans some harassment of their conscience.

The *Völkischer Beobachter* says, "As a result of the progressing stabilization of an extensive system of obstacles, the tendency towards slowing down the Russian advance continues." This is the way they announced a defeat.

Duckworth is the stoogemaster. Any operation of the canary, or any plan of escape, required a great deal of organization on our part, so a full intelligence of the location of every German may be centered to one directing group. The stoogemaster has the job of organizing as many people as is necessary to keep every German in the camp under surveillance.

July 23, 1944 – The Three Ring Circus performs. Meacham reports on losing place and British parcel. (Am not sure what this refers to, unless it was some item of our own internal administration.)

July 24, 1944 – There is much anxiety here in Altbergoon (Schubin.) Col. Drake is leaving and Millet will take over as senior American officer. I am afraid Millet will not be able to stand up to the Germans.

July 25, 1944 – Col. Drake left today and gave me his last box, which was most gratefully received.

July 26, 1944 – Mrs. Drake had sent the Colonel some dried lima beans. I cooked them today and they tasted almost like caramel candy. I ate so many that I became sick as a dog.

July 27, 1944 – There are many rumors of moving and great plans. (This refers to the always-possible problem of what would happen to our security devices if the camp were moved. This might also refer to the fact that some of the moving rumors were started by us. We would drop a hint to one of the German security soldiers that we understood the camp was to be moved and then make bets as to how long it would be before the

German *Kommandant* would call the senior American officer in to find out what he knew about it.)

July 28, 1944 – The Germans made a strong effort to employ POWs as soldiers. They were successful with many of the French, Belgian, and many others, but never with the British. I understand that they organized an army to free Britain and were able to obtain one officer and seven enlisted men. I have also been told that they offered Col. Drake a commission as a Major General if he would attempt to raise an army to fight the Russians.[4]

July 29, 1944 – Maw and her kittens are just about as cute as you would ever find any young animals.

July 30, 1944 – The Hitler *Jügend* are being moved out and the civilian population is being used to build trenches, fox holes and other fortifications in the area. You will have to admit that the Germans are very thorough in their planning, and should they have to fight in this area the foxholes will already be dug.

July 31, 1944 – Col. Cooler gave a very interesting talk on his experiences with the British Army in Tripoli.

August 1, 1944 – We are reorganizing, and the parcel department is placed under Meacham, of all people. I immediately talked to Johnny Waters and told him that I did not care what field officer was in charge of the hut provided he stayed out of my way. We had too many necks out over a sharp axe for anyone to come down and disrupt anything we were doing in the parcel hut. In my book, Meacham was just about green enough to upset the apple cart at the wrong moment.

August 2, 1944 – Lt. Walter Werner and Lt. George Reavy left for home. (I believe this refers to them being repatriated.)

August 3, 1944 – Morale is high. The Russians are expected in this area in the very near future. We have sealed up our

---

[4] General John K. Waters – This is true.

tunnel so that it can be used at a later date.[5] The bets are that the Russians would be here before we could get it completed.

August 4, 1944 – Three new POWs in from Rotenburg.

August 5, 1944 – Read and played cribbage.

August 6, 1944 – A picture brought in and shown to us. Lewd as hell.

August 7, 1944 – A huge caravan of horses and refugees arrive in the area from Stalingrad.

August 8, 1944 – More American orderlies (enlisted men) are due in. Had some fun with the Germans today and have really left them in a sweat. (Told Knorr that a Russian paratrooper had been dropped in our camp. He was in direct communication with the Polish underground and with the oncoming Russian Army.)

August 9, 1944 – There are rumors of a search by the *Gestapo*.

August 10, 1944 – As usual, the search is conducted first by the local Germans.

The caravan of refugees with their Russian Cossack hats, moved out again. They made a great display and it looked like a picture from some newsreel.

The Germans, with their yen for propaganda, have made a large display of a picture showing an American girl thanking a soldier for a Japanese skull.

August 11, 1944 – The German papers make a big to-do about "We are not going to crack as we did in 1917." I believe it is dawning on everyone in Germany that they are losing the war.

---

[5] Lt. Col. Maynard W. Files – Directive because of *Stalag Luft III*, where the *SS* recapture and killed all but 7 escapees out of 63 I believe.

August 12, 1944 – August 24, 1944 – Had to hide this during a search and was unable to get to it until now. Col. Millet has been taken away by Flexler, a German, and we believe that he is in Frankfurt am Main.[6]

Some French officers in American uniforms have been brought in. One of them is a pretty sharp character.

Larry Allen has been heard from.

The American Army is in Paris.

Bulgaria has folded, and the Germans are really getting jittery. The Germans still think we are hiding a Russian paratrooper in the lager.

I am using my German to get bets, order the guard at night to chase cats. (Don't recall.)

I have started studying my Russian again. It is the most difficult languages of all to write in a script form.

August 24, 1944 – Some of the tales of the invasion are whoppers. It is very interesting to hear of the new changes in our material. We now have about 650 POWs and 60 orderlies.

August 25, 1944 – The Germans give us pay in *lagermarks*. We can spend them for nothing and a large amount of this money has been sent to the *Stalags*.

August 26, 1944 – Col. Millet was taken away for several days for requestioning.

August 27, 1944 – Betty writes that she heard from Larry Allen.

August 28, 1944 – Recheck our parcel hut. (Believe this refers to a search by the Germans of the entire parcel hut. Somebody had disturbed some dirt underneath the building and they have great ideas that we are building a tunnel from the parcel hut.)

---

[6] Lt. Col. Maynard W. Files – Millet–God rest his soul. He is dead now.

Figure 13-1 Captain Lumpkin's POW ID. He distorted his face whenever photographed by the Germans in order to make later identification more difficult.

<u>*August 29, 1944*</u> – The head German can be reached. (Not sure what this refers to.) The German attitude is cracking. They simply do not have the snap they had six months ago.

<u>*August 30, 1944*</u> – The news is good, and the Germans are really getting jittery. Flexler says he doesn't like to argue with me or with Col. Schaefer. Flexler was a German who came back to Germany from the Philippines when he thought Hitler was going to dominate the world. My path crossed his even after I escaped. The Russians had captured him and I know that he was sent to Siberia – or was headed in that direction. He was a very shifty person and gave one the impression that he wanted to be friends just in case we won the war.

<u>*August 31, 1944*</u> – The German papers say "We cannot expect a great change in the fortunes of war from a new weapon". The German papers were always talking about a new weapon that Hitler was going to bring out that would

completely turn the tides of the war where it was employed. I am sure that he put great store in V-1 and V-2 rockets which were not known at that time.

September 1, 1944 – We have orders not to discuss anything with anyone when the war is over. This came from our G-2 section in Washington.[7]

September 2, 1944 – Harry Schultz is back. He was the one who took the identity of Heathcoate. He had been caught in Prague and sent to a *Gestapo* prison where he saw many brutalities. One of the favorite tricks was to beat prisoners with a hose. He reports the Jews there were a pretty sad lot. Some were almost too weak to stand up in the food line. He says that his dog tags and the efforts of Col. Drake saved his life.

Col. Millet is now waking up to the fact that a fuss with the Germans is worthwhile now and then. (Not sure just what incident this refers to.)

September 3, 1944 – Meacham and I go round and round in regard to the issuance of parcels. He still does not understand about the security parcels.[8]

September 4, 1944 – Waters finally explained to Meacham to leave the parcel hut alone.

September 5, 1944 – Millet apparently has difficulty making up his mind. This indecisiveness can cost us.

September 6, 1944 – The S.A.O. repeats a German order that we are to turn in all cards. Surely this will not be carried out!

September 7, 1944 – I regret very much to think it, but it is evident that Millet is afraid of the Germans.

September 8, 1944 – The news is good. We are in Belgium.

---

[7] General John K. Waters – Kill this. People will wonder how we were able to communicate with Washington.
[8] General John K. Waters – Kill reference to security parcels.

September 9, 1944 – The Germans really got stewed up by their order, as no one turned in their cards.[9]

September 10, 1944 – Schultz gave the field officers a talk today. (Do not know the details.)

September 11, 1944 – Millet really messed up today. He told the Germans of one of the orderlies being here under an assumed name. How dumb can he be? (Believe this refers to a British enlisted man staying with us as an American enlisted man serving as an orderly.)

September 12, 1944 – Millet just will not put his foot down to the Germans. (Do not recall the details.)

September 13, 1944 – We have great preparations for a track meet. The Germans are getting nervous.

September 14, 1944 – No parcels coming in now. Doesn't look good, and yet it has its good points as it is evident the German railroad system is breaking up.

September 15, 1944 – Mail from home was good.

September 16, 1944 – Our track meet a big success. The Germans change the *appell* to 4:30pm without a protest. Millet certainly missed an opportunity by not laying the Germans on this matter.

September 17, 1944 – Read most of the day. 98 officers came in. We now have a total of 770.

September 18, 1944 – Issued parcels. Millet talked with Col. Schneider and gave in on all counts. The guy is just weak.

September 19, 1944 – We have been ordered to eliminate the tin store in two weeks. The tin store is the residue from the parcels that a POW could leave and obtain from day to day. By eliminating the tin store, everyone would have to eat everything during the week. We should never have lost this.

---

[9] Lt. Col. Maynard W. Files – We all hid them in rolls of toilet paper.

September 20, 1944 – 2,000 parcels stolen by the Germans. No protest by Millet, and finally Col. Waters jumps in and writes the letter.

September 21, 1944 – I don't know what is coming over us! It has been suggested that we hide all of our tins of meat, but everyone seems to be afraid.

September 22, 1944 – In eliminating the tin store we are making every attempt to get every can out without it being opened. These, of course, are taken out and hidden in various places around the compound.

We have some new workers in the parcel hut and some are most interesting. One is a hotel owner from Bohn, and another was a University of Berlin student who had been majoring in astronomy.

Chapter 14

Gottfried Dietze: An Unlikely Friend

September 23, 1944 – The new interpreter, Gottfried Dietze, has been attached to the parcel hut. He is a graduate of the Berlin University. His father is in some kind of political service and he is very interesting to talk to.

September 24, 1944 – Our little theater put on the play, "You Can't Take it With You." A very good performance.

September 25, 1944 – Issued parcels, and able to get out almost 500 tins of food without being opened.

September 26, 1944 – Schopert has apparently been back for some time, as the diary reports he is up for a medical exam. 800 cans out of the tin store without being punctured. A good job.

September 27, 1944 – The Germans are greatly excited about having to go to the front. I accused Zimmerman of digging up an excuse to stay here.

Sgt. Ayers, an orderly, jumped the truck and is loose; he had worked with Standard Oil Company before the war.

September 28, 1944 – No news of Ayers, but the story we hear is that he is out, living with a woman.

September 29, 1944 – Millet lets the Germans walk over him again. We now have an order to clean out the kitchen tin store and leave only one week's issue of parcels in the camp.

September 30, 1944 – Six copies of the International Red Cross Convention arrived, and the Germans refused to *geprüft* them. A kick made about this, but to no avail.

October 1, 1944 – A hot argument today with Zimmerman. I insisted that enough parcels be returned to us for an issue.

October 2, 1944 – The Germans returned 800 parcels. Many private parcels arrived, including some security parcels.

October 3, 1944 – After much arguing the Germans take a copy of the Geneva Convention out and return it *geprüft*.

October 4, 1944 – More private parcels arrive today. I got a tobacco parcel dated in July.

October 5, 1944 – Studying astronomy. Made a raid on the German warehouse and really loaded up with sugar.

October 6, 1944 – Dietze, the new interpreter, is a good lad – has a good mind. He is a loyal German but is definitely not a Nazi.

October 7, 1944 – The power which drives the water pump for the camp water goes out. We have no water for three days. Each man is issued three cups each day.

October 8, 1944 – This is a black day. The Germans came in and took all tins and forced an issue today rather than Monday. Millet just simply will not stand up to them. In my own personal store of tins I insisted on and finally obtained a receipt for every tin they took.

October 9, 1944 – Started a hot argument going about the parcels and the tins. The Germans finally have Lt. Haynes, a hospital attendant, and two orderlies, and go over and draw our cans.

October 10, 1944 – 2,280 private parcels arrive and are held up by Zimmerman and LeViseur at Dietfurt. We immediately protest. Also, 25 sacks of mail have come in by *Reichspost* and are held at the *Kommandanture*. The Germans repeat that they have an order saying that we may have only one week's supply on hand, and later say that we can have only one day's supply of food or cigarettes. We protest.

October 11, 1944 – The Red Cross Commissioner here, and the Germans promise us our private parcels when we want them.

October 12, 1944 – *Oberst* Schneider has a Lt. Col. in as an executive officer. I do not have his name unless it is LeViseur. I am quite certain he is a Nazi and probably an undercover man for the *Gestapo*.

I go over and make a plan with Zimmerman to issue all private parcels. He promises to see the Lt. Col. Later I go over and see *Hauptman* Derring regarding the issue of parcels. Derring is not a half-bad egg. He is fat and has a head just like a pig. He is very loud but has no bite.

October 13, 1944 – The Germans bring in 10 sacks of parcels to the Russian barracks (a building which had been occupied by the Russian orderlies and was now vacant). They offer to issue them but we refuse to accept them under the conditions of the clothing to us and the food to the German warehouse. There was much argument. The German interpreter, Crinkle, tried to get me to confess what Col. Millet had said. I am certain that Crinkle is a *Gestapo* agent.

One of the guards at the gate is quite a character in his own right. He inspects all wagons, water tanks, vehicles, and everything that comes through the gate. If anything passes his inspection he bellows in a very loud voice *"est Stempt!"*. Today he took off a POWs hat, looked under it, and hollered, *"est Stempt!"*.

October 14, 1944 – A carload of private parcels were taken to Dietfurt by the Germans.

October 15, 1944 – *Oberst* Schneider back but apparently he and the Lt. Col. were unable to get together on the parcels.

October 16, 1944 – Col. Paul B. Goode and 100 officers arrive. I believe Col. Goode is going to handle the Germans better.

October 17, 1944 – Col. Goode understands these goons. He is very aloof and refuses to talk to anyone except other full colonels. This leaves the *Gestapo* Lt. Col. foaming at the mouth.

October 18, 1944 – The Germans are commencing to be fed up with the extra work involved with the Red Cross parcels.

October 19, 1944 – Zimmerman says that we are to move the tobacco store, and I say "Like hell we are."

October 20, 1944 – We start issue of private parcels, and Schneider has given an order that I am to remain in the parcel hut. This comes as a relief to me as I am certain that Zimmerman was delighted to have me move out of that position. What a battle!

October 21, 1944 – The Germans have been making many searches and every POW has his own places to hide things.

Col. Goode really on the ball. He ignores all Germans, especially those who are present when the Red Cross or the YMCA are seeing him.

October 22, 1944 – We issue the last full parcel to each POW.

October 23, 1944 – Have another big fight with the Germans regarding the issue of parcels. (Don't recall the details.)

October 24, 1944 – Win the debate and we are to issue regularly, but to keep the excess food in boxes.

October 25, 1944 – Issue 67 sacks of parcels, and the Germans thought we could not do it!

October 26, 1944 – Hard work on issue.

October 27, 1944 – I get two tobacco and three food and clothing parcels from Mrs. T. D. Drake, 2252 Adams, Indianapolis, Indiana; one from APOW Headquarters, 1205 Delaware Avenue, Buffalo New York; and one from home.

October 28, 1944 – More issue of private parcels.

October 29, 1944 – The Germans slow up the issue of parcels. I squawk, and find that they fear an inspection from the SS Commission. We may have to lose this argument in order to protect them.

I raid the pickle warehouse again. They are delicious.

October 30, 1944 – The Germans order that we can have no inks or indelible pencils.

October 31, 1944 – Tobacco parcels from Betty. I am really set up right, now.

November 1, 1944 – No parcels for the officers, but each orderly issued one-third of a parcel.

November 2, 1944 – There are four more security parcels yet to come in. Hope the Germans do not pick them up at Dietfurt.

November 3, 1944 – We have a big battle in regard to some records – a gift from C.B.S. Col. Goode tells the Germans to either *geprüft* them in the parcel hut or break them up in our presence. This really confounds the Germans. Goode is going to be a good man.

November 4, 1944 – Col. Goode has placed the parcel hut entirely under his jurisdiction. This makes it much better for me.

November 5, 1944 – We definitely have a thief in our group. No one knows who it is, but we will find him. He is stealing food.

November 6, 1944 – The *Gestapo* come in and start a round of searches, with plenty of help – about 60 Germans.

November 7, 1944 – The Germans find much food and we had a scare over our own personal hides. I lost nothing, but the thief stole a can of milk from Lt. Robert Oshlo.

November 8, 1944 – Captain Dicks lost to the Germans as well as to the thief. Lt. Col. Louis Gershenow, Walters, Alger and Schaefer lost over 100 cans. Quite a loss!

Hauptman Merck received word today that one of his sons was missing on the Italian front I truly feel sorry for him, as it has broken him up considerably. I assured him that if he was captured by the Americans he would be well treated. Merck was not a bad egg. He was an athletic coach in his University at Nüremberg.

November 9, 1944 – Merck feels a closeness to me. He brought me a piece of good white bread. It was delicious. However, I do not believe I will be able to get much valuable information from him. He is completely fed up with the *Gestapo* and all Nazis.

All of the cans are turned in and are to be handled by Major Crandall.

November 10, 1944 – Col. Goode put on quite a show with Zimmerman. It was almost ludicrous to see how he browbeat that German. (Do not recall the details.)

November 11, 1944 – We are still set up to frame *Hauptman* Zimmerman with the can deal, but Col. Millet vetoes it. (This refers to a plan which we had: We would tell the *Kommandanture*, especially the Lt. Colonel, that these cans had been taken out with the approval of Zimmerman. I am quite certain this would result in Zimmerman being transferred to the

East Front. It probably would have been a favor to him, as I understand he was killed in the last days of the war.)

November 12, 1944 – Read most of the day. Rumor has it the *Gestapo* is due here Tuesday.

November 13, 1944 – The local Germans are still sweating out the *Gestapo*.

November 14, 1944 – The *Gestapo* arrives on time and very quietly start a search, but find nothing. I find that they can be bribed just as well as the others, as I gave one of them a cigarette to leave my log book alone.

November 15, 1944 – The old argument starts again with the Lt. Colonel. He wants to move the parcel hut out of its present building.

November 16, 1944 – The argument continues about moving the parcel hut.

November 17, 1944 – The Germans are digging many holes around the camp. Are they getting ready to blast, or is this for a seismograph device to learn if we are digging tunnels.

November 18, 1944 – Protests are being made regarding the retrial of POWs previously tried. The German courts have not heard of double jeopardy. (This refers to the case in which Captain Smith and Colonel Schaefer were tried on some minor charge and acquitted, then the German People's Court retried them by shifting the prosecuting attorney to the judge's chair and the judge to the prosecuting attorney's chair. They were found guilty and sentenced to death. The sentence was never carried out, as they were liberated by the Russians before the final papers were approved in Berlin.)

November 19, 1944 – We finally lose the argument about moving the parcel hut, and so the movement gets started.

November 20, 1944 – News is good; however, the Germans are attempting to create an incident. (Don't recall details but believe one of them was attempting to get me into a hot argument and make an accusation as to his pedigree.)

November 21, 1944 – Col. Schaeffer is charged by the Germans with obstructing the path of a German soldier who was in the main building. The *Wehrmacht* had issued an order that anyone obstructing a German soldier in the performance of any of his duties was to be immediately shot. They framed Col. Schaefer on this matter, and later on included Captain Smith. These men were tried by the People's Court and defended by a POW lawyer. The result of this trial was a stalemate. The trial was then reconducted according to the usual plan of changing the judge and the prosecuting attorney. This time they were found guilty and sentenced to be shot. Smith received his sentence with almost an Indian-like stoic attitude. The sentence bothered Schaefer somewhat. All of Captain Smith's forebears had been in the Army for at least three generations.

November 22, 1944 – We are still moving the tobacco store in a building that used to be a work shop.

The Germans are blasting near 3B. They think they have found our tunnel.

The Germans have come in with an order stating that a definite number of articles of clothing were to be taken.

Did have one comical thing happen. The Germans are attempting to store some cabbage in the basement of one of the buildings. As the orderlies were bringing the cabbage in under German guard there was a blind spot which we quickly located and stole about 400 or 500 heads of cabbage. Our problem then was to eat as much as we could of it before it was found and had to be turned in. Cabbage is most difficult to hide.

November 23, 1944 to December 19, 1944 – Much has happened, and this had to be hidden for many days. We have been without parcels for some six weeks, and then three cars came in. They are storing some of the parcels at Dietfurt. I insisted on going over to Dietfurt to see where they were stored. It turned out they had confiscated a Polish Catholic Church, moved out the pews, and that was our warehouse. I unloaded some of the parcels and had a chance to talk to some of the Poles.

The camp is very much excited relative to the issue of parcels, and the new POWs are to be issued a full parcel on arrival.

There is a bomb-launching device southeast of there that goes on a spree every few days. I recall one night there was a most reverberating thunder sound almost over the camp. (I am quite sure this was a testing of the V-2 rocket.) Northeast of the camp we could see the rocket trails on a cold day. I later found out these originated at Peenemunde, an island off the north German coast.

One POW has developed diphtheria. Lt. Charles Burns and his barracks are quarantined. This hurts me considerably, as Lt. Amon Carter is in that barracks and Carter is the key man in solving the problem of getting out the security parcels. Without Carter, it is most difficult to watch these parcels closely enough.

After much arguing, we are able to get a number of parcels for each week in excess of the daily allowance. We change the issue so that they are issued by barracks with the special Christmas parcel. Several POWs are very suspicious and believe the worst of any man regarding these parcels.

Lt. Wright (Baldhead) Bryan arrives here. He is a graduate of Clemson and Missouri University. He used to date my sister, Martha. I hardly recognized him when he came in, but was able to identify him immediately.

We have all been deloused, and it was a pain the neck. (As I recall the details, this involved us taking off all of our clothing and being given a very hot shower. Just before the water was turned on, we started kidding each other that the gas would come first. It was extremely cold and the clothes were being deloused in another building.

The Germans are trying to move the tobacco store again. They are continuously blasting holes in the ground to discourage tunnels.

Many of the German soldiers are fed up with the entire matter. Their morale is deteriorating rapidly. They want to quit and return to their families and their cellars.

December 24, 1944 – Very busy today, getting out the Christmas parcels. There are many ideas and arguments relative to the issue. It seems that each Senior American Officer has tried a new policy. None seems to work quite as well as that instituted by Col. Drake.

December 25, 1944 – Christmas Day, and what a day of memories! (I am quite certain this refers to each man thinking of his family and the many happy Christmases they had had in the past.)

December 26, 1944 – We got into quite a hassle in the big building. There are 159 men in this barracks and there are 6 toilets. The 13 field officers have 3, and the other 146 men have the other 3. Believe this is stretching privilege just a bit too far.

December 27, 1944 – The Germans announce a special order sentencing Lt. Col. Schaefer and Lt. Smith to be shot for obstructing a German guard in the performance of his duty. If this book ever gets back to Washington, the only obstruction they gave was to protest the posting of an order on a bulletin board. (This order was an announcement that "if you try to escape you will be shot." I brought one of them back home in my scrapbook.)

January 1, 1945 – The weather is extremely cold. We can see many vapor trails of the rockets to the east of here.

January 2, 1945 – We receive some Red Cross parcels.

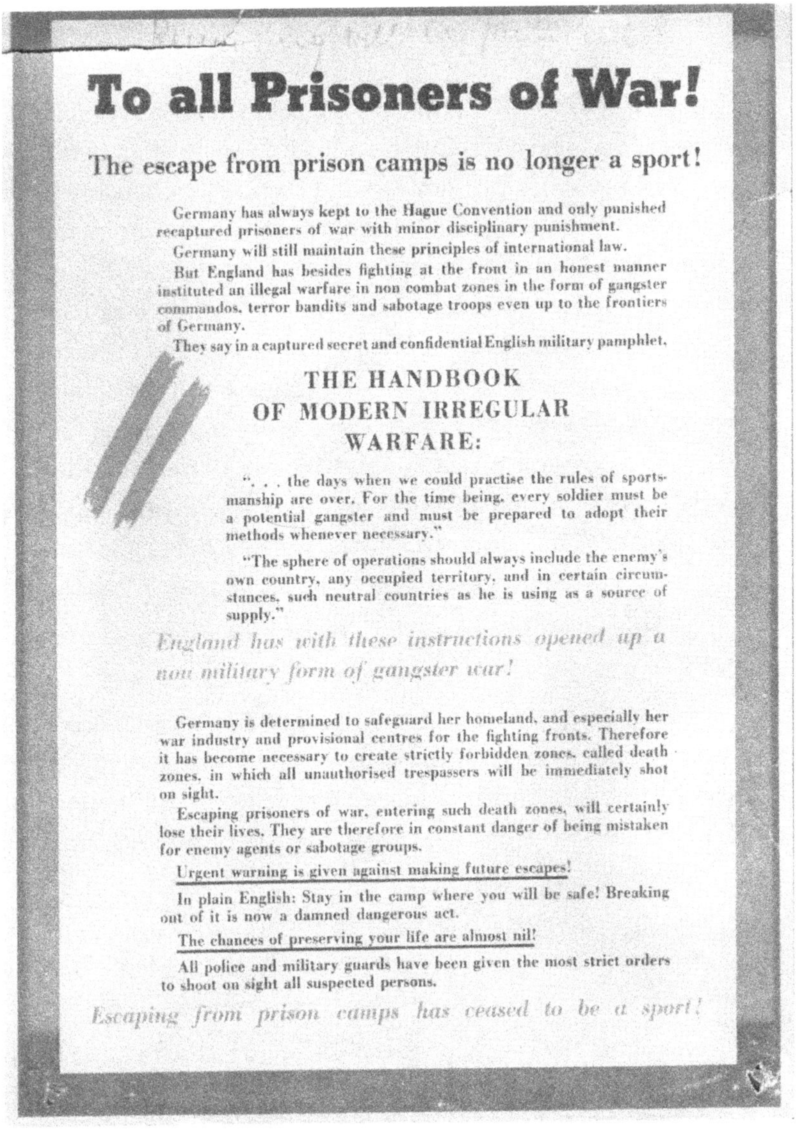

To all Prisoners of War!

The escape from prison camps is no longer a sport!

Germany has always kept to the Hague Convention and only punished recaptured prisoners of war with minor disciplinary punishment.

Germany will still maintain these principles of international law.

But England has besides fighting at the front in an honest manner instituted an illegal warfare in non combat zones in the form of gangster commandos, terror bandits and sabotage troops even up to the frontiers of Germany.

They say in a captured secret and confidential English military pamphlet,

THE HANDBOOK OF MODERN IRREGULAR WARFARE:

". . . the days when we could practise the rules of sportsmanship are over. For the time being, every soldier must be a potential gangster and must be prepared to adopt their methods whenever necessary."

"The sphere of operations should always include the enemy's own country, any occupied territory, and in certain circumstances, such neutral countries as he is using as a source of supply."

England has with these instructions opened up a new military form of gangster war!

Germany is determined to safeguard her homeland, and especially her war industry and provisional centres for the fighting fronts. Therefore it has become necessary to create strictly forbidden zones, called death zones, in which all unauthorised trespassers will be immediately shot on sight.

Escaping prisoners of war, entering such death zones, will certainly lose their lives. They are therefore in constant danger of being mistaken for enemy agents or sabotage groups.

Urgent warning is given against making future escapes!

In plain English: Stay in the camp where you will be safe! Breaking out of it is now a damned dangerous act.

The chances of preserving your life are almost nil!

All police and military guards have been given the most strict orders to shoot on sight all suspected persons.

Escaping from prison camps has ceased to be a sport!

Figure 14-1 Poster warning that those who attempt escape will be shot

Thank Goodness!

January 3, 1945 – We have several Polish officers here as POWs. Every effort is being made to protect their full identity, as some of these men actually came from this same general area of Poland.

January 4, 1945 – I am relieved from work in the parcel hut. After the second warning, Col. Goode and Col. Waters said they appreciated my work but would take no further chances. They were to promise me a commendation. (This was the result of Dietze coming in and warning both me and the SAO that the *Kommandanture* had decided to frame me as they had framed Col. Schaefer. I am certain that I could have dodged any type of frame-up, but the S.A.O. was determined not to take any chances. I told Dietze that I appreciated very much what he had done and I requested that he memorize my name and address and I have his written in code in this book. (After the war, Dietze told me that Zimmerman had said, "I don't know what Lumpkin is doing but we must get him as he is sly as a fox.")

January 5, 1945 – Spent the entire day cleaning up and studying.

January 6, 1945 – I believe I forgot to mention that the parcel hut was turned over to Files, who had been with me since we were captured, and had worked with me in the parcel hut as head of the tobacco department. We spent most of the day getting his books set up.

January 7, 1945 – We are still trying to run things as in the old set-up of 300 men. (Do not recall the details of this comment.)

January 8, 1945 – Two of the German censors have been transferred to Posen. I believe this was an indication that *Oberst* Schneider felt that the camp would probably be moved towards Berlin.

January 9, 1945 – I am enrolled in a class on Security Analysis conducted by Lt. Seeman. He is really good.

January 10, 1945 – Heard a very good talk on jewelry by Capt. William Whorley of Columbia, Missouri.

January 11, 1945 – Lt. John B. Shinn, Jr., of 3916 Kilbourne Rd., Columbia, South Carolina. He works for Jeff Hunt Co. He is making a handbag for his wife, and is quite a bull-slinger. He was a most interesting conversationalist.

January 12, 1945 – They have removed some of our group to Schocken (sic?) to start a camp with the Italians who were picked up as part of the Badoglio group who were anti-Mussolini.

January 13, 1945 – I am playing lots of chess, studying and reading quite a bit, particularly about our western U.S.

January 14, 1945 – The news is not good, as the Germans have driven us back somewhat in the west. (This was the Ardennes offensive.)

January 15, 1945 – Louffler, the "weasel", and Capt. Merck gave me a personal search, as we had quite a hassle in slipping out a garden tool sent to us for camp use. This made quite an argument. Col. Cooler says he does not understand my way of handling them (the Germans). (Actually, it was just simply arguing with them at every opportunity.)

January 16, 1945 – I am using lots of coffee with Shorty (Capt. Whorley).

January 17, 1945 – Started some more classes, this time on money and banking and war finances.

January 18, 1945 – Still studying Security Analysis under Lt. Seeman. He really is good.

January 19, 1945 – The mighty *Wehrmacht* is really cracking up. Today the Germans refused to go to Dietfurt, stating there was no wood for their wood-burning carburetor-truck.

January 20, 1945 – We have no inspection, but do get an alert order to move. The road in front of the camp is filled with refugees, all of them heading east. It looks just like what one sees of war pictures on the newsreels.

Chapter 15

Forced March and Escape

January 21, 1945 – We walk to Exin and sleep in a barn. Very tired. I am with Lt. Col. Jim Skells from South Dakota.

This was the day in which the Germans attempted to move everyone to somewhere near Berlin. It was evident they were highly excited. I had a lot of fun kidding "the Weasel", Louffler, Merck and others that we expected the Russians there within two hours. Before moving out, the old German colonel gave us a lot of barking about how he would march us out safely to escape the Russians. I never heard such a bit of hogwash in my life.

The march starts about 9:00 in the morning, although we had been rousted out about 6:00. Each man was issued a half loaf of bread, and he carried whatever he wanted of his own personal possessions. In my own case, I put on two of everything I could possibly get in the way of shirts, socks, etc. Old newspapers were stuffed between the shirts, and these papers actually contained the cartoon drawings that are now in my scrapbook. There were no hourly halts, but we walked as slowly as possible without getting the German guards too mad. My estimate was a mile and a half an hour. The guards were spaced about every 50 feet. At one point in the march, a refugee column overtook us and this really created confusion. I threw my knapsack and blankets on one of their wagons and had the wagon pull me. Believe it or not, it is easier to have someone pull you along than it is to make the effort to walk.

It was extremely cold; there was a very heavy hoar frost on the ground which had puffed up almost four inches. The frost had also blown on many of the trees so that when you looked in one direction all the trees appeared white; if you looked in the opposite direction they stood out with each little black limb showing individually.

We walked until about one o'clock the next morning, when we were bedded down in a very large barn. We walked probably 15 to 18 miles that day.

In dictating this some 20 years after it happened, I find that many of the details stand out very vividly, while others seem to get mushed up in the background. I recall thinking about the effect of the frost and my chances of escape. If you were viewed from one direction any dark object would stand out like a lighted sign and you would have to lie flat on the ground, whereas if you were viewed from the other direction your best bet would be to cling to a tree as closely as possible and blend into its outline. Another incident comes to mind; anyone who had any sense at all would understand that you were in for some hard days. One of the things that any foot soldier – or anyone who had ever done much trailing – should know is that he should carry nothing in his hands, as this makes the shoulders extremely tired. Things carried in a condition like this should have some immediate use – either for consumption or for clothing or for comfort. I recall one officer carried out, in his hands, about an 8 lb. book of Shakespeare's works. Our tempers were rather short, and I remonstrated with him that it would be better to carry 5 pounds of bread and buy Shakespeare later. I noticed about 10 miles later Shakespeare had been thrown in the ditch.

Some of the POWs were rather ingenious and had worked out a system of dragging all of their belongings on some sled-like affairs. These were made with and without runners. These were of a great deal of use, because when we were overtaken by the column these characters merely hitched their sleds to the wagons.

While I have commented on this before, it was evident that the nervousness felt by the Germans was multiplied by the hour.

In the cold air it was very difficult to determine the difference between artillery fire and demolitions, but one could feel the tremor in the earth and knew that some type of explosion was going on in the east. I thought they were bombs, but believe now they were merely demolitions.

Also noted on this march were truckloads of German soldiers who were unarmed, going towards the west. My G-2 of this situation was that these were base section soldiers and the withdrawal was rather general along the entire line for these boys to be moving in the numbers that they appeared.

For the day or so before, we had had our canary operating almost around the clock, and by changing the wave lengths we were able to switch into the Red Army command channels and were able to listen to the Russian commands. The officer operating the set did not understand Russian well enough to follow just what they were saying.

In the break-up of the camp, all of the security items which had been sent over in the security parcels were taken out, allocated to many of the POWs, and the remainder of it was destroyed. We burned about $90,000 worth of allied currency (English pounds, Belgian francs, German Reichsmarks, etc.) There were several hundred American flags distributed, of which I was fortunate enough to get one, and each man was given a small compass. By the way, this compass is so small that it could be hidden underneath the eraser of an ordinary pencil, almost too small to use, but could be of help at night. We had, as I recall, some six or seven radios by this time, two or three cameras, some wire cutters, and my own knapsack arrangement consisted of a blanket which could be thrown over the shoulders. On one end, I tied a bundle containing a needle, thread, buttons, food; and on the other end I balanced the weight with my second blanket. Betty had just sent me a copy of Lee's Lieutenants. While I valued it very much, I did not wish to overload myself, and left it on the table. Col. Skells came in about that time, and, believe it or not, Col. Skells carried the book for several days that I know of.

To go back and pick up the events of the day, we finally were bedded in this huge barn, and everyone started scouting around for a place to get warm. In the barn were some cows and hogs. I slept with the hogs that night, as they really felt warmer, to my way of thinking, than the cows. A Polish hog looks very much like our Poland China swine, but they are extremely narrow of beam and very tall. They almost resemble a calf. As I recall, Skells and four others were with me in the pigpen, which, by the way, had just been freshly filled with straw. The hogs were large and there was some apprehension about how much rolling around they would do during the night. We did get some rest, and possibly some sleep.

About 4:30 or 5:00 in the morning I went to the barn door and had an opportunity to talk to Merck. Merck was extremely worried. He was sure the Russians were going to overtake us. While we were talking, Knorr came up and I do not believe I had ever seen him as nervous or as frantic-looking as he appeared at that moment. He was sure the Russians were going to catch him.

I went back and talked it over with Skells, along this line: These Germans are ready to panic. If anyone makes a move to escape, they will be shot without any question, but on the other hand they are not going to wait around looking for anyone if he does manage to get out of sight. I suggested to Skells that this would be the time to fade out of the picture, and since he was my platoon leader I wanted him to know that this was my intention to do it this night. Skells then went over and talked it over either with Johnny Waters or Col. Goode, and said he was going with me.

A rather peculiar thing happened about this time, and it is something that is hard to explain. I had the idea of remaining behind when the Germans marched out. This could be done either by hiding in the loft, in the straw, or somewhere in the building, as it was a very large barn and they could not possibly search every nook and cranny of it in less than five hours. I explained this idea to several officers, and was amazed to find that they were more afraid of the Russians than they were of the Germans. Regardless of what one might think, the Russians were our allies at that time, we were prisoners, and the worst that could happen to us would be prisoners under another detaining power. I probably should have argued with these men a little more than I did. I do not think it was done from a standpoint of fear so much as it was done from a standpoint of remaining with the herd. A good lesson could be learned from this – that the herd is not always right. As it turned out, I was home three or four months before these characters arrived in Boston.

January 22, 1945 – At about 6:00 the Germans called an *appell* to count the prisoners for another day's march. The Germans have difficulty in counting above several hundred, as they have to repeat each number and when you get up as high as 1,983 they sometimes get confused with their own words and have to start all over again. So, I was quite sure that whatever count they determined would be incorrect, but since none of them wished to wait around and check on any laggards, everyone would report the right number of men present. Some German officer, and I think it was Merck, smelled a rat and

Oberst Schneider detailed a German soldier to remain behind to pick up the stragglers.

In the meantime, Skells and I went back into a large room filled with straw and buried down in the straw about three or four feet. While I could not see anything, you could hear the usual barking and ordering right and left by the German guards in rousting out the POWs. You could hear the counting and finally there was a move out of the head of the column. We kept very quiet in the straw for about an hour and a half to two hours. I cautiously worked my head out to see there was no one else in the room, then I got Skells out and we approached the entrance door, where, lo and behold, I saw the German soldier, luckily, before he saw me. We went back into the straw room and decided we would have to sweat it out a little longer, or at least until this goon decided to leave.

During the rousting out, I heard Zimmerman and Knorr discussing whether or not to burn the barn down. We were in a general government area and the farm was operated by the Reich. This made the barn the property of the government. As it turned out, this was our salvation, as Zimmerman was afraid he would be tried for destroying government property. Again, this is an illustration of the German correctness of doing everything in the proper manner. If the shoe had been on the other foot, I would have burned the barn down and worry later, as I know the American Army would not want a bunch of prisoners loose in the rear.

I then went down to the room where the cattle stalls were, and a Polish boy about 16 years of age came in. While I had a great deal of apprehension about what he might do, I explained to him that I was an American and that I would appreciate it, and my government would appreciate it, if he would help me get away. He told me not to go out, as they had a guard on the door. When he told me this I felt sure that I had a friend; otherwise he would have said "Yes" and gone and fetched the guard. All of this conversing was done in my rather broken German. We then rigged up a plan whereby this lad would go out and tell the German soldier that he just came from the kreis (the local community) and that he actually saw some Russian soldiers in the community. They were drunk and shooting at everyone. The lad did this very convincingly. Through a crack in the door we could watch the soldier talking and could see that it was working on him almost minute by minute. After about 25 minutes he stamped his feet three or four times and took out towards the west.

Skells and I then starting shouting with glee, after the German guard had gotten out of hearing, for we were free at last. All of this commotion made quite a bit of noise in the barn, and this led to our discovery that there were others who had had the same idea. This was an unorganized escape in which several people had the same idea at the same time. The following people were present at our "roll call":

Lt. Col. Skells	Lt. Palumbo
Capt. Richart	Lt. Salmons
Capt. Bond	Lt. Anderson
Maj. Dobson	Lt. Reffetto
Capt. Chizanowski	Lt. Marnien
Capt. Manual	Lt. Wisniewski*
Capt. DiFrancesco	Lt. Crocker
Lt. Szczerbinski*	Lt. Gaich
Lt. Goleash	Lt. Winton
Lt. Kodziolka*	Lt. Cooney
Lt. Thomas	Sgt. Massey
Corp. Votaw	Priv. Grisson
Priv. Walker	

*Polish officers – more on this later

It was evident that this was too large a group to stay together. There were many debates about what each man would do. Since Skells and I thought of our idea together, we decided that we would stick together and take out towards the southeast. We chose the southeast rather than the east, as we were certain the Russian Army would penetrate Germany in columns. Our best chance to make contact with the Russian Army was by crossing one of the columns. If we had gone east we felt that we might walk many days without realizing the Russians were on either side of us.

It is hard to put down on paper the true feelings one has when it dawns on him that he is entirely free. I recall even now what a joy it was to realize that I could walk in one direction as long as I wanted to without being curbed by the barbed wire and the guards.

Skells and I walked cross-country. While the ground was plowed and uneven, it was frozen so hard that it was not too difficult. I don't know what distance we covered, but about sundown (I would guess it was 4:30) we started looking for a place to spend the night About 600 yards in front of us was a settlement consisting of several buildings, and we decided to take a chance and see if there wasn't some building or haystack near there that could be utilized by us for a night's rest. As it turned out, this set of buildings was really another large barn with several smaller buildings built around it. At the last moment we decided not to contact the buildings, but to open a mound. These mounds were nothing but huge trenches that had been filled with sugar beets, turnips, etc., and then covered over with dirt. This was the method used by the farmers to protect their own food and the feed for the cattle during the winter. However, the ground was frozen so hard we could not break through the dirt to throw out any of the beets and turnips, so we were forced to seek shelter in the barn.

Rather stealthily we crawled up to this large building and determined there was no one inside, but you could determine some movement being done by the animals. In scouting around this barn I found a hothouse where they actually had asparagus growing. I was so hungry that even this raw asparagus tasted almost like boiled peanuts. After getting a good fill of this type of food, I then moved into the cattle stalls and attempted to milk one of the cows. I had not milked a cow since I was 12 years old, and I do not think the cow appreciated the way I was handling her. Anyway, I got very little milk.

While engaged in this, the door behind me opened and as I lunged to the entranceway I saw the most dried-up, wizened little old man that I have seen in some time. He was one of the Polish workers on the farm and quickly explained that he had no use for Germans; that he had watched Skells and me come across the field, and that he wanted us to come up to the house (one of the small houses) and spend the night.

When you are living by your wits you are very suspicious. I was sure that it was a trap and told him that I would just as soon spend the night in the barn, talking loudly so that Skells could overhear me. After much discussion and argument, as he was not a person to be put off easily, Skells came out and we both went up to the house. His name was Jarosz Michal, Kcynia, Powiat, Wągrowiecki, Poland. From questioning some of the Poles on the farm it appears that the Russians are both north and south of us in fairly large masses. One Polish man had walked to the main road and had actually talked to a Russian patrol.

I have never felt so much warm hospitality as I have with Jarosz. He is quite a character, having been at one time a prisoner captured by the Russians, and also a prisoner captured by the Italians.

Two more officers came in – Lieutenant Murrell E. Thomas of Concordia, Kansas, and Daniel E. Crocker, c/o Mrs. Georgia Parks of Sheldon, Iowa.

Colonel Skell's address is: 3 Farnum Road, West Hartford, Connecticut.

The weather is extremely cold, very bright, and there is a heavy frost on everything. The frost is so thick that it appears to be almost like snow.

January 23, 1945 – Had one hell of a good night's sleep in a feather bed last night. Skells and I debated a long while as to whether we should stay in Jarosz' home or go back to the barn. If the Germans were to return I know they would execute Jarosz for hiding an American POW.

This morning I had my first sight of a Russian. A patrol of four men in a small truck and a G.I. motorcycle drove up. All of them were pretty well stewed. One tried to give away everything that was in the schloss. I did not have much of an argument with him proving that I was an American. These characters searched every room in the schloss, the farm and Jarosz's hut. Out of plain orneriness, they broke a huge plate glass mirror in one of the rooms of the schloss.

January 24, 1945 – During the early part of the afternoon a tank column appears on the road about 400 yards from Jarosz's hut. We leave the hut to make contact with this Russian column. These vehicles were not tanks, but were self-propelled antitank batteries. There was quite an argument with the battery commander, as Thomas, a paratrooper, had a homemade parachute emblem embroidered on his shirt. This led the Russians to believe that we were actually German paratroops that had been dropped back of their lines. It was indeed unfortunate, also, that in speaking with the Russians I would forget and lapse into German. I think that actually I was trying to speak Russian while I was thinking in German. I was about at the end of my rope in explaining the situation to the Russian Commander, and asked Skells to take over and try an explanation in French. This did not work too well either, and there were some anxious moments. We finally overawed them by demanding that we be sent to the next higher headquarters.

Incidentally, we had an American flag which I brought out to further illustrate my argument that we were *Americanski*. We were finally taken to a Division C.P. where we spent the night.

A G.I. is always a G.I. (This is a key to some incident which happened with the Russians, but for the love of me I cannot recall it right now.)

At the Division C.P. we were treated courteously but were kept in close confinement.

In the morning we went into another conference with the commander of self-propelled battery, and it was decided that we would be taken elsewhere, apparently to a higher headquarters. It turned out that this was larger than a corps headquarters, as there were small observation planes attached directly to the headquarters vehicle park. At this C.P. we talked to a short, stout, well-built Russian Marshall whom I take to be Zhukov[1], who gave us a lot of words about Malenkov being to the south of him and being to the north of him, and there being two other columns beside these – all of them heading for Berlin. He told us that they had thrown patrols across the Oder, and as far as he was concerned the war was over.

The intelligence officer at this command post was a pretty sharp individual. He scurried around and made sure that every bit of the operations map was covered by canvas while we were in the room. Later on I found that he was actually a Naval officer and had spent quite a length of time in Murmansk.

He left the room and a big argument started up as to whether we were German paratroopers or American POWs. Finally an officer, whom I took to be Zhukov's Chief of Staff, said, "These men are *Americanski*," and from then on we walked on a bed of roses. We drank some vodka. He gave us some

---

[1] Marshal Zhukov was the leader of the Red Army through its advance through much of Eastern Europe and into Berlin. He remains the most decorated general in the history of both Russia and the Soviet Union.

cigars, which were delightful; I gave him a tank emblem off my shirt collar and he gave me a red star with scythe and hammer, off his headpiece. Not to be outdone, one of his aides also gave me his headpiece and I gave him the "US" off my shirt collar. Everything was hotsey totsey, and everyone just a little bit drunk.

The four of us then go back to Schubin in a Russian scout car, where we find that about 20 others had arrived before us.

Rehash of the last few days:

On Sunday we were formed at 9:00am to march out ahead of the Russian Army under Zhukov. The Germans have difficulty in getting the proper head count and we lose about two hours while they fume and fuss with the adding of the numbers. Going out, each man was issued a portion of a loaf of bread. However, there was not a sufficient amount of bread to cover the entire group. *Oberst* Schneider gives us a strong speech, saying that march discipline would be strict, that we would march in a column of threes, and that he would lead the way to the very end at Berlin. We start out, and within a hundred yards the discipline breaks down and the column of threes occupies most of the road. Accompanying us was a more or less steady stream of refugee wagons, each wagon completely filled with the family and all of its goods. The wagons were apparently grouped together with groups of 30 or 40, under the command of a Nazi party leader. I later found out that these wagons were to travel on schedule and had definite times for halts, thus keeping the distance between the convoys constant.

The walk was terrible, in that everyone was loaded with entirely too much and we were in such poor physical condition. It was extremely cold and the road was slick with ice and dry snow. Several of the group had built sleds to assist in carrying their loads. Some of the POWs had selected the oddest things to carry with them. One man left carrying with him about an 8-

pound volume of Shakespeare's plays, which was tossed away in the first five miles. In my own case, I tried to carry nothing that could not be eaten, keep me warm, or be used to repair my clothes.

There was no water, and the snow was dirty and so cold that it would not melt easily.

At Exin we were passed by truckloads of German soldiers of the 70th Regiment, also moving in our direction. One of them was a Frenchman who whispered to me "*L'guerre est finie*" ("the war is over".) The Poles all gave us a big happy smile. Many of the POWs had tied their sleds to the wagons.

Capt. Merck was screaming and I told him to take it easy. (I do not recall this incident, but do recall that all of the Germans were highly excited and threatened to shoot anyone that delayed them. One almost got the idea that the Germans were anxious to get rid of us.)

About one hour after dark, we drew up in a farmyard that was apparently a tourist hotel for farmers, as there was a very large place for mounts to be watered and fed. There was still no water, the air was very cold, and our muscles were sore; all in all we were a very tired group. After about an hour and a half my platoon was assigned to one of the barns for sleeping quarters. The first place was too small and I finally found a good room with plenty of hay. Lieutenants Robertson, Murphy, Cory and Fabian had remained in our half-completed tunnel at Schubin, and Lieutenant Aten had hidden in the shower room.

I paired up with Skells at this time and tried to catch a little snooze under the straw with my overcoat. We were finally able to find some water at the pump in the barnyard. When the noise quieted down we could hear distant artillery fire and demolitions going on to the east. The sound of the rumble of the refugee wagons continued until well past midnight. There were stragglers under German guards coming in until 3:00am. This is a point that was interesting, in that many of these groups could have fled but they were under the psychosis of the "group-herd" instinct.

Early in the march, Schneider had said that we would march only to Exin. We were very much disappointed after passing a large factory in the town and going about four miles further. The total distance walked that day estimated about 25 kilometers.

Early the next morning, Skells and I debated and finally decided to hide back under the straw. A local Pole helped us hide and the column left about 10:00am.

After watering up and re-packing our gear, we head out southeast across country. The ground is frozen dry, and the air is extremely cold. We pass Lieutenant Crocker and Lieutenant Thomas. Many times we stop and talk with the Poles in wagons, and in houses. There is no sign of the Germans or the Russians.

After dark, we near a collective farm, and are taken in by a friendly Pole who gives us real hospitality: real eggs, milk, tea, and, above all, warmth. His friends drops in for cigarettes and keeps us posted. A Russian patrol had entered the nearby village about 8:00pm. Neither Skells nor I are quite sure where the German soldiers are, as the front is very fluid. The cook at the schloss brings us a bottle of wine. That night we sleep – Yorozs, his wife, Thomas, Crocker, Skells and myself in a small room with no ventilation.

Yorozs tells me that as a farmer he gets one-third of the wheat he raised, the Wehrmacht gets one-third, and the city people get one-third.

In the morning, we take a tour of inspection of the schloss and the farm. It is an extremely large, well-operated farm, tenanted by about 150 workers. Yorozs said there was 23,000 hectres – approximately 30,000 acres. There were no tractors in evidence. However, he did take me down and show me one of the largest draft horses I have ever seen. It must have weighed

3,000 pounds. It was larger than any beer horse I have ever seen – a beautiful animal, in perfect condition.

At this moment, as we concluded our tour of the farm, the Russian patrol shows up and immediately gave the farm and the contents to the cook. The patrol was looking for gasoline, Germans and arms. All of their motorized equipment was made in the USA.

After we made contact with the tank destroyer column the Russians did not permit us to go back to Yorozs' hut and I lost my package of food.

The intelligence officer at Zhukov's headquarters was actually a marine – not a naval officer.

While at Zukhov's headquarters, we argued several times to have the five columns make contact between each other, with the connecting patrols. We explained that there were about 2,000 American officers in between two of the columns. Since they spoke no English, and my Russian was so very poor, I was never able to get this idea over to Zhukov's chief of staff. This one thing bothered me a great deal, as I was sure that we could have saved the rest of the boys from a great deal of discomfort in their march towards Berlin.

One incident which sticks in my mind is the extreme care the Russians took of their weapons. I recall a Russian soldier having on as dirty a uniform as I have ever seen, cleaning the frozen snow off of his burp gun with his shirt

My impressions of the Russian soldiers is that they are extremely friendly and very kind. They have a readiness to shoot at any possible target. They do a great deal of reconnaissance with small arms weapons. Their discipline was good and there was quite a bit of esprit de corps in the group which I contacted. While I never learned the exact unit I was with, I do know that it was a part of one of the "Guards' Divisions of Zhukov's Army". There was a difference between their officers and the men, but it is different than it is in our

Army. One incident points this up, in that I recall Max, the battery commander, cutting the hair of his own orderly.

Their staff work is apparently quite good. I know their intelligence section is extremely alert, and took absolutely all precautions that we never see an operations map.

The Russian G.I. is not a person of all thumbs. One of them made a light out of a raw potato sitting in a pan of gasoline. On the other hand, they can be very destructive, as there was one incident in which we were quartered in a school house and since the fireplace was not big enough to give off enough heat, they started a second fire on a piece of tin in the other corner of the room. Finally the room was so full of smoke that you had to feel your way around to keep from falling into one of these fires. Most of the fuel for the fires was schoolbooks, printed in German.

I am quite certain that I forgot to mention that at the corps command post we had been interviewed by the Russian Army Press, and pictures were taken. Later I received a copy of the Polish newspaper showing my picture in a Russian scout car.

The Russians were greatly interested in all rings and watches and placed great value on them.

They have an almost fatalistic view of death and dead people. When they entered a house they would kick the door open, start their burp gun firing, and walk in. Like all soldiers, they had no use for civilian snipers. While going to the corps C.P., the Russians had knocked a sniper out of the church belfry. The body fell in the street, to remain there as a lesson to other snipers. Three or four days later I was in the same spot and saw that so many vehicles had passed over this body that it was stretched for a good 200 yards.

There were Russian women as soldiers in uniform in the combat area of the Russian Army. One of the radio operators, and a machine gunner, were Russian women.

Chapter 15 – Forced March and Escape 279

Figure 15-1 Captain Lumpkin's photo in a Polish newspaper. The caption reads: "Soviet troops liberated from German camps a thousand British and American prisoners of war. On the photo: Soviet officer talks with US officers."

The ammunition in the anti-tank column was very unique. It had a normal ogive, with what looked like a cut in it through about 30% of its diameter. Its penetration of armor was terrific, and when I asked for details as to its range, effectiveness, etc., they would not tell me. I did see them knock out a Panther tank, a Panther being heavier than a Tiger tank, at about 2,000 yards. The Russians told me that the highest point that the shell rose above the line of site was about two meters. This would make a muzzle velocity as great if not greater than our M-1 rifle.

I have these items mentioned in the diary but do not recall the anecdote: "War Correspondent at Corps C.P. and at

Schubin, Millet out, Drury out, Pole cleaning Col. Skells and me."

January 25, 1945 – After much discussion with Max we finally agreed that we should go over to Dietfurt to see if we could locate any of the Red Cross parcels. We rode over on a commandeered farm tractor and found that the Germans had taken all of the parcels. There was plenty of sugar at Dietfurt. (The local industry was a sugar industry, extracting sugar from sugar beets.) Also beans and pickles. In the meantime we commandeered a farm wagon and hitched it onto our tractor. When we returned to Schubin we found that the Russians had provided trucks to take some of the sick and wounded out to Moscow.

A Polish family is brought into our old camp at Schubin, where I get a chance to see Russian interrogation at first hand. There was no threat of violence, kicking, beating, etc., but the family was sure that the Russians were going to shoot them. All the Russians were trying to do was find out if any of them had seen the senior German officer in any of the government area. I do not remember his name, but found out later that the Russians wanted him as a war criminal.

January 27, 1945 – I tried to determine if there were any wrist watches for American officers at the Post Office, and had an opportunity to see what the Poles did to the buildings and property of the collaborators during the German occupation.

About one-third of the buildings in Schubin had been burned down. Strangely enough, it appears that the *Bahnhofmeister* (station agent) at Schubin was actually a leader in the Polish underground, as he was now apparently a *Bürgermeister* for the village of Schubin. Willie Krick's printing shop was burned down and there was no sign of Willie or his family.

That night I saw the Russian film, "The Rainbow" which is about the German invasion of the Ukraine.

A German woman being interrogated by the Russians was very brave and self-reliant during the time they were questioning her as to the whereabouts of the German general they were seeking. I am quite certain that she knew nothing, but the Russians were taking no chances.

The Russians brought in three cattle which they slaughtered and fed the heterogeneous group now occupying the old Army quarters in Schubin.[2] In the meantime, Max picks me up and we return to his battery. He had gotten most of his vehicles to the banks of the Oder, but was down to about a gallon of gas per vehicle, so we were now in a spot where, if the Germans counterattacked they would annihilate us in short order, as we could not maneuver for more than 10 or 15 minutes. We solved part of this dilemma by throwing patrols across the river and getting the guns in as good a "hull-down position" as possible. There is no sign of any German activity. If we had gas we could move out.

Upon querying Max and some of the Russians, it is apparent that there are no American observers in the forward area of the Russian Army. It is doubtful whether I can get out of this place unless I do it on my own initiative or unless the war should suddenly end and an Armistice be declared. So I decide then that the best thing is to head east on my own until I find a military observer who can get me out of this, or until I get to someone who can speak sufficient English to understand that I am anxious to get home.

---

[2] Wright Bryan – I well remember the slaughtering of the cattle. In quite a number of speeches I made just after the war, I recall stating that we were not too hungry at this stage because of recent arrival of Red Cross parcels, but that, when the Russians asked us about food, we said we wanted meat. With that, they "liberated" and slaughtered the cattle.

January 29, 1945 – Some Russian trucks arrive in front of the old *Oflag*, and we leave about 1:00pm. It is very cold and a blizzard is raging across the countryside. These Russians beat anything, in that they can certainly stand the cold. It does not bother them to answer a call of nature or attempt to cook a meal right in the middle of a blizzard.[3]

All of the remaining American and some French, British and Belgians leave in this convoy. That night we are billeted at a Polish house in Hohenzohlza. There is plenty of food. The head of the house is a rather elderly man and his wife and they have a small daughter, Yadwiga. These people are very kind to us and apparently are used to having soldiers billeted on them. They take our occupation of their house in a rather matter-of-fact manner. There are several of us billeted in one room, and by common consent everyone sleeps on the floor and no one in the bed.

January 30, 1945 – We travel all night. The Russian driver is a good man, but absolutely careless with fire. In order to keep the cab of the truck warm he burned some alcohol cubes on the let-down door of the glove compartment. During the night our vehicle had a tire cut in two by the rail of an old roadblock. We repair this tire, using wire from a fence there for an "outside shoe." This is done by wrapping the wire around the cut, and we are able to hobble along.

The Red Army operates on Moscow time, regardless of what longitude they are in.

---

[3] Wright Bryan – That was truly a blizzard in which we travelled from Schubin to Warsaw. I remember how glad we were to share the body warmth of all who were packed in a truck; but that we were so crowded everyone was constantly getting cramps of arms and legs and having difficulty in shifting positions. The temperature, I think, was at least ten or twenty degrees below zero. I was wearing two suites of G.I. long-handled underwear, flannel pajamas, trousers, two woolen shirts, sweater, combat jacket, and trench coat. No wonder we could not move in the truck body.

The notations in the diary state "Stopped in a small village – Polish naval officer – two Russian soldiers – Russian couple – before this was with a Russian sergeant and teacher from Leningrad who understood German but spoke none. We get to Kriestadt about 15 kilometers from Kutno for the night and are fed an honest-to-goodness hot meal of borsch and tea".

<u>January 31, 1945</u> – The next morning I get a chance to shave with honest-to-goodness warm water. The cute little Yadwiga is 2 ½ years old and watched me shave. She is very much like Anne. Her mother is Helena Link, address: (I am reading this from script) Yacewska 22, Fnownoclaw. Her older sister is Maria Lewandowska.

They reported that when the Germans moved out they attempted to move the family and gave them 5 minutes' notice to pack up 15 kilos of possessions. This family merely hid.

Russian WACs are used as M.P.'s in this town and appear to be most efficient. Was invited to a Russian USO but was just too tired to attend.

I am leaving for Warsaw – it should be more comfortable and more room. We have quite a number of French and British escapees. We stop in Lowick, a town of about 20,000, where we have an opportunity to speak momentarily to an American woman. She had married a Pole and had been living in Poland for 25 years. Also met an American soldier of fortune who apparently got lost from World War II. He tried to join our group. The Poles are very friendly and invited all of us in for a cup of coffee. We stopped at a restaurant kitchen operated by the Red Army.

From what I saw of Warsaw, it is in total ruins – not a building left. One huge bomb had penetrated the pavement in the street but was unexploded.[4]

---

[4] Wright Bryan – The truck in which I was riding went through Warsaw late at night and crossed the Vistula on a pontoon bridge. All I recall of Warsaw

We crossed the Vistula River on a bridge supported on ice. The original bridge very beautiful but had been damaged. We are bedded down in a huge building about 5 or 6 miles west of Warsaw.[5] There were two Italian generals, and more US, British and French join us from Wallenstein. The French came in and tried to take over the operation of the camp but they were told off by the British G.I.s. The French, as usual, were screaming for their share of the food. The facilities here are somewhat limited, but it is nothing to gripe about. The friendship among the group is very warm, except for the French.

February 1, 1945 – Slept well. The food service is poor. The Russians wear a very nice felt boot called a *"valin."* Instead of socks, your feet are wrapped in ankle cloths made from an old blanket. There is some straw in the bottom of the boot. They are excellent for frozen ground and snow, but are very poor when wet. They must be taken off when you come inside. I received a pair and they have done wonders in keeping my feet warm.

More refugees come in. I have no idea of the number, but estimate there are about 3,000 in the building at this time. The building is four stories high, and at one time was used by the

---

is the snow in the streets and many substantial buildings gutted by fire and shelling.

[5] Wright Bryan – Wasn't the huge building where we were billeted east of Warsaw, rather than west? Wasn't it in the town of Rembertov, which you mention earlier? If so, the directions from Warsaw could be located on a map. We were told (whether accurately or not, I cannot say) that the building where we quartered had been a Polish military academy. Of course, I did not stay in this spot long, because I was taken with three infantry captains (DeLand, Gibson, and a third whose name I cannot recall) to a Russian army hospital, set up in some former school buildings. We stayed there until put on the train for Odessa. A sergeant of medics, Andy Stermchek (spelling not guaranteed) from Pittsburgh, was sent with us to be helpful and to be an interpreter, since he came of Ukrainian parentage; but he did not have much more Russian than the rest of us.

German Army as a training center for SS troops. There is a huge parade ground which is literally covered with "acres of diamonds." Since the toilet facilities have broken down completely, I hate to think of the odor when these "acres of diamonds" start to melt. Col. Drury, the Senior American Officer, is also bothered, and it is estimated that some slit trenches will be dug.

The Red Army has many kids who are orphans attached to each unit. Some of the Commanders have brought along their wives.

The spirit of some of these refugees is excellent. In particular, there was one Russian soldier who had both legs off at the hip. He had been left behind from one of the POW camps near Danzig. He had built a wooden platform, with a wooden axle and wooden wheels. His body was on the platform and he propelled himself along, using blocks of wood to grip the ground, and his arms as a source of power.

I am struck by the fact that every Russian seems to be completely sold on winning this war, and each one feels that he has a personal interest in gaining the final victory.

Had a bath, and must admit that it was the best since leaving the States. The bathhouse is operated by the Red Army and is run by the Russian WACs. Father Brock was blushing through his beard.[6]

Many women are employed in the Red Army. Many are attractive and some have very pretty features. As an average, they seem to be somewhat smaller than American girls.

Many of the tales told us have been exaggerated, as I find that the average Russian is just another person.

---

[6] Wright Bryan – Apropos, Father Brock: I quoted him many times as saying he had decided the war was being fought for watches and fountain pens.

February 2, 1945 – Marshal Zhukov has ordered that we be placed in better quarters. In Russian his name is spelled: Маршал Жуков правописание.

Yesterday we were joined by Lt. Col. Cheal and Major who were in Schocken.

There are approximately (180?) British G.I.s with the group, in the charge of a British medic officer whose name is Geoffrey Allen, M.D., c/o Dr. Allen, Shotiey Bridge, Durham. He appears to be a pretty good egg.

I go into Rembertov, the nearest town, where I find that there are two SS officers due for hanging. The method of hanging seems to be somewhat cruel, as wire is used for the noose. These men were to be executed in retaliation of some German guerrillas having killed three Russians and two Poles.

February 3, 1945 – Col. Drury orders an inspection, to get the quarters cleaned up. The Russian commandant for the area requests that we stay out of town (Rembertov), or go in with a Russian.

Capt. Bond comes in. He had been left behind at the first halt. I am studying Russian very hard, trying to increase my vocabulary.

Wash two towels in some very cold water. The towels froze before they dried.

It is the consensus of all of the Russians locally that the Germans will halt on the Oder.

A Russian doctor from Mongolia is in charge of the area and is excellent. He has treated my feet, which were frost bitten, with some type of salve made from the fat of a goat. It smells like something awful but seems to be very efficient.

Some of the British G.I.s are shacking up with the French refugees. This caused Max a great deal of consternation and he has insisted that the men and the women get separated.

It is starting to warm up a bit, as there was some melting of snow today. With no lights, since the power was very much rationed and used only for certain things, it makes the going at night very messy.

The *Bürgermeister* of the town comes out and pays his respects to the American and the British. The local baker originally had been a banker, and when the Germans occupied Poland he left his family on a 15-minute notice, and has not seen them since.

We have a League of Nations dance tonight, with Russians, British, Americans, French, Belgians, Serbs, Czechs, Slovaks, and Fins in the group. The Russians are great dancers. If there are not enough women to go around, then the men dance with each other. The dance consists of a great deal of stamping of feet and hurling themselves in the air. A very picturesque effect.

February 4, 1945 – The SS are already swinging from a light pole in the town Square.

Capt. Bates? and another officer turn up last night, and two others came in today.

I repacked my possessions and got into a long argument with Max in regard to Russia and the organization and aim of the Communist Party and Russian Nationalism. (Will explain more of his position later.) The winter is starting to thaw and it is extremely messy outside. I walk to the village, as I have become more or less the trader for the group. Trading for a loaf of bread is very interesting. Their loaves are somewhat smaller than ours, and trade for whatever price they can get. This morning I traded a small cake of soap (hotel size) for some 30,000 *zlotys*. Bread was priced at 50 *zlotys* a loaf, but after much haggling, the price came down to approximately 20 *zlotys*. Soap is a great medium for trading.[7]

---

[7] Wright Bryan – I did not recall soap being such a good medium of exchange; but, of course, I could not move around as much as you did. Cigarettes were the favorite medium everywhere I was. My memory may be vague but I think one of my pals got 450 zlotys for a G.I. shirt and paid

There are so many new graves about.

The person in charge of the bakery is named Klara. She is trying to learn English and seems to be definitely upper class.

That night I heard a Polish sergeant play the accordion. At one time he was a big name musician with the the Warsaw Conservatory of Music. He could play anything from the classics to the very latest, and was good with all of them.

Quite a number of soldiers in Russian uniform who are Poles from this area. An add this, but it seems this same thing could be said of the German soldiers in that there were a number who were Poles from this same area. The Polish soldier seems to be a better soldier when he is fighting for some place other than his own country.

Our building looks and smells about like an unkempt Ellis Island, but at least it keeps us out of the weather.

February 5, 1945 – I bind up mail.

It is rumored that *Hauptman* Minner surrendered the POW column to Col. Goode, and all were recaptured by the Germans. This later turned out to be false. There are many officers drifting in, each one reporting that the main column had been freed and later recaptured.

February 6, 1945 – Go in to town to trade for bread, and find that the Poles are great traders. They are truly a nation of small shop owners.

Many sad stories, particularly one concerning some Czechs. (Don't recall.) Beating of Jews. (Don't recall.) One lady, Klara, who worked in the small bakery shop, looked as if she was at least 65, but her actual age was 32.

---

250 zlotys for a liter of vodka, from which we had our first alcoholic drink since liberation. Correction: the Russian correspondent who came into *Oflag 64* and dined with Colonel Drury and me had some champagne with him and we helped him drink it.

There have been no small luxuries such as chocolate, soap, etc., in Rembertov for the last 5 years.

The Mayor of the town of Rembertov is very friendly toward Col. Drury. Col. Drury is sweating out Col. Goode.

The Polish soldiers in the Russian Army have a concert and invite the entire community to a dance.

Remember the Czech walking for 5 days with no food and then passing out. (Don't recall details.) Talked a long while with a Russian nurse who spoke almost perfect British English and a Parisian French.

At the dance it was immaterial whether men and women were dancing together, as there was a great deal of stamping, etc., in time to the music. Everyone had lots of fun.

February 7, 1945 – In this large building we occupy a cubicle. In my cubicle is Lt. Col. Thomas J. Riggs, Jr., of Huntington, West Virginia, Major Dobson, Lt. Col. Cheal, Lt. Col. Skells, Col. Fred Drury, and Max, the Russian liaison officer. [8] Major Ralph E. Pennick, of West Baden Springs, Indiana, is also here. Pop Amerill and another officer drifted in from Exin. He thinks that about a thousand of the POWs from Oflag 64 were loaded on trains for Germany. Why more did not escape, I cannot figure out.

Late in the afternoon, Dobson and an Italian General and an Italian Admiral and I go to dinner at a Pole's house. Col. Drury was sick and he asked me to express his regrets to the host, Bielab Pavel, Alexandrowsha Street, N26, Rembertov. Some Russians were also present there. The host had some very

---

[8] Wright Bryan – Post-war note: Tom Riggs lived for two or three years in a house just around the corner from where we lived in Cleveland. I did not realize at first that he was the Riggs of Kriegie days; but when I did realize it, we had quite a reunion. I do not know where he went from Cleveland. Also, I've had correspondence recently with Jack Dobson. His address is: Brigadier General John W. Dobson, HQ Antilles Command, USARSOUTHCOM, A.P.O 851, New York, N.Y.

interesting details to tell us of the anti-German activities during the last 5 years. He escaped the work camps by throwing his hip out of place. His wife allowed herself to become unattractive, disheveled, and very dowdy looking during the occupation. She was a very attractive lady at the dinner. Most of the conversation was in French and was conducted too fast for me to follow too well.

Later that night the other Russians invited us over to see a film on Africa.

February 8, 1945 – We are about 18 kilometers east of Warsaw.

The latrine in the parade ground is a mess.

About 14 more POWs showed up.

Many of the officers have the itchy foot. Cheal left this morning. Max says that we are to go to Moscow via Brest.

Major Dobson is a real character; has lots of guts and does not mind telling off Drury if it is necessary.

"Weeks rations – Italian generals and cigarettes and bread." (Do not remember details.)

A German boy about 17 years of age has appeared among us, and we are carrying him along as an American G.I. It is rather dangerous, but for the love of me I cannot see where this kid could be any great German criminal. His name is Herman Wedel, Waterhock 1945, Annheim.

February 9, 1945 – Two enlisted men AWOL today.

Went to town with Riggs and Dobson and traded for some bread. Riggs got quite a bang out of my arguing with the shopkeeper on the cost of bread.

Rembertov, Poland at one time was a town of about 20,000. It looks considerably beaten up now, many wrecked buildings, etc.

At the station a Russian troop train came through with the big hammer and sickle on the front of the engine. Just a block away from the station, remember the wrecked Sherman tank.

Major Crandall and about 40 or 50 more POWs come in. It seems that the main column marched for nine days between two Russian columns and were taken into Berlin. I certainly hope that everyone is O.K.

"Remember shooting in straw, killing pigs, dogs and burning." (Do not recall details.)

Later in the day I go over to the Russian Army Hospital to see Wright Bryan and his group[9]. All are O.K. The British enlisted man, Hazelton, is much better.

Reports are that *Oberst* Schneider was a true fox in handling his column of POWs. The sick and wounded were carried by trucks in leaps and bounds. (The non-walking sick were hauled by truck to the estimated position where the column would be that night, and the column walked up to this point.)

All of the Russians say that the Lublin government is here to stay. They have apparently changed two laws, in that only 300 hectares of land may be held by any individual. The same value is true with money and banking. The political question is as hot here as the religious question was in Ireland. The Poles are still trying to get the Americans in the frying pan by siding with them individually in their arguments. Col. Drury is invited to wine and dine by all of the factions (of which there are at least nine) so that they may sell the American government on their form of government.

Economics are the same the world over. We have pooled our cigarettes and have a monopoly on American cigarettes. We

---

[9] Wright Bryan – Thanks for coming to see me in the Russian Hospital.

have boosted the price, and before I could get out of the store, bread had gone up likewise. You can't win![10]

February 10, 1945 – We are still waiting for word for a move. Rumor now has it that we will go to Brest-Litovsk, then Stalingrad, and out to France. Frankly, I doubt it.

While bargaining today, one Polish woman thought that I was being gypped and pitched in to see that I was given the fair price. Her name was Klara Kalinowska, Aleja Pietsudskiego 55, Rembertov. Before the war she had been a coffeehouse operator and refused to open her shop only for Poles. She apparently had been a very beautiful woman, as she had pictures to prove it. She had not seen her husband since the surrender of Warsaw.

Had a long talk with Max regarding Russia, Poland, and the *Bolsheviki*. He could not go to bed because his roommate was having a liaison with a Russian WAC.

Max is an unusual person. He speaks at least five languages fluently, he had been a movie director prior to the war, and I noticed that all Russians listened very attentively to him. While he swears that he is not a member of the Communist Party, I am certain that he has something to do with the political section.

The big question for all us Americans now is how to get out of here.

February 11, 1945 – As I have said before, this building is four stories and a basement, and was built as a dormitory with eating facilities for approximately 250 to 400 men. When the Germans pulled out, they sabotaged the building rather effectively by placing a grenade in the boiler. We have since gotten it repaired by scrounging some spare parts from one of the buildings in Warsaw. Incidentally, on one of these trips into

---

[10] Wright Bryan – This confirms my memory of cigarettes as a medium of exchange.

Warsaw I saw one of the A.P. Green[11] firebricks lying in the street.

One of the pumps on the boiler is operated by use of a belt made from some webbing which has been sewed together. Again, you can do almost anything if you will use your head just the least little bit. While the building is not as warm as the hospital, we can keep everyone from freezing. At the present time there are about 175 Americans and British here. All of the British are enlisted men, with the exception of the officer medic. Our group, together with about 4,000 refuges, makes this place look like an Ellis Island.

In the he afternoon I go down to the village and strike up an acquaintance with Klaus. He was about 22 years of age and before the war had been an owner of a small haberdashery shop. He reports some hard times during the German occupation – families being broken up, rough treatment for not working, and forced labor while sick. His war experience consisted of about three months as a pilot in the Royal Air Force in England.

When I returned to the barracks there was a Russian Major General there in answer to Max's letter. (Do not recall the details of the letter.) He was quite a pompous old fellow with his *astrikan*. Still, Max gave him a pretty hard going over, and it looks like we will move out before long.

Col. Drury has made the suggestions, and I think we can do it, of purchasing the next train that goes east through Warsaw. (This is what was actually later done.)

February 12, 1945 – Was able to obtain some soap from a Russian WAC and washed my jacket in the morning. Soap a very poor grade.

---

[11] A.P. Green was a brick factory in Captain Lumpkin's hometown of Mexico, Missouri.

My knowledge of Russians is increasing slightly. Major "Wirlaway" (Haggard) comes in; also a Polish Naval officer who had been fighting in England. With the number of Poles I am dealing with, I am finally picking up some of their language.

Napoleon's Polish girlfriend was Ksiezna Walewska, pronounced kar-ee'-nya-Va-lev'-ska. Koscuszko is pronounced kos-choos-kar. Paderewski's name is pronounced Pad-rev-ski.

Down to the village and met with Klaus. He is trying to improve my Polish. Everything the Poles wear is something that has been remade from something else. His trousers were 7 years old, and his shirt was 5 years old. The shirt had been made from an old Polish Army blanket.

Major Haggard is some youth. He is trying to operate the showers (don't recall details) and at the moment is creating quite a problem in that he wants a British enlisted man who came with him to remain with the Americans.

We have been warned to be ready to accept between 100 and 500 more American officers. I sincerely hope this is true.

February 13, 1945 – Wrote myself a letter, addressed it to me in Mexico, Missouri, and mailed it in the Red Army's postal service.[12]

At the village today I bargained for a candle, and had a long talk with a group of Poles. If you can get five Poles together, you have a political party.

The Poles are trying to learn English – Lost a U.S. – it seems we did not accept a Russian who was worn out with an escape across Germany. (I don't recall what this meant.)

The Polish Workers Party came in with some bread and some cigarettes, which were gratefully received.

We also have a few Central Americans in among the refugees.

---

[12] Wright Bryan – Did the letter ever reach Mexico, Missouri?

A Swedish farmer was sent here to be sent home by the Russians. The Poles lack experience in such matters. (Do not recall what that could have meant.)

Coffee was seen by some Poles for the first time.

<u>February 14, 1945</u> – Air is poor when we sleep, as we are too crowded. We are visited by a Russian general on an inspection tour, and it is somewhat of a lousy inspection.

The ratio on cigarettes has gone up. We get 80 *zlotys* for a cigarette and are able to buy a small loaf of bread for 55 *zloty*.

Some Russians gave me some Polish and Russian coins for my coin collection.

Wonder what the story is behind her? (The lady at the bakery shop.)

I wrote to Elmer Jackson, Toady Barksdale, S.W.H. and Betty. Each of these was a card showing a scene from Warsaw.[13]

Another inspection by a lieutenant general in the Polish Corps and a Russian Lt. Col. Max is still the question in my mind, as he certainly had these two men jumping through the hoop.

Our host at dinner the other night contacted me and wants me to be sure and tell his brother, John Bielak of Highwood Avenue, Southington, Connecticut, that he is O.K.

Remember Dr. Prey, who lost his Jewish wife during the German occupation of Lithuania.

My picture appeared in the Warsaw paper.

Lt. Cols. Louis Gershenow and Gaines Barron and what appears to be the remainder of those who escaped at Exin, came in.

---

[13] Wright Bryan – I should have taken this to Orangeburg to show Toady Barksdale the reference about your card to him. Did he ever receive it? And what did you finally conclude about Max? Any news of him since the war? Am I correct that he attended City College of New York and spoke excellent "American?"

February 15, 1945 – Times are commencing to be a little tough. We now have 13,000 refugees in the building, and from the appearance of things we will be here at least 20 days more. It is suggested that we get up a regular drill schedule and get set for a big reorganization.

Col. Drury's talk to new officers is good. (Do not recall the details other than that we should make the best of a poor situation.)

Capt. Dicks is here.

I go down to the village again and sell my extra pair of cotton socks for 700 *zloty*. One Pole told me a story of a frustrated love with a rich family and a later marriage. (Do not recall the story.)

We are really bulging at the seams in this building. Within our own American organization, Drury had made me the intelligence officer. On the other hand, I am assisting Max in the administration of this Ellis Island type hotel. It is enough to keep everyone busy. Yesterday we served at least 40 seatings for each of the two meals. The first seating for breakfast started at 1:00 in the morning, and we kept the seatings going through to the following midnight. During these 23 hours, everybody got two meals.

Col. Yardley, the paratrooper from Texas, is in. He tells of being strafed by a *Heinkle*. (Do not recall his story.)

Went with Max to where there was much German dead. These men had all been battle casualties, as they were mangled up quite a bit. The Red Army, assisted by the Poles, were burying them as the ground softened. Also saw some ovens which the Germans had operated to make soap from Poles, Jews, and teachers.[14]

Beating of Cloyber. This was in Torun (Thorn) near Colan.

---

[14] During WWII, the Germans developed a process to make soap from human corpses.

Chapter 15 – Forced March and Escape

February 16, 1945 – Our meal schedules are really off. There is just simply not enough time or equipment to prepare the meals. Today the boilers of *borsht* were never clean. We just kept adding water and cabbage. Col. Drury has asked Max if the Americans could run every phase of camp life and be responsible for lights, water, mess, interior discipline, cleanliness and everything.

Money is still the best bet on trading. (Believe this refers to the fact that I had 4 or 5 script dollars and have been able to trade these for sums as high as 15,000 *zloty*. One of the Italian admirals had a blue seal $100 bill for which the Poles would not give him more than 25 *zloty*, as they were sure that the bill was counterfeit.)

February 17, 1945 – My calendar is wrong. I have missed several days. Each day is somewhat like the others, with our main effort being used to obtain food or warmth.

Picked up some old Republic of Germany coins today.

We are having trouble with one of the pumps on the boiler, and it looks like we can send a detail into Warsaw to scrounge around. I am hoping to get on this detail, but Max would rather for me to remain in the barracks. In case I do go, everyone is donating his extra cloths, as I am doing the trading for the group. In the final showdown I was unable to make this trip.

February 18, 1945 – I was able to trade $10 for 1,300 *zloty* and a shirt for 40,000. We now have plenty of Polish money and are able to eat white bread.

Had a long talk and discussion with Max. I think that we will be able to leave in two weeks.

Marshal Zhukov has sent us two huge kegs of wine. These tankards are about 12 feet high and 15 feet across. With our enrollment now being about 14,000, I can see there will be quite a problem on the distribution. All of the Americans got drunk on the German wine.

February 19, 1945 – We actually dig up an issue of cigars, tobacco and soap for everyone.

February 20, 1945 – Today was the day set aside to issue wine to all, and we do this by giving each person about a half-pint of wine. The Yugoslavs were the only ones who tried to take advantage of the few and they attempted to go through the line twice.

February 21, 1945 – In the village today I found out that there is a train which we might be able to obtain. Bought 50 loaves of bread for our group.

February 22, 1945 – The deal went through. We have purchased the train on reverse lend lease.[15] We get everybody up at 3:00am for the walk to Warsaw. I rush down and spend the last of my money buying 50 loaves, 2 kilos of butter, 6 or 7 candles, some matches, etc. We then find out the train is to leave at 10:00am. At 6:00pm, we still have not moved. I ate with Tom Riggs, Jack Dobson, Yardley, and an American major whose name I do not recall. I tell Klaus and all of my Polish friends good-bye. They seem to be really sad about the entire matter.

Max has messed up the records and everyone works all night (I believe this refers to the fact that he had to write everybody's name in Russian, and it is most difficult to put down an English name in the Russian alphabet.) Max goes out and gets 5 or 6 Russian WACs to come in and assist us.

---

[15] Wright Bryan – I well remember the train to Odessa, but this is the first I heard about purchasing it on reverse lend lease. Tell me more.

Chapter 16

Warsaw to Odessa

February 23, 1945 – We issue the American officers their rations after much accounting with a Russian staff sergeant who was really a good soldier. He tried to get cheese, candy and chestnuts for his group.

We moved out on the main track and are prepared to stop the next train that comes through, regardless. At the present time there are between 200 and 300 Americans and British in our group. The Russians guarding the rail station are undisciplined according to our standards, as they think nothing of dismantling their rifles and cleaning them while on duty. They also called to each other at night by firing their rifles.

Col. Drury is a very patient man. (Do not recall this incident.)

Col. L. Gershenow has arrived with one enlisted man. (Do not recall the story.)

The train finally connects up at 8:30pm. Half of the town is down to tell us good-bye. A Russian major medic is aboard, and he speaks perfect German. He is O.K. The Russian colonel is a much-decorated soldier, and he is the train commander. As I recall, he was a veteran of Stalingrad.

<u>February 24, 1945</u> – The train actually moves at 2:00am and we go to Siedlus, a small village east of Warsaw. During the

train halt I wash and re-gather my equipment. We loaf about the place for the remainder of the day.

February 25, 1945 – The Russian major, who is the medic, and the Russian colonel gave me their names.

We are now in Brest-Litovsk where two nurses are placed aboard who are being sent back for a bit of rest. Both of these girls were decorated with the Order of Stalingrad. It seems that the Russian language has many dialects and that the best Russian is spoken in Leningrad.

There is much shifting about of the empty cars in the marshaling yard.

The train passes through Kukov, Brest and Kovel. All show gaunt evidence of war and destruction. Remember the prepared holes for explosives.

The Red Army served us a Russian cake baked like a turnover, with cabbage inside. Not bad! However, our main dish is a boiled porridge similar to kasha.

One G.I. fooled around, attempting to get water, and was left in the Pripet Marshes. The train had stopped and he had rushed over to a farmhouse, hoping to draw water from an abandoned well.

February 26, 1945 – We pass through Równe. The country is very flat and there is evidence that it is starting to roll. Much of the architecture in the village is Russian, with the onion-type trimming on the buildings. We had one whale of a long wait after arriving in a small town east of Rowne. We leave at dark, but have many halts during the night. Col. Drury has asked me to contact the engineer at every halt and ask him how long we will be here, and invariably the answer is "23 minutes." The engineer's idea of 23 minutes is extremely variable. One halt was for less than a minute, and another halt was for almost 20 hours.[1]

February 27, 1945 – We arrive at Kozyatn. I wash my face and hands in the snow. There is a very large rail yard in this town. We are about 450 kilometers from Odessa. During the day we pass through Vinnytsia and Ameniker. There had been some extremely heavy fighting in this area. Many buildings busted up.

There is much snow. The Russians have a unique idea of making snow fences from snow itself.

A long halt at Rudnytsya. I strike up a conversation with some Russians in the rail yard, and they give me some parched sunflower seeds to eat. The seeds are very aromatic.

There is a beautiful moon in evidence.

Col. Drury has promoted some Russian chewing tobacco – very strong, but not too bad.

February 28, 1945 – We start moving early in the morning, and roll along very well. Bernie Bolton gave me 35 rubles.

Here is Max's address:

максим коровочин, камяевская уп д5 к6 185

There is also a chess-playing major aboard, and his name and address are:

Демидов владимир казначбйская ул Домз к9

We pass through Karstan and roll on into the night.

---

[1] Wright Bryan – My chief recollection of the country we traversed en route to Odessa was the number of burnt out houses, towns, tanks, and military vehicles we saw in the snow swept landscape. It seemed truly scorched earth.

Someone had a short wave radio on the train. I remember once hearing Robert Magidoff of NBC, whose wife we have known in this country since the war, calling BBC from Moscow Central Radio to get a trans-Atlantic circuit and then going into one of his news broadcasts. That was interesting to me because I had done similar work for NBC from England and France.

March 1, 1945 – We arrive in Odessa about 10:00am. There is much evidence of Russian architecture. Many people in the streets. Homes and apartment houses appear to be modern, but many of them have been wrecked by the war.

We are quartered in four old Czarist homes that are near a sanitarium. Russians very strict on letting too many of us go into the city.

The water has an odor and a taste and is very hard.

Col. Drury is to fly to Moscow.

Query re: Waters, Rossback and Bryant.

Remember the two Russian WAC's who acted as interpreters. (One spoke English with a British accent, and the other spoke French just like a Parisian. Neither of them had ever left the country.) Wright Bryan to fly out with Col. Drury.

We are given a chance to get a bath at a bathhouse operated by a bunch of Russian women, and our clothing was deloused.

Much, much, much rearrangement of the staff duties. (Do not recall.)

Send one radio with Major Crandall and have one for our use. (Do not recall.) Sleep between sheets for the first time in 2 ½ years.

March 2, 1945 – Got a haircut from a Russian woman barber. Had bacon and eggs for the first time in almost three years. Sat around in the morning and shot the breeze with Sage, Wright Bryan and some of the others. I am in a room with Bryan, Dobson, and Tom Riggs.[2]

The weather is cool – not cold – and beautiful.

Classic remark: "We will get there with a reasonable percent of what we started with." This refers to the fact that Drury, while a good officer, was sometimes insistent upon telling his subordinates how to do his orders. Dobson and I

---

[2] Wright Bryan – Interesting that since the war I have seen all three of my Odessa roommates: you, Dobson, and Riggs.

were attempting to move the convoy, containing ourselves and some Frenchmen, into Warsaw. Drury was riding us pretty hard until Dobson told him, "Colonel, just leave us alone and we will get there with a reasonable percent of what we start with."

Remember "I can get it for you wholesale – on a package of cigarettes." (Don't recall.)

We promote some powdered coffee, but it makes a terrible drink, as the water here has considerable salt. All of the drinking water is distilled, as the Black Sea water is briny.[3]

Major Dobson is appointed S-4 and I am his assistant.

The Russian colonel has an interpreter. She speaks perfect American English, is very polite, and reads Dickens, Thackery and Dreiser. Theodore Dreiser, by the way, is an extremely popular novelist with the Russian G.I.

Dobson and I go down to get the mail. It is awfully cold. Odessa must have been a beautiful city at one time. Most of the buildings are stained a suntan.

<u>**March 3, 1945**</u> – Worked with distribution of supplies to other two camps. This third camp, downtown, has plenty.

Col. Drury is all set for Moscow. Cans to the hospital, and Kelly to be senior American officer.

My box of "iron" rations is just about finished. These are odds and ends of trading materials which I have accumulated in dealing for some of the luxuries of life. In addition to its bad taste, the water here acts as a mild laxative.

The Russian USO shows us a Russian film with U.S. actors. The story is about the retreat through the Pripet Marshes.

---

[3] Wright Bryan – I can still shudder over the taste of that coffee made with brackish water. I wanted the coffee so badly: the first swallow or two wasn't so bad, but after that I just couldn't take any more.

Have tried my best to buy dolls for Martha and Anne, and get something for Tony, but it is extremely hard to get out of the gate to go to Odessa.

<u>March 4, 1945</u> – The Russian supply officer and myself are developing quite a friendship. He is quite a chess player.

Had some trouble getting out of the gate to contact the other camps. Remember the sugar. This refers to an incident which illustrates the Russian mentality. The Red Army is composed of many nationalities, and covers at least five distinct languages. They have a guard on our gate, and rather than change an order to the guard they merely change the guard, but be sure that the new guard understands what the orders are. Dobson and I heard of some Liberty ships being in the harbor. We got the *palkovnik* (the Russian colonel) to permit us to go down and promote flour, sugar and cigarettes. The order to the guard was that we could go out and return. We obtained the supplies from these boats and made a distribution to the three camps. (By the way, I have since run into Ted Supplee and in comparing notes at a Dairy Queen Convention which he was attending on behalf of his interests in Dairy Queen; I find that he was the wireless operator of one of the boats we contacted.)

After we arrived back at the camp I found that I had shorted the next camp by one sack of sugar. I went down to the gate and asked the guard if I could walk 200 yards to the next camp and deliver the sugar, and he said *"Nyet!"* I then go back to the compound and get about 15 or 20 Americans to volunteer as a drill squad. We marched down to the gate, counting "One, two, three, four," in a very military manner. I gave the Bessarbian guard a snappy military salute and called out "Hungen, gokolen, jackeben, ensogum, humbusk." He then comes to "present arms" and we march out of the gate to deliver the sugar next door. Upon our return to the compound I merely repeat the process and we march back in through the gate. All of the gibberish which I gave the guard was merely counting to

5 in Seminole, which I learned from one of our students at MMA.[4]

I stripped down some of my cards. (Do not recall.)

Got into a heated discussion with three Russian interpreters regarding the Communist way of life vs. the Capitalist way of life. One of the interpreters, Olge, is very attractive and has the boys jumping through the hoops.

At night the Odessa theater comes out to entertain us with singing and music. The contralto was unusually good.

Cans is sent to the Russian hospital.

Odessa was quite a resort area before the war.

<u>March 5, 1945</u> – Dobson gets a haircut and a hat, for a pair of trousers. I am trying to promote a belt for my fur coat.

One of the interpreters has promised to translate "*vasbillis.*"

The weather has turned very cold, and with the dampness it penetrates our clothing. My Russian coat is good and warm.

Major Paul Hall is the U.S. Military Commissioner in Odessa. After much wrangling around we are able to get a British boat to haul us out. Hall says that we should be prepared to load on Wednesday and leave on Thursday.

<u>March 6, 1945</u> **(Tuesday)** – A Cuban girl, Juliet D'Mesa, her brother, another woman, and an old G.I. from World War I have shown up, requesting us to claim them as U.S. citizens and take them back with us. They have not been in the States for the last ten years. Miss D'Mesa claims to be a friend of Tony Biddle. Frankly, I think they are attempting to take advantage of a situation.

---

[4] Wright Bryan – The "ensogum humbusk" is my favorite story of the war. You remember our wives comparing notes on it that night in Missouri a few years ago?

Col. Drury could not leave, so Major Hall stiffened his backbone and grounded the entire Russian plane.[5] We are to leave in the morning for the docks to board the British boat.

---

[5] Wright Bryan – I thought it was an <u>American</u> plane with an <u>American</u> crew which had come down from our military mission in Moscow to check up on our condition and to bring some medical supplies. It was my understanding, as you indicate, that Colonel Drury was to fly to Moscow when the plane returned and that he had permission from our people in Moscow to bring me along. Be that as it may, the Russians wouldn't let Drury or me on the airport and the plane, American or Russian as the case may be, departed without us.

Chapter 17

Odessa to Newfoundland

March 7, 1945 – Up at 6:00am and pack all of my gear. I was fortunate in being able to throw my possessions on Major Hall's jeep. The Russians furnish us a band, and we march to the docks. We must have made quite a sight with the palkovnik marching at the head, the Russian band playing British music, and the most nondescript-looking marching body following them. After half a mile or so, the band gave out of British tunes and played Russian marching tunes. The only one I could remember was a slight variation of a tune that sounded like the Beer Barrel Polka. We join in and sing some good old G.I. songs and some British songs. The songs and the band were not necessarily in step with each other. It must have been quite a sight!!

We finally arrive at the docks, where there is another big bunch of rhubarb. It appears that the Russians had lost one sheet of the passenger list. After much arguing back and forth between Dobson and myself on the American side, and the Russian *polkovnik* who was trying to help us, and the Commissioner of Docks in Odessa, we finally get aboard. The boat pulled out almost immediately.

On board the boat I am quartered at first in a dining hall. There are not enough beds, blankets, or anything, for the group that is on this boat. Later, I was able to get in a cabin with 5 others, and this was not too bad.

Some of the boys are having a hard time trying to get civilized again. Some of them had sunk to rather low levels.

We pass through a mild snow flurry after leaving Odessa.

There is a great need for these men on board to receive some money. We work out a deal with the British commander whereby every man will get the equivalent of $25.00 and every officer will get $100.00 paid in Egyptian pounds. Foolishly or not I have signed a slip as to who this should be charged against. (Believe it or not, this $100.00 was deducted when I separated at Jefferson Barracks. The record had come half-way around the world at the same speed that I had.) The rate of exchange: $1.00 = .241635 Egyptian pounds.[1]

---

[1] Wright Bryan – On my transport, I think we drew just 20 shillings to spend in the ship's canteen instead of the $100 you mention – or maybe it was a few pounds, sterling, and I had twenty shillings left when we got to Naples. The memory gets fuzzier and fuzzier. However, I am sure we did not draw anything like as much as $100. Whatever the amount, the bill for reimbursement also reached me quickly – while I was in First General Hospital near Paris just a few months later.

When I came ashore in Naples I had only a few shillings and no finance officer from whom to draw pay – because I was on The Atlanta Journal's payroll and not Uncle Sam's. With wartime control of communications and my credentials confiscated by the enemy, I didn't' know how long it would take me to get expense money cabled from Atlanta. Fortunately, at the Terminus Hotel in Naples, which was a billet for transient American officers, I encountered a friend from Atlanta, a major in military government who was a banker in civil life. He advanced me $100 worth of lira and I was in business again.

I left Odessa on a different ship from yours. Mine was a Canadian Pacific liner, one of the "Duchess" boats – *"Duchess of Bedford"* or *"Duchess of Richmond"*, I think it was. We did not touch in Egypt. We anchored a day in the harbor of Istanbul but no one was allowed ashore. One American correspondent came aboard, talked to me, and relayed messages through his office to my family. Later we touched at Marseilles and unloaded all our French passengers there. I tried to jump ship at that point to get back

March 8, 1945 – The name of the boat is the *Moreton Bay*. As we near the Dardanelles, I notice that the water from the Asian side shows a distinctly different color than the water on the European side.

I am interrogated by a British agent on board the *Moreton Bay* regarding the behavior of the British enlisted men on their trip from Warsaw.

Got some pills from the boat hospital.

We reach the Bosphorous and dock just inside the Sea of Marmora to take on water.

I am able to buy a limited supply of chocolate candy from one of the boats from Constantinople.

I forgot to mention yesterday that we passed by three floating mines. The crew, who couldn't hit the side of a barn, fired 500 or 600 rounds of ammunition, trying to sink them, but were unable to do so.

Have been appointed ship's duty officer. It seems to be a title but no work.

Slept in the orderly room.

March 9, 1945 – The ship stood by opposite Istanbul all day. We could not go ashore. It certainly is very pretty and picturesque, with many minarets and light colored stone buildings. Could see the cathedral established by Constantine in the distance.

Get underway about 6:30pm. Have a terrible cough and cold. Wind is strong and goes right through you. Not much sleep last night.

March 10, 1945 – We are making good time, but the weather is still cold. We are interrogated by Major Sommers of the Intelligence section.

Everyone is reading old U.S. magazines found aboard.

---

to Paris or SHAEF headquarters, but no British or Americans were allowed ashore. For some reason, they backtracked to Naples and landed us there.

March 11, 1945 – We pass by Crete in the morning. The British say that they sacrificed as this was the narrow part of the Channel. Part of Crete is still occupied by the German soldiers. As far as that is concerned, I know that there is a large force of Germans – at least 100,000 – that are in the Kuban – Caspian Sea area. There is no chance of them ever getting back to Germany.

The boat makes good progress all day, and we expect to be in Port Said at 10:00 tomorrow morning. The British enlisted men are all sprucing up their clothes for leaving. We Americans simply don't have anything to spruce up. I am in a pair of British battle dress trousers, but the rest of my uniform is all Russian.

I take a bath in seawater and write a V-letter to Betty and to mom.

March 12, 1945 – In the morning we repack all of our gear. Everyone of course has too much. Some of the officers had drawn battle dress. This had to be returned. We are taken off the boat in lighters and go to a camp just outside of Port Said. There are many temples about. The camp is right on the edge of the Suez Canal.

Go to an ENSER (British USO) show at night. The performance was only fair. See a write-up of our arrival in the Cairo papers, but am unable to read the Arabic.

The American Red Cross is on the job and gave each man an invalid kit. It was very nice of them, but I did not need it. There are many forms to fill out for this issue. This is just another illustration of the effect of the Army on anything that it touches. There is a form for everything.

March 13, 1945 – Everyone draws more clothing. I draw a new shirt and a pair of American trousers, but kept my Russian coat and hat. Also got $100.00 from the paymaster. Capt. Bolton and I go to town with two or three British officers, where we had a good party with wine and excellent food. Bernie Bolton and I are finally chased out of the Kasbah by the British police.

Talked to one of the natives, and bought some perfume for Betty at one of the bazaars. Get back to camp about 5:00am.

<u>March 14, 1945</u> – Had a smallpox shot, and returned to town, where I met some Maltese soldiers. These people are white Arabs. They assisted me in buying some jewelry and obtain some rare Egyptian coins. Everyone very sober, although we enjoyed some excellent wine.

Saw Hughes dance the rhumba with an M.P. (Believe this refers to a small fracas Hughes had with British M.P.'s. Do not recall too much about it.)

General Ritter, the commander at Cairo, has called for Capt. Coles. Coles was one of Ritter's favorite company commanders.

There is a rumor that we will all be sent back to the States by boat.

<u>March 15, 1945</u> – I fill out many forms, and we are restricted to the area. However, it will be difficult to contain this group, as they are not in the mood to be restricted anywhere.

Remember the Arab who, in perfect Brooklynese, said:
"Say Joe, giveyouahelluvagoodshineforabuck."

I make an attempt to buy three of the fezzes but was unable to do so. I go to bed fairly early after packing up all of my gear.

<u>March 16, 1945</u> – About 6:00 in the morning I find that we are not going to move. I then bum a ride to the docks and, and on my own, get aboard a boat, the *Samaria* (Liverpool). This is a much larger boat than the *Moreton Bay*. After much yakking with the captain he agreed to take me to Naples. So Bernie Bolton and I take out. Conditions aboard the boat very good. We have more time for eating, and the food seems to be better. I find that several G.I.s, as well as officers, have had the same

idea. There is a USO troop aboard and they seem to be almost continuously under the weather.

Had a hard time in a bombing raid at Marrakech. (It is hard to understand this.) One of our group is helping them in their performance, as they have lost one man. John Hanlon is helping the USO.

After much checking around, they placed six of us in one cabin, which makes it crowded but still O.K. Aboard there are many Frenchmen and many women. Some are wives of British POWs. One POW wife had a baby 2 months old.

The French are somewhat "feelthy."

Remember the grandmother hauling her two dead grandchildren around in a baby buggy. War is sure hell.

<u>March 17, 1945</u> – In my cabin are:

Capt. James T Maher, Jr.
652 E. Market Street
Huntingdon, Indiana

William H. Jarrett
2251 Jackson Street
Philadelphia, Pennsylvania

Harris O. Macus
1031 Madison
Birmingham, Michigan

William P. Kielmeyer
490 Sheldon Ave.
Columbus, Ohio

Vladimir B. Kovac
634 Second Ave.
Columbus, Ohio

(His brother is **Ivan K. Kovac** of Flushing, L.I.)

Loafed about all day in the shadow of a lifeboat with "Bumstead" Bolton, and we try to find something to do. He had a long story to tell on how he used to raise capons.

<u>March 18, 1945</u> – On board, all clocks are retarded a half-hour. We sight land on the starboard side about 0700 hours. The USO troop is truly an international organization. The individuals can hardly talk because of their different mannerisms, speech and acting which they put into everything they do.

The refugees are doing a land-office business, telling their tales of woe. A girl and two sisters, all that was left of a Hungarian family of eight, asked me to mail a letter to kin in New York City. I smelled a rat, in that it could be that these people were merely trying to get into the country, so I got one of the Hungarian G.I.s to give me a translation. Here is the letter translated:

Dear Lulu and Maurice,

I have written one letter to you and thank God that we escaped from the Germans. We have been here three weeks. There are also British and Americans here. In a few days we will be going home, if we still have a home. Out of the whole family there are three of us left – Gisi, Alonki, and myself. (Her name was Aranka.) Here in Poland they have separated us from the rest. What is the matter with us God only knows. We have suffered a lot. We have run out of everything.

I am asking you now to help us as much as possible so that we can start anew. The only clothes we have are the ones we are wearing, and they are rags. The Kells family has been written but up to the present we know nothing.

We do not know as yet when we will be leaving for home. When we arrive we will write from there.

It seems like a dream that we could go through as much suffering. Let everyone know of our sorrow, and find out if possible about the family.

Lots of kisses, and write. (signed) Aranka, Gisi, and Alonki"

The story back of this family is that the father was a prominent banker in Budapest. He had no sons but many daughters. When the Germans came in the entire family was sent to a concentration camp. The women, who had never done a hard day's work in their lives, were part of 2,000 sent into the woods to cut lumber. Of the 2,000, not quite 50 of them survived the ordeal.

March 19, 1945 – The boat passes through the straits of Messina and past Stromboli during the early evening while the volcano was erupting. It was a very pretty sight.

We loafed about the dock all day and kidded some of the refugees about life in America.

Many rumors.

March 20, 1945 – We arrive in Naples harbor about daybreak, and about the only change I can see is that there appears to be a few more sunken boats. I get off the boat at 10:00am and wander around the town of Bolton. Joined with some Americans who are quartered in an area west of Naples. Bolton and I are in Russian uniforms, and we are taken as part of General Anders' Polish Corps.

Saw my first American WACs, and it is hard to believe that these girls are in the Army. Capt Whaley joins us, and we go into Naples where we rent an apartment for some 8,000 lira. Everything seems to be high, but the cost of things are always relative. Later we find out that our apartment is in the "off bounds" area of Naples. At night we bring in many bottles of wine and some excellent Italian sausage. Bernie gets a drink or two too much, and we apparently create a nuisance with so much noise. We are picked up by the British M.P.'s, as they are sure we are British enlisted men. We finally admit to the British provost marshal that we are actually Americans.

March 21, 1945 – The American provost marshal has been looking for us, and he seems to be a pretty good egg. There are many forms for us to fill out. The paymaster here is about as dumb an ox as I have ever seen. We are taken to an American Hospital Officer's Club for food and lodging.

March 22, 1945 – Loafed about in the morning, and have about decided to leave here on my own for the First Armored Division, which is north of Rome. Jewelry here is very expensive, and the only thing worth taking home is some cameos.

We received an order from the commanding officer that we are to remain within the grounds of this hospital unit until arrangements have been made for a plane to take us home.

March 23, 1945 – "Stars and Stripes" the Army newspaper, came out for an interview and was very much interested in how we escaped.

The base section people in Naples do not know the war is on. I go to bed early.

March 24, 1945 – Of all people, I run into Capt. Buckner, from Mexico, Missouri. He was one of the Medics examining all of us and giving us some additional shots.

The darn fool paymaster finally paid us $150.00 each, and agreed to take back all of my Egyptian money.

A funny thing about the rate of exchange: I thought I had spent most of my equity, but I find that I actually made 15 cents by not taking occupational lira when I landed in Naples.

I go to Caserta, where I buy some slippers and a jacket.

The medics had a dance for us, and a colonel tried to pull his rank on Bolton. We told the Lieutenant Colonel where to head in, but fast. The dance is very poor. These people simply do not know there is a war.

I rest most of the day, and that night go to a cabaret with a medic who is a good friend of Col. Ginn. These base section people beat me! They conduct business as if there is no war!

March 25, 1945 – I am interviewed by another doctor, and report my scratch at Maknassy. We are invited by General Mike Daniels to visit his command post. Trip very dusty; scenery is beautiful.

March 26, 1945 – Go to Pompeii. Pompeii should be visited by everyone, as you find that the old Romans had central heating and air conditioning, even during their time.

Everything that is purchased from the Italians should be bargained for.

<u>March 27, 1945</u> – Run into Elam and Suhm – two old MMA graduates. Johnson Hagood, a classmate at the Citadel, looked me up. He is in the G-2, or Intelligence Section in Washington.

There are more forms to fill out, and we are further restricted. The base section group are a bunch of nuts.

Bolton and I still hang together. Remember the urchins and how they all tried to sell everything from coat hangers, peanuts, or what-not to any G.I. or American who would listen to them.

<u>March 28, 1945</u> – More forms to fill out, and we are further restricted to the building, or must be accompanied by an officer of the base section. Here are some of the prices:

cigarettes	180 lira per pack
meat	1000 lira per pound
lace	500 lira per yard

Some of the merchants are as bad as the "gilli" men in Port Said. I write many letters, and we are given instructions on how to behave when we get home.

<u>March 29, 1945</u> – The paymaster and I tangle again. I sold my private blanket, and "Bumstead" and I go AWOL. We go to a cabaret show and come home with a good snoot full. We find that the M.P.'s have been searching for us and the orders are out to have us picked up and flown to Washington.

<u>March 30, 1945</u> – We are awakened early in the morning, and I am told that Bolton and I had our names scratched from the order and that we have been given A-1 priority and are to be flown home immediately. Bernie and I go back to Naples for one final fling, where we run into some Air Corps characters who were lodged in the Hotel Terme. I also get a haircut.

March 31, 1945 – As we suspected all along, the air orders have been canceled, but we are told that we will leave at 10:30 tomorrow.

They have a system of permits and tickets here which Bernie and I have been accumulating to where we can get sufficient leave to stay in Naples for a week, if we can get by the administrative office.

April 1, 1945 and April 2, 1945 – Today is Easter! We are taken to the airport and leave Naples at 1:30pm.

We fly to Tunis and then to Casablanca. At Casablanca, a general tries to bump us, but his priority was only A-2. Since Col. Roosevelt had made the news by shipping a dog back as an A-1 priority, we made the general very mad by barking like a dog. We land at Casablanca about 3:00 in the morning. Here I turn over all of my occupational lira, black market lira, for Moroccan francs, as I thought we were going to be there for several days. We are taken through the streets to very nice quarters, and had no sooner flopped down on the floor to rest than we are awakened and told that our plane is leaving for the States.

On the plane are three old nurses, who smell to high heaven, and an Air Corps general. Flying over water is very boring. We land on one of the Canaries for about a two-hour refueling operation.

Chapter 18

Debrief, Visit Fort Hunt, and Finally Home

April 3, 1945 – Early in the morning we land at Stephensville, Newfoundland, and have breakfast. Leave at 5:10am and arrive in Washington at 1:00pm. We are all very thankful to be back in this country.

They pass us through customs and a medical examination. The War Department sends a jeep over to take me to the "Country Club" in Virginia where I see the other end of the parcel business. They are extremely clever -radio, balls, etc.[1]

Chief and I have a room at the Ambassador Hotel at our disposal.

At the Pentagon, I run into Bill Jones and Hagood M. I am finally turned loose and get a chance to call home.

Chief and I have a few drinks and he really gets plastered. He thought he was in Naples.

<u>April 4, 1945</u> – Spent most of the day in the Pentagon being queried by our Intelligence section. They were very much

---

[1] Refers to a visit to the MIS-X operation in Fort Hunt, Virginia where the security parcels originated.

interested in my report on the Russian anti-tank gun. Major General Henry was the most complimentary.

Saw Col. Cochrane and Bill Nutter of the First Armored Division.

<u>April 5, 1945</u> – Back to the Pentagon for questioning by the Adjutant General. I go to Towson and spend the night with my mother and my sister. We talk until 4:00am.

<u>April 6, 1945</u> – Buy some clothes, and leave on the train at 6:30. Train very crowded, so I get off of that and catch the next section, which is 30 minutes behind.

<u>April 7, 1945</u> – Shave and wash. No sleep last night, as there were simply no bunks available. I am still amazed as to how these people do not know there is a war being fought.

I was to meet Betty in St. Louis at the Mayfair Hotel. The hotels are very crowded nowadays. Fortunately, the manager had been an old patron at the Academy and he got me a room. Betty, in the meantime, had gone to the station, had missed me and returned to the hotel where she ran into Jumps Cauthorn. I had spoken to Jumps after checking in, and he took her up to my room, where I saw her for the first time in 35 months.

Both the *Post-Dispatch* and the *Globe Democrat* were pestering me for an interview, but for fear I would say something that was classified, I begged to be let off, and they finally accepted my request.

<u>April 8, 1945</u> – In the morning we just missed the train and loafed around Union Station, catching the 7:00 o'clock train which arrived in Mexico, Missouri at 10:00pm. <u>It was a long time!!</u>

Afterword

Figure A-1 *Tony B. Lumpkin*

Tony B. Lumpkin

After the war, Tony Lumpkin left the Army and went on to a successful career in the Dairy Queen business and had the franchise for several states. Tony retired and traveled the world with his wife Betty. He died in 1979.

He got in touch with Gottfried Dietze after the war and "vouched" for him with the authorities in the U.S. and brought him to the country and helped him get enrolled in college.

In the 1960's, the Central Intelligence Agency got in touch with Tony and asked him to make contact with "Max," whom they believed was then operating as a spy in the U.S. Tony politely declined; stating it would be very suspicious if he were to somehow get in contact with Max after so many years.

Several other subjects of this diary had notable post-war lives.

Figure A-2 General John Waters

General John Waters

General John Waters (December 20, 1906 – January 9, 1989), was a United States Army four-star general who served as commander, U.S. Army, Pacific from 1964 to 1966. He was also the son-in-law of General George S. Patton. During World War II, he was taken prisoner while fighting in Tunisia in 1943. While he was initially at *Oflag 64* with our grandfather, he was later transferred to *Oflag 13-B* where Patton set up the controversial attempt to free him. The disastrous maneuver was later chronicled in a book titled, **Task Force Baum.**

After World War II, he served as commandant of cadets in West Point. He was promoted to brigadier general in 1952 when he was deployed to Korea.

During his career, he received many medals including the Distinguished Service Cross, the Army Distinguished Service Medal, the Bronze Star, the Purple Heart and the Korean Service Medal.

Amon Carter Jr.

Figure A-3 *Amon Carter Jr.*

Taken prisoner in Tunisia, North Africa, while serving as a forward observer, he was initially held in Italy, then transferred to Poland by the German Wehrmacht. During the twenty-seven months he is a prisoner in *Oflag 64*, a camp outside Szubin, Poland, he managed to contact his father and tell him he was alive and that he was with other Texas prisoners of war.

His father, Amon Carter, Sr. began publishing updates for all the families in the Fort Worth Star-Telegram. Carter Sr. sent his son supplies and information through an underground contact in Portugal. Carter Jr. used these materials to "publish" on toilet paper a newspaper for the camp. He also included news from a friendly Polish contact at the train station that clandestinely listened to British radio and left news items in a wastebasket for Carter Jr. to recover later.

His role at *Oflag 64* would be notable enough, but his accomplishments went well beyond World War II. With his father, he published the Fort Worth Star-Telegram and was instrumental in getting American Airlines to put its headquarters in the Dallas Fort Worth area.

When he died in 1982, he was given a twenty-one gun salute by the Fort Worth Police in recognition for his support – only the second civilian to receive such an honor. The Amon Carter Museum of American Art in Fort Worth continued to be run by his sister, Ruth Carter Stevenson, until her death.

Henry Söderberg

Figure A-4 Henry Söderberg

Swedish lawyer Henry Söderberg, as the representative of the International Y.M.C.A., was responsible for the region of Germany in which *Stalag Luft III* was located. He visited the camp regularly and went to great efforts to procure and deliver items requested by the various compounds. As a result, each compound had a band and orchestra, a well-equipped library, and sports equipment to meet the different British and American national tastes. Chaplains also had the necessary religious items to enable them to hold regular services.

In addition, many men were able to advance, and in a few cases, complete their formal education. Söderberg remained in touch with many of his American friends by coming from Sweden to attend their reunions until his death in 1998. He kindly donated his rich collection of official reports, photograph albums, letters, and other materials documenting his work on behalf of the prisoners of many nations to the U.S. Air Force Academy Library. It is available to scholars, other researchers, and cadets alike. While not actually in the camp as a prisoner, he had frequent contact with them and was admired by them as well.

Gottfried Dietze

Figure A-5 Gottfried Dietze

Dietze was an American political scientist of German origin. He grew up as the son of the mayor of Goldberg in Silesia. His father, because he was a Freemason, was dismissed in 1936 from his post. Growing up, Dietze was a member of the German church youth, one in 1929 by Eberhard Koebel.

Dietze studied after the end of World War II foreign science, law, philosophy and politics in Berlin, Göttingen and Hamburg. Immigrating to the United States he acquired in Princeton his PhD with a dissertation on the concept of "free government" in America. For over 50 years, from 1954 until his death, he taught Comparative government (Comparative Politics) at Johns Hopkins University in Baltimore and its field office in Washington.

Characterized in his obituary as a "Prussian through and through", he considered himself as an "anarchic conservative". His research has been repeatedly through external funding conservative think tanks such as the Earhart Foundation.

Of particular interest to Dietze and his country of origin, the "Hitler complex" – also the title of a book published in 1990 – he saw as the source of the self-destructive foreign and domestic policies of Germany. He wrote several books on this topic and articles, including one of Hans-Dietrich Sander issued government bonds.

Dietze was actually a camp interpreter that my grandfather liked and respected. Their friendship extended well beyond the war. He met our parents and I (Tony Lumpkin III) also had the good fortune to meet him when he came to Missouri to visit. He died in 2006.

Wright Bryan

Wright Bryan (full name William Wright Bryan, Sr.) was a leading American journalist and newspaper editor. He was a lifelong Clemson man, as a faculty brat, graduate, administrator, and historian of the university.

Born August 6, 1905, he was the son of Arthur Buist Bryan, also a Clemson graduate and faculty member. Growing up in Clemson, he attended Clemson and graduated class of 1926, serving as editor of The Tiger 1925-26. Additionally, he attended graduate school in journalism at the University of Missouri.

Working as a reporter for the Atlanta Journal, he rose quickly through the paper's ranks to become managing editor in 1973. As a World War II correspondent in London and France, he achieved the high point of his career, being the first to broadcast the first eyewitness account of the D-Day invasion. It was during this mission, that he was wounded and captured by the Germans in France. He was sent to *Oflag 64*, where he met our grandfather.

Following the war, he became editor of the Atlanta Journal and later, the editor of the Cleveland Plain Dealer. In 1964, he returned to his alma mater, Clemson, to serve as the Vice President of Development. During his tenure, he wrote, Clemson: An Informal History of the University, 1889-1979. After retiring in 1970, he remained in Clemson. He died in February 1991.

Awarded the nation's highest civilian decoration, the Medal of Freedom, by President Eisenhower, as well as the Clemson Medallion. Honorary degrees from Clemson and

Wooster College (Ohio). A Clemson scholarship was established in his honor.

A journalist – one who studied at Mizzou, no less (our father's alma mater and where I (Dr. E. Noel Lumpkin) went to medical school). Of course, the Clemson angle would appeal to more in the Carolinas!

Max

Max is a puzzle. He was one of the Russians that my grandfather spent some time with after leaving the camp. We know that he was a colonel in the Russian army and that he was a film director, and there was a mention in the diary that he attended Columbia University. I have tried to figure out what his last name is, but I have not had any luck. His theories are one of the appendices of the diary, so it would be nice to know exactly who he is (or was), but for now, he is simply "Max".

Georgy Zhukov

Figure A-6 *Georgy Zhukov*

Georgy Konstantinovich Zhukov (1 December 1896 – 18 June 1974), was a Soviet career officer in the Red Army who, in the course of World War II, played a role in leading the Red Army drive through much of Eastern Europe to liberate the Soviet Union and other nations from the occupation of the Axis Powers and, ultimately, to conquer Berlin. He is the most decorated general officer in the history of the Soviet Union and Russia.

While serving among many other notable generals during World War II, Zhukov maintains a top position due to his numerous victories. Other military leaders such as Montgomery and Eisenhower, recognized his significant contributions during the war. His influence extended well beyond the Soviet border.

Like some of the others, there are actual books written about Zhukov, so there is plenty of information available via the internet. Obviously, he is one of the Russians that my grandfather met, but to my knowledge, there was not any communication after the war.

Ernie Pyle

Figure A-7 *Ernie Pyle*

Ernest Taylor "Ernie" Pyle (August 3, 1900 – April 18, 1945) was an American journalist who was known for his columns as a roving correspondent from 1935 for the Scripps Howard newspaper chain, especially during World War II, when he reported both from Europe and the Pacific, until his death in combat on a Pacific island. He won the Pulitzer Prize in 1944.

His travel articles, about the out-of-the-way places he visited and the people who lived there, were written in a folksy style, much like a personal letter to a friend; many were collected in Home Country (1947). By the war, he enjoyed a following in some 300 newspapers and was among the best-known American war correspondents in Europe.

There are numerous books about Ernie Pyle so I won't go into a lot of detail about him. Our grandfather did develop quite a friendship with him before he was captured, so it is a proud memory for all of us. Even those who are not up on their WWII history have heard of Ernie Pyle.

Ernie featured Captain Lumpkin in one of his national columns following his capture. He also mentions him several times in his book, *"Here is Your War."* Following our grandfather's capture, Ernie donated his ID bracelet to a war drive in our grandfather's hometown of Mexico, Missouri. The family that purchased the bracelet then presented it as a gift to our father.

THE ROVING REPORTER
A Captain Is Captured,

BY ERNIE PYLE
Free Press Special Writer

NORTHERN TUNISIA—By Cable)—Another friend whom I've mentioned before in these columns is now among the missing. He, too, we know almost definitely is a prisoner.

He is Capt. Tony Lumpkin, of Mexico, Mo. Tony was headquarters commandant of a certain outfit—a headquarters commandant being a sort of militarized hotel manager.

NICKNAMED 'NOAH'

Just before he disappeared Tony got to going by the nickname of "Noah" Lumpkin, because he always seemed to pick out such a miserably wet place for a command post. On their last move before he was captured, the commanding general — a swell guy with a sense of humor—called Capt. Lumpkin over, stood with him outside a tent looking out over the watery landscape and congratulated him on locating them in the center of such a beautiful lake.

Tony Lumpkin needn't have been captured at all if he had been content to stick to his comparatively safe "hotel managing." But he wanted to get a crack at the Jerries himself. He is an expert gunner, and he finally talked the commander into letting him take five men and a small gun on wheels and go out to see what he could pick off.

The first day they got one German truck plus something that turned out later to be a camel, although it looked like a truck at the distance they were firing from.

LIVED WITH DETROITER

The second day they moved farther into the mountains to get into a better shooting position, but bagged nothing that day.

On the third day they went even farther into the hills, hunting a perfect spot for firing.

Capt. Lumpkin used to share a tent with Maj. Chuck Miller, of Detroit, and with their assistant, Corp. William Nikolin, of Indianapolis, both of whom I've written about before. They formed an intimate little family.

That third night Maj. Miller came in late. He was astonished, and a little bit concerned, to see Tony's cot empty. When he woke up next morning there was still no Tony.

SEARCH STARTED

He knew something had happened. He went to the general and got permission to start out with a squad of his own military police and hunt for his lost companion.

They covered all the ground Tony had covered, and finally, by studying the terrain and talking with others who had been near by and interviewing German prisoners, they pieced together what had happened. The hill that Capt. Lumpkin had been trying to get to had simply been lousy with German machine-gunners.

The Germans saw him all the time. They sent out a party that worked behind and surrounded him. A German who was captured later said that a captain with a Tommy gun killed one

Figure A-8 "A Captain Is Captured" – Ernie Pyle (continued next page)

THE DETROIT FREE PRESS — MONDAY, MAY 5, 1943

Breaking Up Perfect Trio

German and wounded another before being taken. That is all we will know until Tony comes back to us.

A TERRIBLE VACANCY

There isn't grief in the little Lumpkin - Miller - Nikolin family, but there is a terrible vacancy.

"We were a perfect team," Maj. Miller says." Tony was slow and easy-going, and I'm big and lose my temper too quickly. We balanced each other. I'd keep him up and he'd calm me down. We sure miss him, don't we, Nicky?"

The two who remain, the officer and the corporal, seem drawn even closer together than before. When there are guests Nicky is called in to be part of the company. Nicky waits on the six-foot-four-inch major as though he were a baby, and the major treats Nicky with an endearing roughness.

TALK BOTHERED MAJOR

Maj. Miller went on:

"Nicky always woke us up every morning by bringing in hot tea. Then the damned intellectual would ruin the day for me by sitting down while we drank the tea and starting an argument along the line of who was the greater writer, Tolstoy or Anatole France. That kind of stuff throws me.

Tony would argue with him and relieve me of the horror of such a subject at such an hour. But now that Tony's gone I have to bear the load all by myself. It's awful.

And Nicky stands and grins while the major talks.

Our conversation drifted off onto other things, and a long time afterwards, out of a clear sky, Maj. Miller said:

"Damn it, I'd give a month's pay — no, I'd give six months' pay — no, by God, I'd give a year's pay if only old Tony were back."

And Nicky would gladly do the same.

Figure A-9 Continued – "A Captain Is Captured"

$103,525 for Ernie Pyle's "Dog Tag" as Gift to a Boy

MEXICO, MO., Nov. 28.—Ernie Pyle's dog tag—the one he wore through four years of war in Africa and Europe—brought $103,525 in war bonds at a Missouri Military academy war bond dance here.

Cadet Bruce Avedon, Miami, Fla., made the purchase and immediately presented the tag to Tony Lumpkin, jr., 7-year-old son of Capt. Tony B. Lumpkin, Pyle's old friend and associate in the North African campaign, who for two years has been a prisoner of the Germans at Oflag 64. Captain Lumpkin is commandant on leave from the academy here.

It was through Pyle's syndicated column in April, 1943, that Mrs. Lumpkin, who lives in Mexico, gained the first hopeful news that her husband might be alive. He had been reported "missing in action" and until the column headed "Tony Is Gone" was published, she had heard nothing else. Captain Lumpkin is mentioned several times in Pyle's book, "Here Is Your War," a copy of which recently passed German censors and was eagerly read by Lumpkin and his friends in the prison camp.

More than $150,000 worth of bonds were purchased at the dance and among the other things put up for auction were: Lieut. Gen. Joseph Stilwell's shoulder patch, a baseball autographed by all the members of the 1944 world champion St. Louis Cardinals, a general staff insignia sent by Col. Jerome G. Harris, former instructor at M. M. A., and a picture of Dorothy Lamour.

Figure A-10 Ernie Pyle Donates ID Bracelet

The following appendices are Captain Lumpkin's post-war notes on his diary and general observations he made during the war.

Appendix A – The Germans

German Security

The Germans, I thought, were rather ingenious in the methods they used to contain prisoners. The camps that I observed showed that there was a perimeter composed of a fence about 12 feet high and the poles about 6 to 10 feet apart. Stretched between these poles were barbed wire strands about 4" to 8" apart, Then, to keep the strands from being widened at the midpoint between the poles, other wire was woven through so that the entire mass made a fairly well contained net.

There was generally a ditch about 6 or 8 feet deep. I believe that this ditch was to ensure that the outside perimeter could be flooded in case there was suspicion that a tunnel was being dug. The British were certain that the Security at Eichstädt used a seismograph to pick up any sounds which might be made by digging a tunnel.

The next fence, just 8 or 10 feet inside of the outside fence, was woven with barbed wire in much the same manner as the other. Between these two fences the German had piled a maze of barbed wire, and to give you an idea how thick this maze was, I know that a small dog (about 15 or 20 pounds, I would estimate) was unable to work his way through this barbed wire maze. One of the favorite sports of prisoners was to study the maze to see what could be done to clear this from one fence to the next.

Just inside of the double fence was a small trip wire. This was about 10 or 15 feet inside of the fence. The guards all had orders to shoot anyone who touched or stepped, over the trip wire. The ground "between the trip wire and the fence was always kept bare and raked occasionally so that any evidence of foot prints, etc., would show through.

Mounted at the top of the double fence, and at intervals of about 200 yards, but particularly at each corner, was an observation tower where a soldier sat, with what looked like a machine gun or some other automatic weapon. These towers were placed in such a way as to ensure that the guards could see any part of the camp at any time. Come to think of it, I do not recall ever finding a spot in any camp that could be completely hidden from some guard if he was at his proper place.

Any idea of escape over the fence requiring the physical climbing over, had to incorporate in it some plan of distracting the guards in the towers. Guards also patrolled the outside of the fence at regular intervals, but due to the pattern of their patrols one could predict fairly well as to when a guard would come by.

At night the entire areaway, from the trip wire to the guards" path, was well lighted. The guards in the lookout boxes were always present. I noticed that the lookout boxes were built so that the guard could remain in the shadow if he so desired and it was impossible to determine in which direction he was looking, if he desired to take advantage of this.

The Germans also had a security patrol with small arms who would patrol, wandering about the camp and might show up at any time and at any place.

Any meeting, such as a class or a theatrical production, etc., was attended by a German who could understand English.

The entrance to the compound was invariably through two gates, with an areaway between the gates which would hold up to 50 or 60 men, or would be large enough to hold a truck if it was necessary for the truck to drive into the grounds. This enabled the guard at the gate to inspect any and all people entering the compound or leaving the compound on any detail. While there was no checkup on Germans coming in, and very few on Germans going out, there was always a check made of any vehicle entering or leaving the compound. This even applied to the wagon which came into the compound to empty the latrines.

There were many other precautions taken by the Germans to ensure that the contraband would not enter the camp. The Germans" orders were that every package which came into the camp would be fully opened in the presence of a responsible German soldier, and nothing allowed to enter which could be used to further an escape plan, or which could be made into a weapon. This applied even to such minor things as black pepper (which could be used to temporarily blind a guard).

The Germans had had some trouble with escaping prisoners who had hoarded their food against such a day as they got outside of the wire. To counteract this, no food parcel was turned over to a prisoner without every tin being opened, to ensure that it would be consumed within a week. We were able to work out a plan with the Germans whereby those tins in a food parcel, not for immediate consumption, could be placed in a "tin" store and drawn out as needed. This enabled a prisoner to conserve some of his tins towards a day when there would be no issue of Red Cross parcels.

Another security measure which I think the Germans used was in the actual ration they gave the prisoner. It was bare subsistence under the most ideal conditions, and no one would be able to walk very far on the daily ration issued to a POW.

The Germans were very cognizant of the fact that the more crowded the prisoners were the better guard they could have on them, and of consequence each compound was further divided by barbed wire fences and certain areas and buildings could not be used except for special occasions.

Many of the buildings were light framework, and above ground, with some type of an open area, underneath the floor. In those cases the Germans had a trap door leading to this area, and the ground under it had been raked and brushed so that any movement by anyone in this area would leave a footprint.

Roll call was made at least twice a day and would be held more often if the commandant deemed it necessary. At this time the number of POWs was counted. To further insure that they had the right people in the camp, every few weeks or so they would have each prisoner come by and they would match up the prisoners against the pictures that they had taken of these men when they were brought in. One of the tricks of the prisoners was to screw up his face in such a way that it would confuse the Germans when they attempted to identify the prisoner as described by the photograph.

I noticed that at Eichstädt, Munich, Capita and Schubin there was no building, no massive growth of shrubbery, trees, etc. within several hundred yards of the outside perimeter. At Schubin, the German colonel had his home next to the camp, but I do not think anyone but a nut would have tried to escape through his flower garden.

While I have mentioned the degree to which they would inspect food, they would apply the same meticulous search to clothing, books, or anything else that had been sent to a POW. All books were read and censored. If there was anything in there derogatory to the Germans, the book was not passed. To ensure that no maps, money, etc. had been made a part of the binding, the Germans slit with a knife the cover of each book, in search of anything hidden beneath the cloth binding.

Prisoners brought into Germany were searched rather thoroughly for any weapons, money, maps, etc. Often this would involve an inspection down to the bare skin. Often their search for contraband was made in such detail that they would overlook the most obvious places. I recall a search at Moosbürg (Munich) where I had removed all of my clothing and stood up with my arms outstretched, to ensure that I was not hiding anything with my arms or legs and they failed to find a G.I. compass and a German identity card which I had taken from a prisoner some two months before. They were held in my hands over my head.

Another cute trick which the Germans tried was to send in a detail to inspect a certain barracks, a certain room, or a certain area. This detail would consist of several soldiers who would come storming in and search everything possible about the room, looking for contraband, unopened tins, etc. They never found anything much, and we generally had more fun out of snorting at them for breaking up our property. I recall one funny incident which happened at Eichstädt during one of these searches. Some of the men in my room had been working on a German officer's uniform to be used as a part of an escape plan. To hide this blouse, the officer merely hung it on a nail back of the door, in full sight of everyone. Again, it was so obvious that they did not notice it.

The Germans were apprehensive that they could not find all of our tunnels. One of the objectives of the security patrol within the camp was to look for any evidence of dirt or spoil from a digging. This aggravated the tunnel making to some extent, as it became necessary for us to hide all of the spoil and we had some rather ingenious ways to do this. The color of the dirt about 10 feet below the surface was almost a bright yellow, and could be easily detected.

The penalty for escaping was a sentence to a definite period of time in the "bunker". Here you were on bread and water, but it did not make much difference anyway, as the others were just on bread and water also. Those prisoners who had attempted to escape several times and had been caught were transferred to a "maximum security" camp, which I believe was located in Czechoslovakia. I do not recall the name or location of this camp, but I have heard of it several times.

While I mentioned that some of the buildings had been placed off bounds, I know that we worked out an arrangement with the German colonel to use a small chapel that was within the compound at Schubin. I understand that when this was done we were asked not to use the chapel grounds as a starting point for an escape plan.

Another item which was contraband was any form of lead, (it could be melted into the form of wire), metal wire itself, or anything of metal that was large enough to be made into a knife, a weapon, or parts for a radio. At Eichstädt they even threatened to confiscate tinfoil off of British cigars, as this had been used for making German Army buttons for blouses.

To ensure that no messages were sent out, each POW was given a piece of specially printed letterform in order that he might write his letter home each month. This paper was a slick paper which contained much sulphite and would show any water marking, scratching, etc. Indelible pencils were forbidden, as the Germans found these were melted for inks used in reproducing maps.

In conclusion, I might add that they had not done this at the early part of the war; that many of their restrictions on prisoners came about because of past escapes, particularly in the first four months after Dunkirk. The policy of the Germans apparently had been to determine exactly how each escape had been engineered, and then put in sufficient restrictions to ensure that the plan would not be used again.

German Education

I was constantly surprised at the type of education found in the average German. As a teacher of some 20 years' experience prior to the war, it absolutely confused me to find a

German with 5 to 8 years of schooling who was able to speak intelligently on English history, American history, and speak several languages. One of the soldiers, Willi Kricks, had had 7 years of schooling, he had an I.Q. which I would estimate at 90 to 95, yet he knew quite a bit of Shakespeare, trigonometry, philosophy, opera, and European history. One of the interpreters, *Hauptman* Minner, had been an instructor of Italian and geography at Munich prior to the war. I often discussed this question with him. He was amazed that we had 12 years of schooling in preparation for college. He did bring out that the college education at the under-graduate level did not measure up to the same under-graduate work in the American institutions. He further explained that a student was made to continue in school as long as he was learning, but when the subject matter became too difficult the student was not required to attend. This may account for Willi Kricks having had such a few years of schooling.

The curriculum in the German schools seemed to cover many more required subjects for their students. Whereas in our system we generally have a maximum of five or six, they would have as many as ten and twelve subjects at the high school level.

Wartime Substitutes in Germany

As a prisoner and otherwise, I had an opportunity to study the wartime system of *ersatz* materials in Germany. A list of items and their substitutes is given below:

Mustard	A substance having some vinegar and the color of mustard, but certainly had no sharpness of taste.
Bread	Made from potatoes
Jam	From what appeared to be either beets or carrots

Sugar	Some other chemical, similar to saccharine
Pepper	Looked like pepper, but did not have the sharpness
Worcestershire	Made from what appeared to be walnut juice
Plaster laths	Made from wood shavings
Broom	Made from twigs
Leather	Made from plastic
Combs	Made from wood
Razor sharpeners	A device made from glass, to resharpen a safety razor
Bandages	Made from paper
String, & fabrics	Made from paper. I even saw a suit of clothes made from paper.
Gasoline	From potatoes
Ink	Made by the use of some berry juices
Shoes	Made from wood; also made with cloth sides and wooden soles
Boots	Made from felt. Very efficient against the cold
Cheese	Made dry
Beer bottle caps	Made from Porcelain
Honey	From what appeared to be a corn syrup base.
Coffee	From parched barley
Coal briquettes	Made from tar and sawdust
Scrub brush	Made from stone
Tobacco	Resembled a combination of straw, and smelled like old cabbage
Money	Printed on ordinary paper
Flashlight	Battery was a hand-operated generator
Wood saw	Made from a piece of wire

Soap	Made out of almost any and everything, from pumice to wood shavings. Almost impossible to dissolve in water.
Picture reels	Made from plastic rather than metal
Wire Insulation	Made from beads strung on wire

Appendix B – Rations and the Effect of Hunger

Rations

As POWs, we all learned, mostly for the first time, the value of calories for human health and comfort. In general, a person sitting still requires somewhere in the neighborhood of 1,200 calories a day for his basic metabolism. An active person should have 2,500 calories, and the Army ration was something in excess of 3,000 calories per day.

The German ration for POWs was somewhere between 800 and 1,000 calories. This was supplemented by a Red Cross parcel which was issued one per man per week, when they were available.

The German quartermaster was a fat little pig. He actually grunted with his guttural German, and this, together with his bodily appearance, made one think that he had some swine blood in his ancestry. In one of my arguments with him relative to the insufficient food the POWs received, he told me that the Wehrmacht authorized the following on a monthly basis:

(a litre is slightly over 1 quart; a kilogram is about 1.7 lbs.)
½ litre of milk (when can get it)
2 ½ kilos of potatoes
.2 kilo of meat
.125 kilos of fat (every other month this can be butter)
    (.1 kilo of oil may be substituted for fat)

1.84 kilos of bread .218 kilos sugar
.05 kilos koffee (an *ersatz* coffee made from parched barley)
.075 roggenflocker
1 small cake of soap per month
.2 kilos of soap powder

I am not sure that this is complete, as I do know that we had an issue of dried vegetables, which were about half weeds and had an awful odor when they were cooked.

As I recall, we took some camp money and bought some small quantities of fresh vegetables when they were in season. From this source we obtained some radishes (wormy and very hot) and cabbages, which seemed to flourish in great profusion in the Polish soil. I do know that if it had not been for our supplementary parcel from the Red Cross, many of the boys would never have made it.

The American Red Cross parcel contained, roughly, 1,000 calories, plus some of the luxuries which we were unable to get from the Germans. As I recall, there was in each package a small can of powdered coffee, ¼ lb. of sugar, a can of meat or fish, an Army ration chocolate bar, a small package of cheese or cheese food, and a can of powdered milk. The British Order of St. John had in their parcel: tea, oleo, jam, and oatmeal. The Canadian Red Cross had a parcel which contained canned butter.

It took us about two months of organization as an American camp to get American parcels. Up to that time we were supplied by the British Red Cross Order of St. John, and by the Canadian Red Cross. The Turkish Red Cross also sent us some bulk dried raisins, which were turned over to the sick in the hospital.

The British Red Cross also had an invalid parcel, designed for those who had stomach ulcers or stomach disorders. The British also had a parcel designed for occupational therapy, composed of scraps of cloth, leather, etc. I presume that if the

Americans had been in the camp as long as some of the British, the Americans would have come through with the same type.

Speaking of parcels, we should give full credit to the Swedish YMCA, who made every effort to get us all types of sports equipment and reading material. This resulted in our having a library of some 800 to 1,200 books, and was, in my opinion, one of the finest things we had in our internal organization, as it gave each man an opportunity to become better read and to study those subjects of his choice. While some of the topics were very far afield, there was quite a section on astronomy, reptiles, insects, and contemporary novels.

I do not recall these same types of books and parcels from the American Red Cross, but do know that many American industries sent us some of their products. We received records from the broadcasting companies, musical instruments from some of the manufacturers, athletic equipment from the American U.S.O. through A. J. Reach & Co. and Spalding Co. (I am certain I do not have it all covered.)

The Effect of Hunger

When a person is captured he is disgusted with himself for getting caught, and this disgust sometimes leads to depression. Most of the stories that I heard, and my own experience bore out, was that we were fairly well fed by the German combat soldiers, who realized that we were merely people trying to do our duty. As you would go back for interrogations here, we found that the food was poor and that there was not enough of it. During this period, the stomach started to shrink in size, and this in turn caused abdominal pains. You have a constant hunger, and you can think of almost nothing but food. After two or three weeks of this, you finally realize that the only way to beat this situation is to never think of food. While this helps you mentally, your body never does quite adjust itself to this lack of nutrition.

Probably the most enduring effect of malnutrition is a complete lack of energy for a sustained effort. You could probably walk 5 or 6 miles, but there is no reserve energy to enable you to walk an additional 5 or 6 miles if it becomes necessary. Your body goes through a change, in that the excess fat in all parts of your body melts away, and your muscles become soft because they are not exercised sufficiently. I found that it was very hard to have a recall of details that had occurred in the very near past. As an illustration, you read a text on astronomy, and after you had finished the text you could not recall more than 20% of what you had read, whereas normally you should be able to recall at least 50%.

I also found that you forget things that everyday skill had almost made a habit with you. As an illustration: I forgot how to spell many words which normally a person with any type of school teaching background should never forget.

When you get relief from this lack of food your recovery is terrific. The Russians, I thought, handled it extremely well in that they would feed us several times a day. I recall one day in which we had actually nine meals.

One funny incident: After having gone without white bread for as long as we had, it was impossible to tell the difference between white bread and pound cake. You just simply couldn"t tell from the texture nor the taste.

Some of the forgetfulness could probably be explained by the fact that our diet was extremely short on protein and on sugar. We never had enough of this during any period of our incarceration. I recall receiving some hard candy from home, and for the first time I realized how much body heat could be generated by one small candy ball if you put it into your mouth just before you went to bed at night. Your body would generate enough heat so that you could actually sleep warm that night.

Appendix C – Internal Organization of the Camp

The internal organization of our camp was copied from the British, and vastly improved through the efforts of Colonel Drake, Colonel Waters and Colonel Alger.

Col. Drake insisted that we were internees, and that the authority inside the camp must come from the senior American officer, and that the officers themselves would be responsible for the internal administration. I understood there was quite an argument with the German commandant on this matter, and that Col. Drake told the commandant that it would either be that way or they would not administer any part of the camp. This, of course, could have made a great deal of chaos for the prisoners as well as the German commandant; hence the arrangement worked out very satisfactorily – the Germans had less work to do and the POWs were able to handle things in a much easier manner.

The senior American officer was designated as the camp commander, and he selected his executive officer. Here Col. Drake truly came into his own. He was very aloof in dealing with all Germans. Whether he felt it or not, externally he gave the impression that he spoke to no German other than *Oberst* Schneider. This had a very strong effect on the other Germans. I have firsthand knowledge that some of the German soldiers were really afraid of Col. Drake. This pattern of behavior, I am certain, got our camp started off in good shape.

The executive officer was exactly what the term implies. He acted for the senior American officer, and here Col. Waters did a superb job.

From the standpoint of our administration, the first and most important department was our "intelligence" – or security – and this was headed by Col. Alger. Alger did a superb job with this. He was constantly alert to any unusual movement by the Germans, and suspicious of anything that might have any bearing on the intelligence that might affect our camp security. Under him was a security committee who passed on all plans for escape. This committee and Col. Alger could draw on the resources of any section or any person in the camp for the benefit of any escape plan.

We had a mess officer who had charge of the cooking of the German ration. His helpers were selected from some of the officer POWs and there was a detail of enlisted men assigned to the camp for this work.

We had a quartermaster who had charge of the issuing of any and all clothing, supplies other than food, regardless of what source they might come from. There was a parcel hut division which I headed up that had charge of the issuance of all Red Cross parcels and any private parcels which came from a family to an individual POW.

There was a hospital detail, composed of about eight or ten doctors and a dentist. To the extent of the medicine available and the surgical supplies we could obtain, they did a remarkable job of maintaining our health under these trying conditions.

There was a camp librarian, who had charge of all books.

There was a head gardener, and we were organized so that every available piece of ground could be used to grow what produce we could, in season.

There was a barbershop, staffed by two barbers.

We had a tailor shop which, besides repairing clothes, could also make some limited repairs on shoes.

As to laundry, each man did quite a bit of his own laundry, but at one time we were able to send some of it out and have it cleaned by some of the Polish families.

We had quite an athletic program, with all games in season, and indoor games for the inclement weather, with tournaments in everything from cribbage to baseball.

There were theatrical productions, with talent that has since gone into the entertainment world.

We had a glee club, and as I recall Lieutenant Ford was the prize soloist, having been employed at the Cathedral of St. John the Divine in musical work before the war.

We had a newspaper, printed by Willi Kricks in his local printing shop, on paper furnished to us by the Swedish Y.M.C.A. A complete set of all the editions is in my scrapbook. Everything in this newspaper was written by the POWs themselves and, here again, we had some experts. Larry Allen, a war correspondent, and Baldhead Bryan, the editor of the Atlanta Journal, were among its editors. We also conducted a news bulletin board, on which a translation of the German news was made by Larry Allen and his editorial group.

Appendix D – The Russians

Theories of Max

Max was a very persuasive person in his discussions we had about the Communist Party. He was very intelligent, was multi-lingual, and had been around the world quite a bit. He was a graduate of Columbia University in New York City, and thoroughly understood the American problems.

One of the most telling arguments he had against our capitalistic form of government was that we did not practice what we preached, and of course he brought out the Negro problem, which has come to the front so strongly during the recent years. He also pointed out that our system permitted a very few people to enjoy the labors of a very large number, and that basically our wealth was accumulated individually by employing large numbers of people or obtaining it directly from the ground in the form of minerals or agricultural production.

To his way of thinking, gold was not a metal of economic importance. His favorite illustration was that they would make toilet seats from gold if the metal was in plentiful supply, as it was a good rust-resisting substance.

Membership in the Communist Party was by a very limited number of people and was not necessary to reap the benefits of the Communist life.

Max's father was a surgeon and his mother was a dentist. The mother belonged to the Communist Party, but neither Max nor his father was a member of the Communist Party. On the other hand, I am quite certain that Max was more than just a captain (or *stashloitner*) in the Red Army.

His idea of what were actually penitentiary crimes was rather unusual: murder and stealing from the government were about the only two offenses which should be punished by detention. This belief may be the result of the men in Max's unit, his unit having been organized at the defense of Stalingrad and recruited from inmates of the city jail. I must say, though, that they certainly did not reflect jailhouse characters as I had known them in the United States.

Another phase of Max's philosophy which I could never understand was his extreme doggedness in tracking down anyone who had committed a crime against the Polish people. He was most anxious to get the Poles to testify against anyone who had, in the least manner, helped the German Army while it occupied Poland.

In my own personal opinion of Max, I am thoroughly convinced that he was a dedicated Russian before he was anything else. He was a patriotic person, and certainly demonstrated his willingness to undergo great hardships and privations in order to further a Russian victory. On the other hand, I could not help but think that practically every man in the camp was of the same stripe, so where is the difference between an average Russian and an average middleclass American?

Prior to the war, Max was a movie director in Leningrad, and had done some film cutting in New York City at one of the American film companies. He was a most interesting person.

The Russian Soldier

I was very much impressed by the ordinary Russian G.I. While he was nowhere near as well educated, with book knowledge, as the German soldier, he was almost a master with improvising from the materials available.

Besides the illustrations quoted in the diary of fixing the blow-out, and the potato light, the G.I.s themselves could exist off of whatever food was available, and were at their very best in adapting clothing, etc., for the intense cold. They were firm believers in having many layers of clothing but all of them very light, then wherever possible they covered their clothing with some type of wind breaker that might be made from a piece of canvas or newspapers, cardboard, etc. They were ever watchful to keep their feet dry and did not worry too much as to whether they had socks on their feet or straw in their shoes, as either one would protect their feet from dampness, which would in turn result in frostbite.

As a combat soldier, the Russian was the best I had ever seen in house to house fighting, and they were absolutely fatalistic in their attitude of getting in the first shot. I do not recall ever seeing them approach a house other than with the most direct method, opening the door and walking in with a blast of automatic fire.

On reconnaissance, they made very effective use of small arms fire in determining if there was anyone in a building, a thicket, a haystack, or other places where a soldier would normally be expected to hide.

While they could be accused of liberating everything and anything that was edible, at the same time I do not recall seeing them actually waste food. If there were any chickens in a farmhouse lot, for instance, you could be well assured that they would be liberated, but only to the extent of what was necessary to feed the group that was present.

Max told me of an instance, which I disbelieved at that time but I have since become convinced that it is true: that during the war with Finland, the Russians had experimented with the dropping of paratroopers into snow banks and small forests without the benefit of parachutes. This was done along the technique of using a light plane, traveling slow at a very low altitude. He said that the Red Army had decided that while this produced some casualties, at the same time it did have some very good possibilities.

Areas selected for this, of course, would have to be covered with some type of fairly high vegetation and/or some very deep snow. However, in the Karelian Peninsula this was not too difficult, and was considered a success in that particular theater.

Max also reported that the Red Army had experimented considerably with the use of the parachute technique used by the Germans in Crete, but for some reason they were unable to adapt this on the same large scale that the Germans used, one of the problems being that the planning was so faulty that often the planes would run into the parachutes of the previous flight.

Conversing with Russians

When I escaped I had a German-English dictionary, a Russian-English dictionary, and an English-Russian dictionary, all three of pocket size. When translation would become more difficult with the Russians, I would give them one dictionary and I would keep the other, and we would merely open the pages to the words we were trying to use in conveying our thoughts. It was rather comical, and difficult to translate thoughts in this manner. You find that you get your sentences down to three words: a subject, a verb, and a predicate.

My Russian Overcoat

When I was taken to Zhukov's headquarters and finally questioned by his chief of staff, a heavily built Russian finally exploded with the announcement that these men were *Americanski,* and asked what he could do to help. At that time he picked up a Russian coat made of goatskin and gave it to me. It later turned out that this was Marshal Zhukov, himself. When he gave me the overcoat, I, in turn, tore a tank insignia off my shirt collar and gave it to him as a return gift. We were in like Flynn from then on.

Miscellaneous

A funny thing happened. Skells and I wandered into this house where there were four or five other American officers, including Colonel Drury. Since Colonel Drury was the ranking officer, he had a room to himself off upstairs, and the rest of us were bunking downstairs and preparing for a good long siege of rest and relaxation. Unfortunately, this did not last too long, as the first Russian patrol to come by was a sergeant and three or four soldiers on motorcycles. They started giving us a lot of lip, and since we were in a majority, the four or five of us on the lower floor started arguing back and threatened to throw them out of the house. About that time, Colonel Drury, comes down the stairs and gives us a good dressing down about the Russians being our allies and we should not create an incident but should go along with them.

We finally got the patrol moving on up the road and about 30 minutes later one of the cockiest little Russian officers drove up in a halftrack and two cycles, with about 10 soldiers alltogether. This character was about half-crocked, and you could tell from his walk and his conversation that he was extremely proud of his unit and the Red Army in general. He started talking to us about how much better his automatic rifle was than our submachine gun. We very naively asked him what was the rate of fire, how far it could shoot, how accurately, etc. just to draw out the conversation. When we asked him about the rate of fire he offered to demonstrate and let go a burst of about 20 rounds, right up through the ceiling. These shells all came up through the floor in Colonel Drury's room, and in something less than three seconds flat, the Colonel came pounding down the stairs, ordering us to throw that bum out, incident or no incident.

So it merely goes to show that in any of the incidents occurring between nations, they sometimes develop over whose shoe is fitting the tightest. Colonel Drury at that time certainly had no fear of creating an incident.

We finally got this character back on the road and three of the officers left with him.

Glossary

Acht ball	German: "eight ball", slang for a soldier in trouble or a misfit
Americanski	Russian: Americans
Appell	German: roll call
ARC	American Red Cross
ASDIC	Acronym used to describe sonar devices during World War II. Later dropped in favor of the acronym SONAR.
Astrikan	Russian: type of Russian jacket.
AWOL	Absent without leave
Bahnhofmeister	German: station master
Bolsheviki	Russian: members of the Russian Social Democratic Worker's Party
Borsht	Russian or Polish soup, usually with a foundation of beet juice
Brown shirters	Nickname for member of Nazi paramilitary organization
Bürgermeister	German: mayor of a city
C.P.	Command post
canary	Nickname used by POWs to describe their radio
Cow Gun	Coventry Ordinance Works 37 mm automatic cannon

Draughts	British term for game of checkers
ESU	German Red Cross
Feldwebel	German: military rank most equivalent to a British or American warrant officer
Flugplatz	German: aerodrome or airfield
Frachtbriefs	German: waybill
Führer	German: Adolf Hitler
G.I.	Government issue, slang term used to describe members of U.S. armed forces
G-2	Intelligence
Gefreiter	German: equivalent to Private in the armed services
geprüft	German: checked or inspected
Gestapo	German: State Secret Police, was the official secret police of Nazi Germany
Goons	Slang term used to describe German prison guards
Hauptman	German: Captain
Heinkle	German aircraft manufacturing company
Ilag	Civilian internment camp
Jugend	German: Hitler paramilitary youth organization
Kaput	German: defeated or destroyed
Kommandant	German: commander
Kommandanture	German: commander's office
Kriegy (Kriegsgefangenen) also Kriegie	German: prisoner of war

Glossary

lagermarks	"Camp currency" Alternative money issued by the Germans for POWs
Lord Haw Haw	German propaganda announcer during World War II who claimed he was British
M.P.	Miltary police
M3 (Medium Tank M3)	American tank used during World War II
Mädchen	German: girl
Marks	German: currency of Germany
Mien Kampf	German: translated as *"My Struggle"*, book written by Adolf Hitler
MIS-X	A section of the U.S. Dept. of War based in Fort Hunt, Virginia that operated during WWII. It aided U.S. POWs and those evading capture.
MMA	Missouri Military Academy in Mexico, Missouri
Nyet	Russian: no
Oberst	German: Colonel
Oflag (Offizierlager)	German: officer's prisoner of war camp
Panther Tank	German tank used in World War II
Panzergrenadiere	German: armored infantry
Polkovnik	Russian: colonel
POW	Prisoner of war
Reichspost	German: official postal authority
S-4	Supply officer
SAO	Senior American Officer
Schokolade	German: chocolate

Schützenfest	German: "marksmen's festival" traditional festival surrounding a shooting competition
SS	See *Waffen SS*
Stalag (Stammlager)	German: prisoner of war camp for all ranks
Stalag Luft	POW camps administered by the German Air Force
Stashloitner	Russian: captain
Tiger Tank	German heavy tank used in World War II
Unteroffizier	German: rank most equivalent with sergeant
V-1	German Gieseler Fi 103, better known as the V-1 "Buzz Bomb", an early jet powered flying bomb
V-2	German long range ballistic missile
verboten	German: forbidden or prohibited
Völkischer Beobachter	German: translated as *"People's Observer"*, was the daily newspaper of the Nazi Party
WAC	Women's Army Corps
Waffen SS	German: "Armed SS", combat arm of the *Schutzsaffel* commanded by Heinrich Himmler throughout World War II
Wehrmacht	German Armed Forces
Zloty	Polish: currency of Poland
zu die salz mine	German: "to the salt mine"

www.ingramcontent.com/pod-product-compliance
Lightning Source LLC
Chambersburg PA
CBHW070118100426
42744CB00010B/1853